MUSINGS

ON

LEBANON

ARAB WORLD

PALESTINE -ISRAEL

ENVIRONMENT

Ghassan Karam

MUSINGS

ON

LEBANON

ARAB WORLD

PALESTINE-ISRAEL

ENVIRONMENT

Create Space January 2012

An e book edition of this title is found on Kindle.

Contents

A good traveler has no fixed plan, and is not intent on arriving.

Lao Tsu (570-490 BCE)

The voyage of discovery is not in seeking new landscape, but in having new eyes.

Marcel Proust

Revolutions are the locomotives of History.

Karl Marx

Introduction

The following collection of 141 articles have been chosen from over 350 or so that I have written for a variety of venues over the past 4-5 years. These articles were initially published/posted by AMIN, Arab Media Internet Network, YaLibnan.com, RationalRepublic.blogspot.com and a few academic conferences. Obviously some of these individual postings/articles were longer in their original format but the selection in your hands ranges in length from 700-1100 words each.

Most of the articles, 80 of them, deal with political developments as they occurred in Lebanon, a country that has been beset by a devastatingly bloody civil war and political instability ever since. Lebanon is a country that has been in search of an identity ever since its creation as a result of the Sykes Picot accords. It will not be difficult for the reader to learn swiftly of my strong advocacy and commitment to a secular state and my opposition to the noble right to resist occupation when it is dealt with as a monopoly preserved for a religious sect, financed by foreign funds and acts as if the laws of the land do not apply to it. This is a perfect example of a noble idea that has been sullied and defiled.

Since my formal education is in Economics and since I have been teaching the subject at a university for over 30 years then it is to be expected that a few of the articles; 13 to be precise; are devoted to Lebanese Economic challenges. Economic analysis in countries such as Lebanon, provide a special challenge because of the paucity of reliable economic data at all levels. As the articles will make clear my basic concerns in this area center around the capability of the country to finance its sovereign debt and the lack of a detailed targeted economic plan to reduce poverty and decrease the inherent social inequity in the system. On a macro level Lebanon seems to have performed adequately but the gains have not been shared by most of the people and the reliance on large capital inflows from expatriates and wealthy Arabs has created a real estate bubble that has marginalized most of the Lebanese.

Obviously one cannot deal with the Middle East without addressing elements of the Palestinian Israeli question. This collection contains 12 such articles that in general fault the Lebanese governments and the Lebanese people and institutions for the impoverished and even wretched conditions of the Palestinians living in refugee camps in Lebanon. As for the broader Palestinian Israeli issue I am convinced that the Palestinians have exploited, mistreated, lied to and disinherited. But that does not mean that I support many of the means that have been employed in an effort to establish their own independent and sovereign state on the West Bank and Gaza. Obviously this does not imply that I favour the cruel Israeli policies that border on apartheid. In the final analysis I find it difficult to support any policy that is undemocratic and that relies on random violence.

Over the past 25 years or so I have developed a deep interest in environmentalism as a whole and in ecological economics in particular. That should explain the presence of 18 articles/posts devoted to environmental issues both on a global level and in the Arab world. I do hope that these few articles will inform the reader about the inevitability of the need to create steady state economies if the world is to avoid an environmental and ecological Armageddon.

And finally this compilation contains 12 articles that speak to many Arab issues such as Islamic Banking, Religious freedom, civil rights and obviously the Arab Spring. The last 6 entries have all been written since mid May 2011 and are devoted to the Syrian Uprising. My support for the Syrian people, and all other people, to gain their freedom and liberty is unquestionable. Dictatorships do not have the right to exist in my view of the world.

I sincerely hope that you will enjoy reading some and possibly all the collection and I encourage you to contact at **karam.ghassan@gmail.com**

Detailed Table of Contents

This document subscribes to the principles of copy left: feel free to use without permission but with attribution.

LEBANON

POLITICS

Monday, September 10, 2007

<u>Why Should Personal Faith Be A Qualification For The Presidency?</u>

Ibn Rushd (Averroes) is considered to be the founding father of what became known as secularism or what is known as laicite in France or the concept of separation of church and state in the US model. It is ironic that one of the greatest Moslem philosophers of the 12th century has left an indelible mark on what has become a fundamental inviolable principle of modernity and democracy but the concept of the separation of state and religion is nowhere to be found in the Arab World , not even in Lebanon.

Some might argue that it is not very judicious, when the very existence of the state is in peril, to devote precious time and energy to a seemingly less urgent issue such as the abolition of sectarianism. Obviously we beg to differ. We are of the opinion that a certain outcome is always predicated on the basic structure that underlies the system in question. Furthermore, tinkering with peripheral issues will not result in a radically different result unless the underlying architecture is changed. The human tendency to concentrate on finding a remedy for symptoms rather than addressing the root causes of an

24

issue has not served us well. The best that can be expected from a remedy that avoids the pain associated with adjustments to a new set of fundamentally different paradigm is to whitewash the problems for a while and to slow down the speed at which the abyss is being approached. Yet the inevitability of the crash is still there. On the other hand a radical redesign that addresses the major shortcomings and flaws in the current architecture will deal with the real problem at its root and will provide for a meaningful relief based on sound foundations.

A seminal structural flaw in the current Lebanese political system is the insistence that sectarian affiliation is the main qualification to fill electoral positions as well as appointed ones. Unless one happens to have been born of a certain sectarian belief then many positions are automatically considered to be out of reach for that individual. That is discrimination at its worst. This system essentially places an obstacle that an individual has no way of compensating for and it is also important to add that this so called characteristic that prevents the many from being considered for certain jobs is not related by the furthest stretch of the imagination to one's ability to perform that job well. In fact religious affiliation is as unrelated to job performance as the applicant's color of eyes, the number of cavities in their molars or the make of car that they drive. The mere act of requesting an individual to reveal ones sectarian observances is best viewed as an intrusion on ones right to privacy. A political system that is built on this flawed concept enshrines the notion of religious discrimination, robs the state of the most qualified for various posts, results in unjust and inefficient decisions and winds up in generating a legacy of tensions and recriminations between the members of the same community.

Luckily enough for us in Lebanon, an agreement has been reached15 years ago which stipulates the dire need to create a just and sustainable political system in Lebanon by eliminating sectarianism at all levels. Let us start by electing to the presidency the person that has a deep abiding belief in Lebanon as a sovereign, democratic and modern state, a person who has a platform to initiate and help implement policies that will encourage the promotion of economic prosperity, individual freedoms, social justice and environmental sustainability. None of these attributes is the monopoly of one sect and thus there ought to be no sectarian restraint on who is qualified to seek that office. It is our sincere hope that you are in agreement with us that we should rebuild the Lebanese system on solid foundations and that the most basic place to start is to remove the criteria of sectarian affiliation for those that want to seek the Lebanese presidency . To have a list of female and male candidates that belong to all religious affiliations in Lebanon will be the best demonstration of our love and commitment to this state. And yes, Walid Junblatt should be just as qualified as say Boutros Harb to seek the office of the Presidency.

We would like to hear from each and every single one of you. Please take the time to post your thoughts and plans and suggestions on this matter.

Sunday, November 25, 2007

Lebanon: A Failed State?

It is highly discomforting to notice that not many political analysts, observers, residents or politicians of the Lebanese political scene have correctly identified the root cause of the Lebanese stand-off as being purely systemic. A proper diagnosis is essential if one is to treat the real malady and not merely the symptoms. Lebanon has just observed its 64th anniversary of "independence" although it is clear that the state has always catered to the whims and dictates of outsiders. Ceremonial events are often meant as a cover and as PR instruments to project an image that does not exist. It is unfortunate, but Lebanon seems to relish ceremonial events, empty clichés and hollow institutions.

The role of the loyal opposition is essential for the functioning of a robust democracy. It is, after all, what keeps the ruling party "honest". This does not appear to be the case in Lebanon. Hezbollah and its allies operate not in the national interest but appear to be in the service of foreign powers that are intent on treating Lebanon as a tool to further these powers' own welfare. The current ruling majority as exemplified by March 14, on the other hand, are focused on preventing the "opposition" from gaining more power and control over the increasingly frail and weak Lebanese body politic. Any investigation of the proclamations and policies by the current government reveals that at best their ambitions are at best limited to checking the plans of the opposition and restoring to Lebanon the same old bankrupt system that has resulted in nothing but turmoil, social injustice and divisiveness over the past six decades. It is a shame that no major figure in the current ruling coalition has either the courage or the ability to articulate a radically new paradigm that Lebanon needs if it is to survive as a state. What is sorely needed is a Lebanese identity that is separate from the religious and spiritual one. Lebanon is in dire need of the erection of a strong wall that separates the sacred from the secular. The root of most of our problems can be traced to the fact that we have tolerated and even encouraged religious activity in the public square. That needs to end and the sooner the better.

No time is better than the present. What Lebanon needs, just like any other functioning democracy, is a president who is committed to the national interest, sovereignty and the protection of human rights to all the citizens of the state. The above criteria are not enhanced by a specific religious behavior or a certain method of prayer. Actually it can be argued that by limiting the population from which to choose such an individual then we are in essence limiting our ability to choose the best that we have. Personal religious convictions should never be used as a prerequisite for political office at any level and definitely not for the top positions.

Unless the ruling party is willing and able to show that it is capable of moving the state towards meaningful change in Lebanon then its political victories, if and when they occur, will be vacuous and totally unproductive. Is the present leadership capable of steering the country to safe harbours? The record so far is not very promising:

(i) A collapsed Lebanese economy
(ii) A society that is struggling to survive
(iii) A weak central government that has ceded control over large parts of its territory
(iv) An inability to provide public services on a reliable and consistent basis
(v) Widespread corruption in government offices
(vi) Disintegrated state institution (non functioning parliament and inability to appoint a Constitutional Council)
(vii) Failure to protect human rights
(viii) A dysfunctional justice system
(ix) Total disrespect for law and order
(x) And last but not least, a failed Constitution.

As the above partial list indicates clearly Lebanon which was ranked last year by Foreign Policy magazine as the 21st most failed state in the world should have no problem in sinking to join the "exclusive" club of the ten most failed states in the universe.

Something can be done about preventing that ignominious rank but the responsibility rests with the Lebanese people who have to demand more accountability from their representatives and the ruling group who must forget about their personal interests and do what is good for the country. The only way to prevent a fall into the abyss would be to usher in a new system based on ability, merit, equality, sovereignty, democracy, human rights and sustainability.

Wednesday, December 5, 2007

Cedar Revolution: R.I.P

A genuine grass-roots movement is a very rare event indeed. But when such developments take place they serve as a reminder of how the power of the people, the ordinary citizens, is the only power that matters. After all the raison d'être of a modern democracy is to promote the general welfare of its inhabitants. The Lebanese and millions of people all around the globe were privileged to witness such a rare event on the streets and alleys and public squares of Beirut. Close to a million and a half Lebanese from all walks of life and from all parts of the country converged on Beirut to send a powerful message: "We are Lebanon and we have had enough foreign interference with our God given rights as a free and sovereign people. We demand a sovereign state and responsible governance." Their call for freedom and liberty was heard by the "occupiers" and the traditional politicians alike. The "occupation" forces had no choice but to comply, helped by the threat of US armed action, but unfortunately the local traditional politicians managed to co-opt the popular revolution and to wrest control of it by pretending that they were the real force behind it all along. In fact the only interest of these traditional politicians was to salvage their spheres of influence and resume their game of Business as Usual i.e. run Lebanon as if it is a collection of feudal fiefdoms.

It is easy to assign blame to Hezbollah and its major ally General Aoun for the current Lebanese political morass. Hezbollah has continued to flaunt its power by establishing a state within a state, starting a destructive war, holding illegal demonstrations and above all paying homage to foreign powers while General Aoun is all consumed by becoming a President by any means necessary. These efforts could be judged by some as being misguided but in a sense such efforts can be dismissed as typical acts by an "opposition" in its efforts to gain more power. Obviously Hezbollah can be looked upon as being the antithesis of a grass roots movement and its lofty goals of establishing a modern, secular, democratic and freedom loving state. (Hezbollah is considered by many to be nothing else but an extension of the Iranian National Guards). And General Aoun dissociated himself from the goals of the Cedar Revolution as soon as Hezbollah promised to help him fulfill his life's obsession.

But yet it was not the opposition that has effectively ended the dream of million and a half Lebanese. A group of politicians managed to present itself as the guardian of a revolution that opposed all what these politicians stood for, real representative government, and a modern sovereign non-sectarian state. The leaders of what became known as the March 14 bloc had nothing in common with the aspirations of the brave, youthful, demonstrators of the Cedar Revolution except its name. They forged an electoral alliance with those whose principles are to undermine the state; they could not take any decisive measures either when a war was ignited on purpose by an illegal militia or when a number of cabinet members resigned. They became obsessed with the tribunal , whose work is essential, at the expense of all other governance, they have failed to enforce law and order all across the land and they continued to surrender Lebanese sovereignty . But above all else they have, through inaction, conspired against the Lebanese Constitution by failing to convene the Chamber of Deputies, hold by elections as stated by the law or make sure that the Constitutional Council is fully constituted and is operational. And as if the previous partial list of major failures to lead and govern is not enough they convene again to short circuit the constitution again and to appoint illegally a president . Yes the real and true betrayal of the popular revolution was accomplished and finalized by the unprincipled actions of a majority that either had no interest in seeing democracy blossom or as a result of incompetence.

Yet all is not lost. We the Lebanese citizens must rediscover our "citizenship" (mowatiniah) and throw out all of the rascals in two years time. If we fail to do that then we deserve all what we are getting.

Tuesday, July 25, 2006

War

It is far too simplistic to refer to the current Israeli attack on Lebanon as a "war of choice". This was a conflict that has been waiting to happen for six years. Israel was not going to stand by forever and watch Iran supply HA with more rockets, advanced weaponry and sophisticated armaments. It is true that Israel could have chosen not to respond this time when two of its soldiers were kidnapped but respond it would sometime. Israel knew that eventually it could not allow the HA provocations to go on and that the longer they wait then the greater would be the stock of amassed ammunition by HA. Israel was fully aware that eventually it had to respond and seems to have come to the conclusion that this was a provocation too many and that the sooner they took on the HA threat the better it would be for the northern residents of Israel.

Obviously this does not mean that the savage Israeli response was justified. It only says that it was not a surprise. Would the use of this overwhelming and disproportional force by Israel achieve its original stated objective of rooting out the military wing of HA and getting back, alive, the two kidnapped soldiers? Of course not. Very few conflicts, if any, achieve their stated objectives. But the failure to accomplish all what Israel had set out to achieve is not to be judged as a waste either. The results of the current campaign have changed the rules of engagement already. I doubt it whether HA, or an HA like minded organization, would in the foreseeable future be tempted to test Israeli resolve in such a cavalier manner. Once the dust is settled and the fog of war lifts I am inclined to suggest that the overwhelming majority of the Lebanese and even Arabs would feel betrayed by the adventurism of HA and the Iranian and Damascus regimes. Lebanon has a problem of learning that sovereignty is not free and Israel has a problem finding an acceptable accommodation between it and the Palestinians and the other Arab states. I hope that the current conflagration will end soon and that the lessons learned by all parties would move the region forward towards what has been an elusive stability for almost sixty years.

Saturday, July 1, 2006

The Qana Tragedy

Moral clarity and moral courage have been absent from most of the discussions about the Qana bombing. It is time that we put an end to the purely emotional selectively indignant posture.
That the killings at Qana are tragic is not an issue open for debate. The death of the 56 civilians was not only tragic but also horrific. Having said that we must immediately add that any uncalled for death, Lebanese, Israeli or otherwise is equally tragic. What makes a human life valuable and its demise a crime is neither the nationality nor the religion of the victim but their intrinsic right to life, liberty and happiness.

If we are to apply the above logic, which we must, then as we grieve for the children of Qana, we must also grieve for all the other children who lost their life and as we condemn the Israeli Air Force then we surely must condemn each and every missile fired by Hezbollah since none of them has a guidance system and thus each and every one of them could have potentially caused a Qana like massacre. Frankly, I have been very uncomfortable with the reaction of many of my Lebanese compatriots. They condemn Qana and in the same breath ask for revenge, they condemn Qana and yet they celebrate the death and destruction of their opponents, they condemn Qana but ask for a pound of flesh in return.

32

Yes, we should condemn Qana, in the same way that we have an obligation to condemn all violent acts , but when we condemn Qana let us remember that what we are in essence condemning is war. We need to condemn the act itself and not only the outcome that we deem to be painful. As it has often been said War is hell, violence only breeds more of the same and it is time to hold ourselves to the same standards that we expect of our enemy. The pain and suffering from an adversity would not be a total waste if that occasion is transformed into a learning experience that will help guide our future actions. Maybe, just maybe, this conflict will finally lead us to reexamine, reevaluate and modify our thinking. Enough senseless wars, death and destruction.

Unfortunately, the results of the tragic events at Qana appear to have been compounded. In addition to the unwarranted loss of life we have failed to learn, benefit and grow from this experience. The Lebanese government in particular has thrown caution to the wind and has decided that it is more expedient to renounce moderation and reason .Instead it has embraced the rationale of justifying the actions and ill conceived tactics that have ignited this conflagration in the first place. We have allowed this tragedy to "Hezbollahnize" Lebanon instead of "Lebanonizing Hizbollah" and that is the most tragic possible outcome.

Thursday, January 3, 200

Duplicitous Lebanese Opposition

The admonition , by Socrates, to always beware those who opine about that which they do not know is as perfect of a description as one is likely to get of the demands by the Lebanese opposition. They claim to be democratic but act as authoritarians, they speak of plurality but seek to impose their narrow vision of political reality, they preach the need to establish institutions but scheme to destroy them and they take every opportunity to promote the need to respect rights, law and order when in practice they act as transgressors. It is not the self described label that counts, individuals and organizations are to be judged by their deeds. Let's not forget that the most ruthless dictators on the planet dispense injustice and promote misery under the guise of Democratic republics.

Any political minority is free to make any kind of demands, no matter how onerous or irrational these demands might be, but no minority is ever entitled to impose its conditions on a popularly elected majority. Once the demands set by a minority-political group are not met then the group in question should simply decline the opportunity to join the government and should work through the established institutions and processes to affect legislation, appeal to more voters and hopefully gain more parliamentary seats in the next election.

In Lebanon, unfortunately, such common sense and logical thinking appear to have been hijacked by those that have already hijacked the Chamber of Deputies, the Constitution, citizen's rights, sovereignty and law and order. A demand, any demand, during political negotiations is no more than the "price" that one group is attempting to exact from the other for agreeing to support the overall policies of the larger group. If for any reason the price is deemed to be high then the offer is rejected and the transaction is not executed. Only an undemocratic organization, an underground group mentality, will adopt the view that the buyer has no choice but to pay the price that it is demanding and that the search for a substitute is prohibited. The lack of logic is furthermore compounded in the case of the Lebanese opposition. As if it is not enough that they want to force themselves on the ruling party they also demand that the ruling party offers them the right to veto any legislation. And unless their demands are totally met they will prevent the ruling party from carrying forward its constitutional responsibility to do the people's business. Such behavior is simply tantamount to extortion and must be totally rejected on political as well as rational grounds. At what level of representation does a minority earn the veto power? Is it at 25%, is it at 35% or is it always entitled to the veto power irrespective of its popular support? What are the bench marks that need to be met in order for a minority to earn the right to impose itself? Would the above conditions be operable if the roles were to be reversed, say in two years time and if that is so then what is to be accomplished by holding elections? It is clear that the current opposition in Lebanon has no interest in the Lebanese project but is merely setting up conditions and obstacles in an effort to destroy that which it claims it wants to preserve.

Tuesday, July 15, 2008

Is The Proposed Lebanese Cabinet a "Tower Of Babel?"

The current structure of the just agreed upon Lebanese cabinet is reminiscent of the Biblical story about the Tower of Babel. What most Lebanese politicians and commentators describe as a major significant achievement in the reconciliation process of what divides Lebanon is nothing more than the individual efforts of each participant to build a tower for his/her personal glory without any regard to the common good of the state. Just like the total chaos and inability to coordinate the construction of the Tower in Babel the Lebanese cabinet as constituted is bound to become a cacophonous meeting place between parties that speak different languages and that have opposite goals and aspirations.

To believe that this proposed cabinet will help establish the democratic Lebanese project on solid grounds is tantamount to a strong and unassailable belief in miracles. Miracles are best described as events that defy natural laws and principles and as such the concept is in essence a code word for fantasy and irrationality. No matter how hard we wish for it, when human jumps from any height the path will always be a downward one. Humans just cannot fly; it is a natural law that cannot be violated. A belief in miracles might be acceptable in fictional epics but it is fatal when confused with reality. To even contemplate a positive outcome from the attempts at dialogue between those whose strongly held beliefs are in total contradiction with each other and whose aim is to shape and move society in opposite directions is nothing short of a belief in unrealistic story tales; a belief grounded in miracles. There is still another apt metaphor to describe the inanity of the current formation of the Lebanese cabinet. The pretense of the Lebanese politicians when they describe in glowing terms their achievements in putting together this mélange of cabinet members is reminiscent of the futile efforts by the Captain of the Titanic to save the ship from imminent disaster by giving orders to rearrange the chairs on the deck of the fatal ship.

The Lebanese ship of state has been severely damaged from the tempests that it has had to navigate. But all is not lost. The ship can be steered into safe harbours but not until all the crew starts pulling in the same direction, speaking the same language, ground their beliefs in reality and channel the scarce resources into meaningful activities that go beyond the superficial. What is needed above everything else is the courage to demand a workable political construct instead of the pretense that the same group can be an integral part of the executive branch and yet oppose it at the same time. This combination is bound to fail and the sooner we admit the impossibility of the task being asked of such an incongruous group then the sooner it will be for a responsible and accountable society to get established. To expect Hezbollah to play a positive role in the creation of a Lebanese civil society is to believe in the supernatural and to suspend rationality in favour of miracles.

Saturday, January 31, 2009

What Took So Long?

So the Egyptian government has come to the conclusion that Hassan Nasrallah and his followers at Hezbollah in addition to Hamas and its leadership are in essence Iranian agents. My only question is: What took so long?

Walid Jumblatt declared over a year ago, on January 2, 2008 to be precise, that Nasrallah "is not a free man and his decision-making is not free." Then he went on to say that Mr. Nasrallah and his henchmen are paid Syrian and Iranian agents bent on destroying the Lebanese state in order to satisfy the grandiose visions held by their masters. Even two years prior to that, in the summer of 2006, Mr. Jumblatt explained that "We had been trying for months, to spring our country out of the Syrian-Iranian trap, and here we are forcibly pushed into that trap again."
It is important to note that Mr. Jumblatt was not alone in his assessment. A broad coalition of Lebanese political parties and associations questioned the motivations of the acts taken by Hezbollah by stating: "Is it Lebanon's fate to endure the killing of its citizens and the destruction of its economy and its tourist season in order to serve the interests of empty nationalist slogans?"

Many a journalist, blogger and analyst had arrived at the same conclusion four years ago. It was evident to whoever cared to look at the facts that Hezbollah's interests were not compatible with those of an open, democratic and secular society. In the final analysis Hezbollah is a group of religious fanatics created to promote the interests of an Iranian theocracy. And as the saying goes: if it walks like a duck, if it quacks like a duck then it is a duck.

It is unfortunate but it appears that many in Lebanon and the Arab world have chosen to conveniently forget the clear history of the evolution of Hezbollah. The para-military and illegal militia was established by generals from the Iranian Pasadran, funded by Iranian money, supplied with smuggled Iranian and Syrian arms, trained in illicit bases in Lebanon by Iranian personnel and is structured to serve the Iranian national interests as seen through the eyes of the Grand Ayatollah to whom Hassan Nasrallah pays ultimate homage as he himself has declared in 1987 that "Those who reject the Faqih's authority are rejecting God and the descendents of the prophet Mohammad." Some might need to be reminded that the Wilayat Al Faqih concept started with Ayatollah Khomeini in 1987 and is interpreted to mean that the Grand ayatollah has power over all Shiite in the world and in all fields: religious, social and political.

Those who willingly choose to live in denial do so at their own peril. When would the Arabs, in general, and the Lebanese, in particular, decide to wake up from their slumber and call things by their real name? The Arab- Israeli conflict has been transformed over the past decade into an Iranian- Israeli conflict except that the ones who are doing the dying, the suffering and the fighting are Arabs. Iran has been able to penetrate masterfully the Arab ranks through its creation, funding and support of Hamas and Hezbollah. Iran has hijacked the Arab –Israeli conflict with the express complicity of these two parties and the cooperation of the isolated weakened and desperate Syrian regime. To expect loyalty to a state and support for democracy and diversity by those whose founding charter declares: "We, the Umma of Hezbollah, consider ourselves part of the Islamic state of Iran... We are committed to the orders of one leadership, represented by the Wilayat al-Faqih, the supreme leader" is the biggest of all follies.

<u>Upcoming Lebanese Elections: A Microcosm of the Political Forces in the Arab World</u>

Most of the nation states of the Arab world are, in their present forms, about half a century old; Kuwait was the first to win its independence in 1961. Obviously the current borders for Gulf States were drawn for the first time ever by the British whose protection of the "trucial states" and its various tribes started as far back as the early 19th century. But after WWII the British had already agreed to Indian independence and so the geopolitical needs for protecting the flank of the Indian subcontinent ceased to be applicable. As for the other main countries of the region, Iraq, Syria, Jordan, Lebanon and Saudi Arabia they came into their present form as a consequence of the defeat of the Ottomans; the sick man of Europe; as detailed essentially in the Sykes-Picot accords. Iraq became independent in 1932, soon to be followed by the independence of Lebanon in 1943, Syria and Transjordan followed suit in 1946. No one knows the exact length of time that is required for the inhabitants of a newly formed nation state to develop and acquire a distinctive identity as a people united by a sense of purpose and a common bond. But definitely as time goes on that special bond gains strength at the expense of the traditional racial, linguistic and cultural conditions that existed under the reign of empires.

The relative "youth" of these nation states in the Arab world is a major factor in their respective inability to develop stable democratic regimes. Democracy, after all, is a new idea that has no roots in the history of the region and the inhabitants are not used to the idea of offering allegiance to an abstract concept such as freedom and human rights. Instead loyalty is usually given to tribal chiefs and religious leaders. To the dismay of Pan Arabism the passage of time has helped cement the concepts of statehood and national sovereignty .Even the term citizenship, with all the responsibilities associated with it, have begun to blossom and to play a seminal role in establishing civil rights and democratic practices, albeit at an early and yet unsophisticated stage. As a result it appears that the Arab region is at a cross roads where the forces of statehood , sovereignty, modernity and democracy are becoming more ingrained but are still at odds with the old traditional forces that do not recognize modern state borders or democratic ideas as helpful. These traditionalists are intent on regaining the days of "glory" of the Arab empire of a thousand years ago by reestablishing the purity of the social and political conditions that prevailed then.

Lebanon and its upcoming elections on June 7 2009 is being presented essentially with a choice between those that value and cherish an independent, diverse, vibrant , democratic and modern state and those that have their primary allegiance to powers beyond the borders of the state and who are driven by a vision of narrow interests and reactionary bankrupt structures. The upcoming Lebanese election is in a sense a microcosm of the politics in the Arab world. Lebanon might be less authoritarian and less autocratic than most but a victory for the forces of modernity, moderation and state identity will be a victory for all the other Arabs who share such aspirations. History is by definition forward looking and as such the prospects for peace and the rule of law in the Lebanon as well as the rest of the Arab world are bright.

Wednesday, June 3, 2009

A Rotten Electoral System

A presentation of any idea or model in any field will fall apart if it is not internally consistent. Although no one should take seriously models that suffer from very obvious logical flaws in their construction yet both of the major political factions in Lebanon appear to be robust despite the fact that each of them is built on very shaky logical foundations.

The upcoming Lebanese parliamentary elections are nothing else but a sham. The traditional politicians and power brokers have gamed the system to such an extent that even the EU and the Carter center have sent delegations to watch the elections and lend its results credibility. The recent leaked recording of the private discussions at Walid Jumblatts residence reveal a sorry state of affairs where Mr. Jumblatt describes the process of forming lists of candidates in some regions as if he was a Godfather running the operations of the family or syndicate. Yes, at some moments he was reflective but in the style of a sixteenth century feudal lord. Although the press is not privy to the pronouncements of the other feudal lords I am certain that the language of Nabih Berri, Hassan Nasrallah or Saad Hariri was much different. The elections in most of Lebanon are not elections at all and it is time for people of character and principle to say that the emperor has no clothes.

But even if one is to cast a blind eye on the utter lack of choice in most districts we will still be faced with the claim and counter claim of who is really democratic. The March 14 group has made it very clear that they will not give the opposition veto power again because that is not how the democratic game is played and they are right. But their case falls apart when one takes into consideration the fact that they are the strongest advocates of what they call the power sharing a la Taif agreement. That in essence is an understanding to give the Christian community in Lebanon half the parliamentary seats although it accounts at best for 35-40% of the vote and its share is continuously shrinking for demographic and political reasons; lower fertility rate and more immigration. But isn't offering a block that amounts to 35-40% of the vote a disproportionate representation of 50% of the seats in the national assembly a form of veto power? Of course it is. Then what is the rationale of March 14 when it opposes the giving of the veto power to some but offers it willingly to others? The only explanation is self expediency and logic and principle be damned.

The inconsistency of the opposition is even more glaring. Hezbollah is willing to play the elections game in order to legitimize its essentially authoritarian and religious principles. They are not even willing to pay allegiance to the country in which they are expanding their fiefdom and control through the use of illegal weapons provide to them by a foreign power. They do not need to win any elections because they are already shaping the policies at the point of illegal guns. The elections for them is not the result of a belief in democratic principles which they oppose but it is a means to legitimizing their power grab for their foreign masters.

As the saying goes "Let there be pox on both of their houses". This charade will not end well. It never does. Lebanon can redeem itself only if it is to adopt a modern electoral system that is non sectarian and that is not subject to the control of its political mafia. Lebanon needs to have elections of citizens by citizens without any regard to their religious practices because our current system is rotten to the core.

Monday, June 8, 2009

The Lebanese Elections: Beginning of the End of Hezbollah Hegemony?

The Lebanese Elections: Beginning of the End of Hezbollah Hegemony?
The official results for the recent Lebanese parliamentary elections have not been announced yet. They are expected to be made public in the next 12- 18 hours. If the unofficial results, widely reported by all parties, are to hold then it is time to lose the spin and look for the real message of this electoral campaign. We could be about to experience a sea change in the governmental structure of Lebanon that will have wide ranging impact all throughout the region.

It is clear that the coalition of March 14 has prevailed. They have maintained their majority by winning, in conjunction with their allies, 71 of the 128 parliamentary seats. The victory is much bigger than what the numbers of seats reflects since these results were accomplished against the obstacles and machinations of Hezbollah, its allies in Lebanon and beyond. The Syrian President , Bashar Assad, and his Iranian counterpart, Ahmadinajad , must be quite displeased about the performance of their Lebanese agents especially that of General Aoun. This victory is so much more impressive in light of the fact that March 14 has managed to maintain its majority under two different electoral setups, 2005 and 2009. It did not seem to make much of a difference which elections system is used, March 14 just wins. The rationale for why that is so is simple and straight forward; March 14 is seen to stand for hope, decency, potential prosperity, individual liberty and above all else a firm belief in the sovereignty and independence of the Lebanese state. The opposition, on the other hand, acted as if the Lebanese state is an afterthought, what matters to them were the national interests of Iranian clergy, Syrian Bath and to keep and even increase the size and sophistication of their illegal militia. This militia was used to intimidate the established legal government of Lebanon and was used to drag the country into a war it could ill afford. Furthermore, this military wing is totally financed by foreign powers and established within the country a state within a state including its own unauthorized telecommunication network.

Although Hezbollah had no use or respect for the Lebanese authorities yet it asked the loyal Lebanese citizens to support its acts of weakening and dismantling whatever authority the state has. Ironically they expected the Lebanese people to participate in that destructive and undemocratic game. The rhetoric of their allies did not help either. Michel Aoun, one of Hezbollah's main Christian allies, spent months railing against the old electoral system that he claimed robbed many from choosing their own candidates through gerrymandering electoral districts when in fact he lost in the districts that he helped create and won essentially in the districts that were gerrymandered.

The elections are over and it is time for the newly elected politicians to roll up their sleeves and form a cabinet based on democratic principles. They should waste no time in reforming the election system by adopting a non sectarian system of single districts. That is the only way to give the communities a chance to elect their own representatives and to diminish the stranglehold of the established "feudal" like power of the traditional regional leaders. It would also be very helpful to require the candidate to reside in the district in which she plans to stand for election.

Victory has its own rewards and so March 14 must insist that the majority party should govern and to give a veto power to the opposition is tantamount to desecrating the results of the elections.

Tuesday, June 9, 2009

The Privileged and The Disenfranchised

Democracy is much more than the right to vote. It is about accepting the other, personal freedom, liberty, social justice and equality. The franchise is a seminal part of giving individuals the right to vote in a peaceful and unintimidating atmosphere. But the right to vote becomes diminished when the system is designed to resemble a George Orwell hierarchy where all people are equal but some are more equal than others. Whenever that is the case then what many like to call democracy turns out to be a hoax upon closer examination?

There is lots of truth to the saying that we see the world from where we happen to be standing. We are after all, a product of our history and the sum total of our experiences but yet if we endeavour to be objective them empiricism offers us a reliable tool to overcome our biases and shed away the baggage that we had accumulated over the decades.

So how democratic was the Lebanese election that was held less than 48 hours ago. I am afraid that if we are to use the metric of equal votes then the show of democracy that many are still celebrating is a failure. Let me explain: The official lists of eligible registered voters in Lebanon reflected a total of 3,257,107 potential voters and the race between the various candidates was over 128 parliamentary seats. A simple calculation would easily show that in a state of bliss then each parliamentary seat should belong to a district of 25,446 votes. No country can have such an equitable allocation of seats per voters and so if we are to accept a deviation of = or – 15 % then an acceptable range of registered voters per parliamentary seat becomes 21,630-29263. On that basis then every district that has more registered voters than the upper limit is one whose residents are underrepresented and disenfranchised. The districts whereby the ratio of registered voters per parliamentary seat is under the lower limit of the acceptable range is a privileged district whose residents are overrepresented.

A review of the registered voters and the allotted parliamentary seats in each of the 26 districts reveals an unhealthy pattern. The following table represents the most under represented districts in Lebanon:

Registered Voters

Electoral District	Registered Voters Per seat
Bint Jbeil	41,132
Nabatieh	40,637
Soor	38,265
Meina/Doneieh	32,451
Akar	31,934
Zahrani	30,998

Figure1: Most Under Represented

Electoral District	Registered Voters per Seat
Kesrwan	17,845
Jazzine	18,063
Beirut1	18,552
Koura	19,265
W. Beka'a/Rashia	20,415
Maten	21,343

Figure2: Most Over Represented

What is interesting is that all the other districts fall within the acceptable range with Beirut 2, Beirut 3, Ba'abda and Ba'alback at or very close to the mean of 25,446 registered voters per available parliamentary seat.

So what is to be learned from this simple statistical analysis besides the need to redraw the districts and their respective seat allocations? It is easy and obvious to note that the top three under represented districts are in the south and are predominantly Shia while the most three privileged districts electorally are more diverse geographically but are predominantly Christian. The above observation is accurate but it does not tell the whole story. It appears that disenfranchisement has also a strong element of class besides religious confessionalism. It is easier to neglect the poor and considerably more difficult to dismiss the powerful. But the most interesting observation of all is the fact that the potential political benefit from over representation was dissipated since the two major political groups appear to have split these privileged districts. Even the potential political losses due to underrepresentation were significant but not overwhelming. An argument can be made to suggest that a more just allocation of seats could have netted the opposition another 3-5 seats but in a perfect world there would be no place for an illegal paramilitary authoritarian and undemocratic party would there be?

Thursday, June 11, 2009

But Can They Govern?

Now that the elections are over and the political coalition of March 14 managed to hold its ground, the hard work is about to begin.

It is important for the newly elected members of parliament to remember what their role is in this democratic game. Contrary to what many of them seem to think, they have not been elected in order to cash in their huge paychecks from a government that is practically bust and that survives only by passing the hat at the sight of a dollar. They have not been elected to rubber stamp all the decisions made by their tribal chiefs and they have not been elected to flaunt the law and travel in motorcades surrounded by armed hoodlums even on their way to lunch. In this game they are supposed to serve one purpose only; be an honest hard working representative of the electorate, their concerns and aspirations. They are expected to be accessible, transparent and humble but above all else they have to be principled.

Members of parliament are elected to serve the public, to listen to the people's concerns and to live up to the promises that were made during the campaign. MPs are to be trustworthy and whenever they betray the trust entrusted to them then they should not be reelected. Unfortunately many of them do and when that happens it is not the MP that is at fault but it is the citizen who is equally responsible for the efficient and democratic performance of government. No government can be held accountable unless the public at large is willing and able to judge the performance of that government.
The next phase in the political drama that is unfolding in Lebanon is for the majority to step forward, form a government and submit legislation that is geared to restore to the central government its authority, to promote fair and balanced economic development, to tackle the budget deficit, enact welfare programs geared to spread social justice, to take strong measures that would protect whatever is left of our natural endowment and to make renewable clean energy a top priority.

March 14 is expected by most analysts to form the next cabinet, possibly under the leadership of Sa'ad Hariri. Although that was a partial goal of the elections the greater expectation is to have them govern effectively with fairness and justice. But can they govern? The short answer to the question is a strongly qualified maybe. The major two pillars of March 14, Walid Jumblatt and Sa'ad Hariri have already hinted clearly about their intentions to accept challenges to the authority of government. If that comes to pass and March 14 proceeds to sweep under the carpet the issue of illegitimacy of the arms of Hezbollah then March14 would have to be considered a total failure. Those who are willing to appease warlords and go back on promises that were made during the campaign do not deserve to rule or to be entrusted. Walid Jumblatt seems to have forgotten his own pronouncements about the incompatibility of a Hezbollah and a free Lebanese state while Sa'ad Hariri is willing to call appeasement a compromise.

What Lebanon needs over the next few weeks is a concerted effort by those that value the basic principles of democracy and decency not to allow the political leadership of March 14 to forget its promises and commitments. But can they govern? The answer has to be a resounding no if they are willing to cut a deal with the largest war lord in the Middle East whose only legitimacy and that of his group is the ownership of the most sophisticated and illegal arms cache and who have no respect for the rule of law.

Wednesday, June 24, 2009

How to lose (elections) through winning and win (elections) through losing

"If we are victorious in one more battle ... we shall be utterly ruined." These words are attributed to King Pyrrhus after he won his battle with the Romans in 279 BC. I imagine that this is the origin of the expression "to win the battle and lose the war". But we do not need to be students of history in order to understand what is meant by that concept; all what one needs is to have observed the recent parliamentary elections in Lebanon.

The June 7th elections were won by the March 14 coalition and its allies while the opposition was dealt a few setbacks in a number of districts. The final tally was 71 parliamentary seats for the March14 coalition and 57 for the opposition, Hezbollah and its allies. In any other country, all over the world, the winners would have proceeded to form the government, elect a speaker of the house and take steps to start implementing elements of their electoral campaign. But not in Lebanon, that would be too simple.

One of the most important figures of the opposition and one of the most strident voices that fought tooth and nail to prevent the Lebanese Parliament from meeting to perform its constitutional function is about to be regaled for the fifth term in a row as the speaker of the house that is under the control of the political parties that he has devoted his life in opposing and obstructing. Sa'ad Hariri has the temerity to endorse the election of the major representative of the opposition to the second highest office in the land. I wonder whether Mr. Hariri or Mr. Jumblatt for that matter, would have had the courage to share that desire with the voters during the campaign.

But that is not the end of the story or should I say the tragedy. Another luminary of the opposition, Michel Aoun, was an active participant in the illegal occupation of downtown Beirut for over a year and a strong supporter of the "novel" idea that the opposition needs to be represented in the cabinet and to give its representatives the right to veto any and all measures that are not to their liking. Mr. Aoun, the megalomaniac that has his party's OTV station running promos comparing him to Gandhi, MLK, Kennedy, Einstein and mother Teresa to name a few , is back again with another one of his ridiculous demands. This time around he is not asking for a veto but for a cabinet whose composition reflects the exact proportional composition of the parliament. This demand has not been approved yet by the so called majority but if recent history is a prologue then proportional representation will be offered in the same way that the right of veto was agreed to.

And the beat goes on. Hezbollah under the leadership of its war lord Nasrallah insists that its militia is above the law, its area of influence is outside the reach of the legitimate government, its allegiance is to an Iranian Ayatollah and that the concept of an absolute guardianship by the faqih is a religious one. Yet

Mr. Jumblatt and Mr. Hariri are more than willing to establish power sharing with Hezbollah, the antithesis of Lebanese statehood, independence and sovereignty.

So the only legitimate question is why did we all vote and what did we vote for? It is all a crock where the winners of the elections are losers and the losers of the elections are winners. Go figure.

Sunday, July 19, 2009

Sadly, Sa'ad Hariri Is Not The Answer.

Lebanon has failed ever since its modern creation, over sixty years ago, to act as an independent sovereign nation. And unfortunately that is not about to change. A nation state is an artificial creation, a social, and political and an economic contract between inhabitants of an area of land based on a strong element of a common destiny and strong cultural ties. If the people in question fail to see citizenship as the single most important trait in defining who they are then they would have lost all legitimate claims to nationhood or a state of their own. In that case dissolving the state would be far more preferable than the charade and the pretense that a country exists when in reality it is a collection of irresponsible; immature and selfish tribal lords who have inherited their position of power.

Lebanon is at that proverbial fork in the road where it will either take positive meaningful steps towards acting as an independent responsible democracy that belongs to all its citizens or it will continue its inevitable slide into marginalization, into the abyss of failed states. This is why the task of the designated Prime Minister, Sa'ad Hariri is so crucial. Mr. Hariri has not shown an ability to lead by motivating his fellow Lebanese to renounce the petty concerns that divide them in favour of adopting a singular concern, a Lebanese identity. His efforts to form a cabinet have dragged for over a month during which he has consulted with the Saudi Arabian government, the Egyptian government, the Iranian government, indirectly the Syrian government, the Western governments and many of the leaders of the Lebanese opposition with no tangible results to show for all of these efforts. This strategy of appeasement is a clear demonstration of the lack of vision and determination by Mr. Hariri to stand up for the interests of the country. The primary task that is facing Mr. Hariri is the articulation of a Lebanese identity that is capable of acting on its own and that looks at the Lebanese not as a mixture of different religious sects who happen to co- habitat in Lebanon but as Lebanese citizens who happen to have different religious beliefs. Mr. Hariri must act by forming a cabinet composed of those who are best suited to perform the assigned task no matter who they chose to pray to and irrespective of their gender or sexual orientation. The only qualification to join the cabinet is a strong belief in the nation and the ability to perform the assigned task better and more efficiently than anyone else. Lebanese cabinet ministers must be above all believers in the sovereignty, independence of Lebanon and the equal human rights for all their fellow Lebanese. The prime minister designate must form a Lebanese government that would not compromise with the opposition leaders. Mr. Hariri has to renounce openly and strongly all manifestations of sectarianism in the Lebanese body politic, transform the Al Mustaqbal into a genuinely diverse Lebanese political party and announce his willingness to fight for the implementation of policies that promote social justice, create job opportunities and protect the environment. Sadly there are no indications that Sa'ad Hariri is seriously considering any of the above. His reticence to do the right thing only makes the Lebanese project less sound.

Sunday, July 26, 2009

Cabinet Formation in Parliamentary Democracies.

Parliamentary democracies, as a general rule, assign legislative power to an elected parliament and assign executive power to the Prime Minister. Usually a role is also given to the president that is essentially ceremonial although in some cases the president is given a consultative role and some executive powers. The Lebanese constitution is no different. It follows the above formula to a great extent. Articles 16 and 17 of the Constitution speak to this very clearly:

Article 16 Legislative power is vested in a single body, the Chamber of Deputies.

Article 17 Executive power is entrusted to the Council of Ministers to be exercised it in accordance with the conditions laid down in this constitution.

As for the presidential powers, they are discussed in great detail in Article 53. The powers range from accrediting ambassadors, presiding over official functions, granting pardons to the right to preside over cabinet meetings without casting a vote.

Then obviously there is the judicial arm which is to ascertain that the laws of the land are being applied in accordance to the constitution.

This system of separate Legislative, Executive and Judicial functions has evolved primarily to make sure that the majority do not ride rough shod over the minority and to assure all citizens of equal protection under the law. The right to dissent without the fear of unjust retaliation by the ruling party is an elemental right for a vigorous and robust democracy.

The above schema forms the basis of democratic governments whether they are the mature parliamentary system of the United Kingdom, the German Federation, the state of India or the Russian Federation just to name a few. This nearly universal system of parliamentary democracy seems to work to the satisfaction of most but for one reason or another it is not deemed to be good enough to the Lebanese who I might add have willingly adopted the constitution mentioned above. For the past three years the opposition has waged a well determined campaign that has effectively paralyzed the country to demand participation in the cabinet and to be given the right of veto. Unfortunately the majority gave in, a "national unity" government was formed and new parliamentary elections held. The opposition failed to gain a majority of the seats in the Chamber of Deputies but yet has been waging another determined campaign with the equally absurd interpretation that the cabinet must be composed of all parliamentary groups each according to its share of the parliamentary seats. The previous cabinet, where all factions were represented, turned out to be a disaster as many have predicted. It was simply a tower of Babel. The new demands are equally absurd. A government that represents everyone is a government without any accountability. Which political group is to get credit for effective and popular policies and who is to carry the blame for the failure to act during emergencies or in face of social, political, economic and military challenges? If no one party is to be held responsible for either the success or the failure then why bother and hold elections.

Mr. Sa'ad Hariri, the Prime Minister designate, has not formed the cabinet yet, but he has given every indication that he intends to form a government that has a large proportion of the opposition in it. That will be a tragic mistake not for rigid ideological reasons but for simple logical ones. A member of a government cannot be expected to be an advocate for a position and yet at the same time be opposed to it. If the opposition is to be integrated into the cabinet then that means that there is essentially no opposition and that does not a healthy government makes. Dissent promotes growth.

It is unfortunate that Mr. Hariri is getting all sorts of advice to proceed and form such a mish mash of a cabinet that will not be able to function and whose very essence would be undemocratic and illogical. I wonder why is it that Mr. Sarkozi does not follow his own advice to Sa'ad Hariri by forming a French cabinet that includes all factions represented in the French parliament. And Mr. Hariri must never forget that the advice or pressure that he is under from either Saudi Arabia or Egypt is from countries that might have the best intentions for the Lebanese state but unfortunately this advice does not come from democratic practitioners and so how can they teach that which they do not understand. Mr. Hariri needs to understand that the electorate voted so that the winning coalition can implement its platform, it did not vote to see the winners equivocate and go back on their promises. Mr. Hariri has to realize that a victory margin of 55% vs. 45% is a respectable margin by any standard and that he should not blow this margin away through indecisiveness and appeasement.

And finally let me be very clear about this, Sa'ad Hariri is not to blame for this. The fault lies squarely on our shoulders, the Lebanese citizens. Our whole political culture is at fault. A Lebanese daily ran a great caricature recently which said that the Lebanese political leaders have failed to teach the citizens anything about accountability. That political cartoon would have been so insightful had it been exactly in the reverse. Governments and politicians are a reflection of the values, sophistication and mores of the populace.

Tuesday, August 4, 2009

The Lebanese Political System: A Dream World

In a make believe world reality is not important. Actually it is shunted in order to give reign to phantasies and dreams. When we live in a dream world then we can avoid making the hard choices and the messy solutions because in a pretend world all is good and we are in control. All of that is good and well, maybe as an occasional escape mechanism from the harsh realities of the world, but the dream world must not be allowed to become a substitute for reality. If it does then the pretender is locked up in a psychiatric institution in an effort to put an end to the make believe.

Lebanon as a state has been, ever since its creation, living in a state of denial. If you listen to the Lebanese politicians opine about democracy, freedom, individual liberty, sovereignty, human rights and economic development you would be perfectly justified in thinking that the state of Lebanon is as close to an idyllic place as any nation can get. But then reality intrudes and the listener decides to investigate the rhetoric emanating from the mouths of those whose personal ego, wealth and worldly power depend on perpetuating the myth that they speak off. Slave owners, lords of the manor and imperial rulers would not want their subjects to learn the real meaning of freedom, dignity or personal rights. Why should they? A simple investigation would immediately reveal that the only principle that guides the actions of the Lebanese politicians is that of personal power and wealth. They have no interest in promulgating ideas that benefit the common good. Another fact that becomes very clear is the total abdication of the media, in all its forms, to perform its sacred duty to inform the public and to investigate the corruption and cronyism. Why should they when each is in effect a mouth piece for one war lord or another. Our investigation would also show that there is no such thing as the rule of law. Some, the political leaders and their henchmen, are above the law. They are the privileged and the laws are passed in order to keep us, the commoners, in servitude. This charade permeates all aspects of political life. And the make belief world becomes the instrument of oppression. It is used to indoctrinate the gullible; the public; that right is wrong, oppression is freedom, misery is prosperity, total allegiance to foreign powers is sovereignty and that the constitution matters.

The President of the Lebanese republic performs essentially ceremonial functions, and that is as it should be in a Parliamentary democracy, but all the actors and especially the Christian Maronites, still carry on as if the country has a strong Presidential democracy system. Things get even worse than this, the current president, Michel Suleiman, had to take the regular oath when he was elected "to help protect the constitution". But what were his prescriptions to solve the inability of the PM designate to form a government? You guessed it; he is leading the charge to amend the constitution as if democracy is a game in a sandbox where one can pretend to be whatever one wishes. Think about this, the person who was elected to protect and enforce the constitution has no respect for the document. But then why should he when he was clearly ineligible to seek the office in the first place. Laws have never stopped the Lords of the Manor from ruling the way they wish over their domain and laws will not be allowed to crimp the style of the feudal political elites of Lebanon, they will go on talking from both sides of their mouth in order to maintain the myth that reality corresponds to the untruths that they are always spreading.. Our only solace in all of this is that no dream world lasts forever. Reality always wins in the end.

Monday, August 24, 2009

Lebanese Political Leadership and Nepotism

Nepotism is alive and well in many countries all over the world. But it is so well entrenched in the Arab world and in Lebanon that it renders the terms democratic and elections a mockery. The Syrian Arab Republic was ruled by Hafez Assad for thirty years; 1971-2000; and when he died his ophthalmologist son was asked to come back from London where he had been living to inherit the Syrian dictatorship. Most of the mock elections held in Syria were won by an Assad who usually received 99.9% of the vote. Mohammad Hosni Mubarak has been the president of the Arab Republic of Egypt since the assassination of Anwar Sadat in 1981 and he is already making preparations for his son to take over. Libya has had Muammar Qaddafi as a president for over forty years; since a coup in 1969; and he is also making preparation for his son Saif to take over. As for Saudi Arabia, Jordan, Morocco and the Gulf states they are more honest about family rule since each practices one form or another of the monarchical system.

Lebanon, the pretend state, on the other hand likes to think of itself as a modern democratic republic when in fact it is ruled and controlled by traditional modern day feudal lords whose power is rarely challenged or even questioned and whose sphere of influence is viewed as being rather saintly. Rafic Hariri is assassinated and his Premiership passes automatically to his son Sa'ad who has not lived in the country for a long time and whose knowledge of its policies and social formation is practically nil. As if that is not enough Sa'ad is seriously thinking about bringing into the Government another one or two

Hariri neophytes. The same story repeats itself ad infinitum. Pierre Gemayel who started the Phalange party modeled around Generalissimo Franco's fascist brown shirts passed the leadership of the party, just like any other family heirloom, to his sons who have in turn passed it along to their sons. It is doubtful that either Sami or Nadim Gemayel has any qualifications besides the family name. (Rumours have it that one of these young Gemayels will be given a Ministry to run in the new cabinet) The same pattern repeats itself with the Frangieh clan where the leadership has passed from father to son to grandson. And then there is Walid Jumblatt who not only inherited the leadership of the Druze but also the mantle to the Progressive Socialist Party. Note the irony. A rich feudal lord inherits, based on kinship only, the leadership of a clan and the Progressive Socialist Party that obviously can neither be socialist nor progressive. It's funny how all of these political feudal lords always have next of kin that are ready to assume their role in order to continue the charade that we call democracy.

The names mentioned above might be the most powerful and the most egregious but they are by no means the only unquestioned political dynasties in Lebanon. There are the Arslans, the Salaams, the Beydouns, the Karamis and the new comers of the Aouns, possibly the Beris and Lahouds among others. Why all of this nepotism and undemocratic practices? Is there a special virus in the water of the region or in the air that we inhale?

The current impasse in forming a cabinet is very much related to nepotism. No major party in Lebanon takes a stand dictated by ideas. It is always about personal power and spheres of influence. It is never about Lebanon the state but about the preservation of privilege and the ability to abuse power. This is no fertile ground for democracy; these are the conditions to ensure that any longing for true responsible representation is suffocated at birth. Yet what our feudal lords and abusers do not realize is that one can check freedom only for so long. Eventually the people will rise and the yoke of exploitation will be broken.

Sunday, September 6, 2009

Has The Lebanese Experiment Failed?

It is practically never the case that societies, institutions, business groups or nations are so aware of what is right, efficient and just that they utilize their resources and opportunities as to always operate at the theoretically optimum combination of the alternatives facing them. To ask for that is to ask for a dream world and a theoretical state of bliss. We all know that this is never the case. Yet it is our duty to adopt policies and champion ideologies that would move us as close as possible to that ideal path. Those who neglect to promote institutions and general governance that would promote the common good would end up in the garbage bin of history no matter how determined their misguided leaders are. Where are the colonial powers, the Nazi and Fascist regimes, the Soviet inspired statist systems and many of the personal dictatorships that ruled through discrimination, exploitation and fear mongering? The answer is rather clear, the world that we live in is not perfect but it will not tolerate for long those that are not willing to learn, adapt, admit their mistakes and attempt to correct the past failures; those that insist on being stuck in an unjust, undemocratic and unresponsive past will not survive. They will wither away.

Unfortunately Lebanon has not absorbed the above lesson from history. The Lebanese politicians, on both sides of the aisle, see no problem in perpetuating their petty differences and carrying on as if Lebanon is a modern democracy only because they claim it to be. The Lebanese experiment has been an utter and total failure by any metric. The head of the state, the President of the Republic, is unconstitutional but both sides pretend that they have not breached the law in electing a president that the constitution clearly forbids from holding that office. Then there is the Orwellian game of calling things by what they are not. The Progressive Socialist Party is neither progressive nor socialist. It is in reality a gathering headed by a feudal lord whose ideas about personal freedom and liberty are best described as being backward. Then we must not forget that the majority bloc is headed by a thirty something whose political experience and ability to lead are totally based on the strength of his bank account.

The opposition is not any better. In a sense it is far worse because its major strength comes from Hezbollah who has yet to pay an unconditional allegiance to the state. The other major group in the opposition is lead by a delusional megalomaniac who wants to be "king"/"president". Each of the other minor political parties in the opposition represent at least as much of a feudalistic system as that of the PSP. Then of course there are the Christian parties that are in essence disguised supremacists run by traditional feudal lords. What a deadly combination to lead a country?

It should be clear that no country whose political structure is as ill-conceived, as backward and as out of touch with modern times as the above is to be expected to rule effectively or even to survive. Well the charade has been going on for over sixty years with occasional violent eruptions interrupted by periods of aimless drifting and personal squabbles. This condition cannot be tolerated for much longer. The Lebanese politicians must show that they are mature enough to govern otherwise the privilege would be withdrawn with catastrophic results for all of them. But is the above merely a wish or is there any chance of transforming this group of political dinosaurs into responsive and democratic political leaders?

Lebanon can be saved provided that the President admits openly that he was elected unconstitutionally, provided that the feudal lords give up their inherited power, provided that the leader of the majority has the courage and determination to act as a majority leader, provided that the opposition will decide to fulfill its hugely constructive role of being in the opposition instead of demanding to be in the government and in the opposition simultaneously. But most important of all the Lebanese citizen has to show clearly that she cares about the quality of governance and that she has had enough of all these shenanigans.

Realistically, can any of the above happen, say within a few months or even a few years? If the answer is in the negative then it is time to come to grips with the sad reality that Lebanon stands for a geographical area but does not represent a state, not a modern or democratic one.

Monday, September 7, 2009

Sophistry and Demagogy

Sa'ad Hariri, the designate premier, deserves credit for having finally, after 11 weeks, submitted a proposed Lebanese cabinet along the lines of 15-10-5. Fifteen members from the majority coalition of March14, 10 members from the opposition coalition led by Hezbollah and 5 cabinet portfolios for the president of the republic. The credit is however to be tempered by some criticism for not having taken this decisive step earlier and for encouraging the opposition to proceed in its meaningless and destructive obstructionism. They have allowed and encouraged to make one impossible and illogical demand after the next four years.

There is only one word to explain clearly and objectively the tactics of the opposition, it is simply demagoguery. That is best explained as a political argument that is constructed on half truths, straw men and logical fallacies. Actually H. L. Mencken, the American author might have said it best when he explained that "a demagogue is one who preaches doctrines that he knows to be untrue to (men) he knows to be idiots". Their whole argument for presenting formidable nonsensical barriers to prevent the formation of a cabinet rests on such flimsy arguments that a government of one colour would be disastrous to the country. What they conveniently neglect to point to is that practically all governments all over the world are cabinets of one colour and furthermore that the ruling coalition's in many cases does not have much more than a 51-52%% majority. Could it be that in this case Lebanon is different since they (the opposition) are motivated only by a personal power grab? The man who would be king has no clue what democracy is and what is the meaning of checks and balances. Another example of pure demagogy is the claim that if the opposition is not given the right to dictate the terms for their invitation to join the cabinet then the Christians will be misrepresented. Sectarianism is the refuge of scoundrels, to borrow a phrase. It is as if one is arguing that say a British Labour Cabinet is an act of discrimination against the Conservatives and what is even worse it is a hidden argument to perpetuate sectarianism, the bane of all what is wrong in the Lebanese political system. To put the demands of the opposition in a simple straight forward analogy, their insupportable obstacles are not any different than when you invite a person to dinner and give that person a say about the menu and the time of service but you are told in no uncertain terms that you will not be allowed to hold your planned dinner without their attendance and that they will agree to accept the invitation only if you fire your staff and hire theirs. What logic, what chutzpah what demagoguery!!

As this column has argued often, the Lebanese experiment is practically at the point of no return, a point of disintegration. It is the duty and the obligation of all those of good will to attempt to save the Lebanese entity and that starts with good governance that will not seek short term solutions by papering over seminal and major fault lines. Mr. Hariri has taken the first minor step in that direction.

He must become more forceful in speaking directly to the Lebanese people and in asking the opposition to live up to their historical responsibility. Mr. Hariri has to take a stand for what is right, a stand for the integrity of the republic. He must form a cabinet that will govern effectively, take decisions that are purely in the Lebanese national interest, eliminate political sectarianism and promote a Lebanese identity that measures the worth of a person not by the method of prayer but by their knowledge of a particular area and the strength of their allegiance to law and order Everything else is demagoguery and will hasten going over the abyss.

Saturday, September 12, 2009

So What Is To Follow a Crisis?

A crisis, in any field, is not necessarily an event to be feared. In a sense such a development ought to be welcomed. I say that because I am reminded of the great idiom: "Necessity is the mother of invention". Can you imagine a group of engineers trying to create a new machine that is designed to perform a task that either does not exist or even a task that current technology is easily capable of supplying for centuries? I cannot. No one will fund such research and very few would be interested in "wasting" precious resources on a problem that requires no solution. That would be similar to inventing a drug first and then go shopping for a disease that it can cure. The same logic is also applicable to the social, political, economic and environmental problems. We often need a crisis and a major one for that matter, in order to question and reevaluate the current conditions that have given birth to the present sad state of affairs.

It was only when the challenge of climate change became so large and so challenging that major commitments to find meaningful solutions to our total dependence on fossil fuels has taken off. In the same token, the need to consider adopting new global financial regulations and reform in the financial sector picked up support only after the "near death" experience of casino capitalism. And last but not least, it was the very poorly underperforming Chinese economy that led Ding Xiaoping to start his reforms that have affected the performance of the whole world economy.

So if a crisis in any field or any country could act as a mechanism to husband resources and seek a meaningful solution to the problem at hand should we then welcome the current political crisis in Lebanon? Yes and no. Yes the current crisis could, in theory, force the two antagonists to come together and find an accommodation that would benefit everyone. That would be the traditional application of the idea that whenever two points of view in any field are at odd with each other eventually the two opposing forces will resolve their differences by creating a new synthesis. That is how history unfolds. This ability to keep moving forward is almost an ironclad guarantee that society will eventually renounce feudalism, discrimination, authoritarian rule and move forward towards the ultimate goal of social harmony and justice for all. To me at least, this is the vision of a society that is grounded in the Cosmopolitan ideas of the Greek Cynics and Roman Stoics; the oneness of humanity.

The above is an ideal utopian vision, one that could ultimately take place. It is often described as the "end of history". But aren't we all dead in the long run? as Maynard Keynes said once. Of course we are and that is why it is the moral obligation of each Lebanese citizen to act responsibly, to act as a catalyst that could force the current political leadership to live up to its historical responsibility and resolve the current crisis not by going back to "business as usual" but by adopting a major and radical reform that

65

will serve the welfare of the state for a longtime to come. It should be clear that such reforms must meet some minimum standards chief among them is the total abolishing of political sectarianism, the promotion of responsible citizenship and a society run by the rule of law a society where no one needs fear his/her future because the government will adopt clear working rules that will establish clearly a system of checks and balances, one that considers the welfare of all Lebanese equally irrespective of their religion , place of birth, gender or sexual orientation. This appears as a tall order but in reality it is not if we, the citizens truly want the change. Let us not forget that we are the country and the politicians are only our agents, they work for us and thus we can dismiss them whenever we choose. Let us tell them that we need a Lebanese solution and we need it now. Are we up to the task?

Sunday, September 27, 2009

Sectarianism Revisited.

It is one thing to set up a goal and adopt a commensurate plan that is designed to achieve the objective spelled out in the plan but it is a completely different thing when the aim of the plan can never be satisfied through the chosen policies. One cannot pretend to be in favour of public transportation and yet offer major subsidies and giveaways only to those who are willing to purchase private personal vehicles. But this is exactly the type of misguided policies that the opposition forces in Lebanon have been advocating. In a perfect world, a random sample of a population; say a bag of green, red and blue marbles; will have the same proportional composition as the population itself. That, however, is never the case in the real world and especially when one colour gets a 25% advantage in the likely hood of its selection. The Christians in Lebanon are at best 40% of the population but are guaranteed 50% of the seats in the Chamber of Deputies and by the same logic demand half of the cabinet ministries. That is a behavior that cannot be condoned in a society of law and order, a society based on equality and justice. Nonetheless if we are to begrudgingly overlook this fatal allocative mechanism then we need to ask the question of what are the attributes that create a personal identity. Why are we to choose a sample that is reflective of religious affiliation and not say gender or even economic station?

One more time, even if we are to overlook this equally fatal error, we confront a more flagrant one. The resulting political parties that compete for votes are essentially sectarian and thus, win or lose; each of them will be able to claim the right to be represented in the cabinet otherwise the sect that they belong to will be able to cry foul. Win or lose representation for each party is assured under this scheme. But if identity is defined in purely religious terms, as is unfortunately the case, then who is to decide whether a March 14 Sunni is more authentic than an Amal Sunni or what is more logical that an Orange Christian is more authentic than a Kataeb or even a Christian woman who does not belong to any of the political parties.

A good example of the strange logic that is being applied to erect barriers and prevent formation of the cabinet is best captured by Mr. Basils' pronouncements on Sept 26, 2009 when he declared that the FPM "will not accept except ministries and portfolios that reflect the will of the Christians and their size within the state and its institutions". This is purely discriminatory logic that claims that only the losing bloc can possibly represent a group that happens to be well represented, in this case, by the winning coalition. Get real FPM, you might be the largest "Christian" group in the parliament but this does not give you any special privileges. Stop the denial and accept that you belong to the minority. Work hard, be productive and maybe the electorate will reward you next time around. You simply cannot have it both ways. But what is even more egregious is the statement of MP Nawaf Moussawey who called for "a unified Christian representation on the basis of the parliamentary elections whereby each party is allocated portfolios and ministries proportional to the votes and seats it has won in the elections." How is it under this logic possible to be and not be simultaneously? Mr. Moussawey wants the FPM to be represented when their coalition loses and yet to be represented when they win. Does ideology and principle count for anything, or is it anything goes as long as we participate in power? My, is that strange logic or what?

There is a way out of all of this. An independent sovereign state must work for the good of all its people, males and females, dark skinned and light skinned, old and young, rich and poor, Christians, Moslems or atheists. The only criteria that matters is that they should believe in the Lebanese project .The only way to do that is to create a secular society where everyone is free to worship whoever they want whenever they will since this is no one's business except their own.

Wednesday, September 30, 2009

Internal Contradictions in the Lebanese Political Structure

Does secularism guarantee that its practitioners are democratic? The answer is obviously in the negative since the world is full of secular systems that are not democratic, Syria is a good example of a government that keeps trumpeting its secularism but yet it is arguably the most authoritarian regime in the Arab world. Iraq's Saddam, especially prior to the Gulf war of 1991 was also proud of its secularity but yet was a very cruel dictatorship. Turkey is another country in the region that is a secular state but one whose democratic practices does not always shine. I shall refrain from using Cuba, North Korea or any other Communist state as examples of secular non democratic states since they are neither secular nor democratic. But I want to submit to you the proposition that it would not be possible to be a vibrant democracy unless the political structure is secular.

Does that imply that Lebanon is doomed to continue living in its current state of never land unless it rejects its current system of political confessionalism? The answer to this question is not as simple as the previous one; it is both a yes and a no. Yes Lebanon has to adopt a fully operational secular political structure if its goal is to move as close as possible, in a world full of friction and static, to being a dynamic, functioning democracy. But obviously Lebanon can choose to retain its odd political confessionalism and yet attempt to become more of a functioning democracy for its citizens than it is currently. To improve on the current state of affairs should not prove to be very difficult since the nation is already on life support.

If Lebanon is to settle for the second best option of the above two it would still need to transform radically the structure of its political parties. The current party system in Lebanon is at odds with the clause in its constitution that demands that its cabinets be all inclusive. That clause is generally understood to imply that the composition of Lebanese cabinets should replicate the religious affiliations of the Lebanese population. Normally that should not pose a major problem. Good democratic governments usually form cabinets that are reflective of whatever criteria that the constitution seems to value provided that the political parties are truly national and diverse. The political party system, as it currently stands in Lebanon, cannot deliver on this promise and never would unless it is radically changed.

A simple example should illustrate the point. Assume that the electorate of a country is made up of 50% males and 50% females. Furthermore let us pretend that the constitution demands the formation of a cabinet that reflects the gender composition of its populace and let us assume that this Idealstan has only two political parties. So what is the problem you ask? If Idealstan is similar to Lebanon then one party will be for females and the other party for males. In that case no party will be able to form the cabinet on its own. It has to give 50% of the cabinet portfolios to the opposition that had already lost the national vote. The obvious question at this point is why have an election in this case? Each party is going to get half of the portfolios in any case and the PM is not the chief executive anyway. The executive power resides in the cabinet as a whole. This problem will not arise if each of the two political parties had waged a national campaign and had attracted a diverse, gender wise, following. As you can see this is the Lebanese problem. If the majority party is to form a government from its own cadres then it will not be representative of the population but if the constitutional edict is to be satisfied then the winners will have to form a cabinet in partnership with the losers and in this case elections become a charade. Short of putting in place a secular system in conjunction with diverse-membership then the Lebanese political needs ,as a minimum, to form national political parties if it's second best alternative is to succeed. I guess that one out of two ain't bad.

Saturday, October 3, 2009

Sovereignty

One of the most fundamental principles of modern states is their ability to "exercise supreme authority over (their borders)." This idea of sovereignty became ensconced as a principle of independent statehood by the treaty of Westphalia over 360 years ago. This right to statehood, sovereignty, independence and self determination has become, ever since the American and French revolutions, the most cherished right for a people to become their own masters, control their affairs and gain their independence and liberty. Liberation movements all over the world including those in Lebanon were ultimately successful in dismantling colonialism and creating sovereign states.

Unfortunately a few countries, Lebanon among them, have been satisfied with de jure sovereignty only. The real fundamental aspect of sovereignty for a people is to exercise its own authority without any interference from foreign powers, to combine de fact sovereignty to the legal one. When actual sovereignty is stripped away from a people then the legal one that they are left with becomes meaningless and worthless. That would be tantamount to abolishing slavery in theory alone but allowing it in practice to go on. Sadly, Lebanon is at such a state whereby even some of its most outspoken and respected political leaders admonish those who want to act as citizens of a sovereign state by proclaiming that "do you think that the Lebanese government is formed in Lebanon"? When Mr. Jumblatt made the above statement he was boasting of his ability to be pragmatic and to realize that Lebanese cabinets are not made in Lebanon but are shaped to satisfy the whims and demands of outsiders, he did not criticize the concept but implicitly accepted it, encouraged it and wanted all factions to act by this idea. Mr. Jumblatt has sure earned his new moniker Jump-a-lot. What is the purpose of having a sovereign state that is not going to exercise its sovereignty? It would be far more honorable in that case to relinquish also the de jure aspect of sovereignty and to put an end to the illusion of independence.

What is even worse is that Mr. Jumblatt is not the only Lebanese politician who does not believe in

Lebanese sovereignty. Hassan Nasrallah, the secretary general of Hezbollah made it very clear last year that his allegiance and that of his militia is the Supreme Leader Ayatollah Ali Khamenei of Iran. It is to be noted that Iran has established, funded, trained and continues to count on the loyalty of its illegal Lebanese militia that is nothing else but an extension of the Iranian Passadran. This issue of loyalty to Iran was on display last week when a top Iranian official stated clearly and unambiguously that Iran expects Hezbollah to respond to any Israeli acts against Iran. What that simply means is that Lebanon is not much besides a dispensable Iranian foreign policy tool that borders Israel. Yes, the Iranian empire has reached the Mediterranean and its troops dictate Lebanese policy. Not to be outdone by the opposition many in March 14 , the current majority coalition, are proud of their association with Saudi Arabia and keep on hinting that a Lebanese cabinet that does not enjoy the Saudi blessings will never see the light of day. One should not neglect to mention the other smaller players like Mr. Suleiman Frangieh, Talal Arslan, Syrian Social National Party and others who will never act on anything unless they get their Syrian instructions. As for the FPM they are the willing veil behind which the Hezbollah operates.

It is evident that Lebanon is a nation state whose sovereignty has been limited to the de jure sphere because the concept is of use to many factions both regional and global. Real sovereignty, the one that can benefit the actual stakeholders has been squandered, traded and abused by both major coalitions.

What is troubling is that these political leaders that have brought the country to the state of dissolution have not been recognized for what they are. The acts of trading sovereignty to outsiders borders on being an act of treachery. It is nothing short of being a Quisling. Are there any quislings in the current Lebanese political leadership or maybe more aptly are there any non quislings? You decide.

Friday, October 16, 2009

They Do Shoot Horses Don't They?

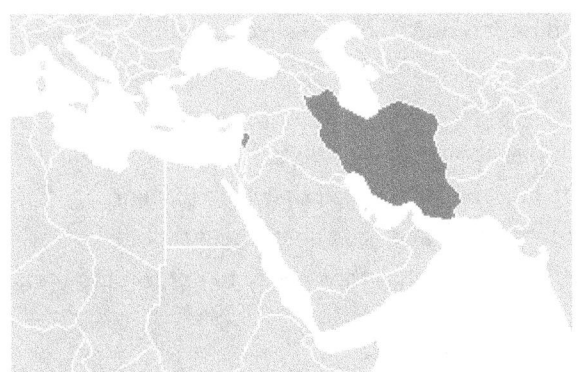

A solid case can be made that any creation, including that of a nation state, needs to fulfill the purpose for which it was originally created otherwise the process that enables it needs to be annulled. Furthermore let us presume, for the purposes of this discussion, that Westphalia is still relevant, which implies that the issue of sovereignty forms the basis of independence and self determination. Government became a part of the social contract only when it agreed to rule in such a way as to serve the governed since it derives its legitimacy and power from them. When the above general conditions prevail then government has a moral obligation to act on behalf of the governed and their interests. These interests are made public through various civil acts designed to demonstrate clearly their views on all important positions and policies. These views are usually best enshrined through the results of a vivid, lively and articulate electoral campaign.

As the above statement makes it abundantly clear the political leaders are in essence only agents that represent the will of the people who vote them into office in order to act on their behalf. These politicians must not misconstrue their political mandate to act on behalf of their electors as an absolute authority to abuse power and privilege and to take measures that will only help further their own selfish interests instead of the general welfare of the public. All acts and regulations are to be judged only in terms of the extent that they promulgate the national interest as expressed by the governed. Any failure by the rulers to promote the desires of the ruled would be grounds for dismissal and retirement.

The duties of the general public are not reserved to the occasional vote, as seminal as that might be. The general public has to take an active role in the operation of the system of governance through constant communication of its views regarding the daily developments and through active demonstrations of their approval or disapproval of the proposed legislation. Accountability rests with them and they have to safeguard their beliefs by exercising it unabashedly.

Once the current Lebanese impasse is viewed through this prism of responsible citizenship and accountable government then the magnitude and severity of the failure on both sides; governors and the governed; appear to be catastrophic. The minority bloc; just like all such groupings; are constantly taking positions to frustrate the efforts of the majority at exercising its mandate. When such tactics succeed then they are bound to help portray the opposition as more capable than the majority whose strategic moves are to be held responsible for permitting such obfuscations to make gains. When the majority fails to govern then it does so at its own peril and has no one to blame save its own incompetence to fulfill its obligations.

The biggest failure, however, is that of the electorate that has abdicated its role to hold the politicians accountable. Instead of showing its outrage whenever the elected officials fail to live up to their promises it maintains a stoical attitude that can be interpreted only as a tacit agreement that all power is to be given to the rulers who are in turn free to act any which way that they chose to perpetuate their personal power, the public good be damned.

Under such circumstances none of the parties is living up to its responsibilities and the best thing that can be said is that they all deserve each other. If this republic is to defy the odds and cling to life then the only path to salvation is for the public to take it to the streets and demand that their rights be respected. That should either cause the majority coalition to take decisive action by learning how to rule or should move out of the way. If all else fails then we would be left with only one choice, to pull the plug on a patient that refuses to take any steps towards wellness. When we act against the original mandate under which we were created then we have given up the right to exist. They do shoot horses don't they?

Sunday, November 15, 2009

Alice in Wonderland or is it Alice in Lebanon?

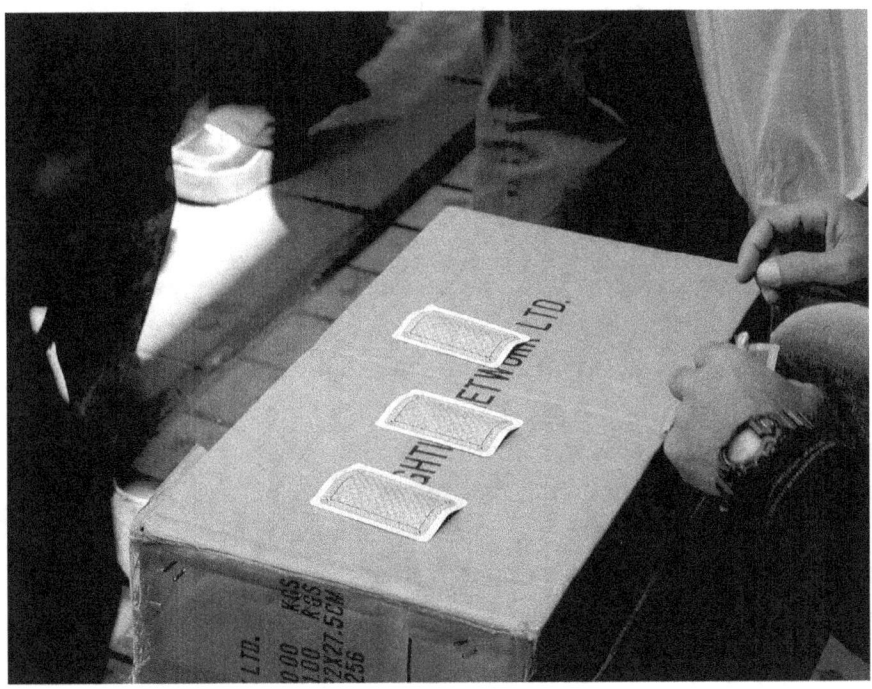

"Things are not as they appear" is as close of a description of the political landscape in Lebanon as a phrase can get. Lewis Carroll could not have had Lebanon in mind when he coined that all popular phrase could he? Nuh, but it sure appears as if he was describing in full details the current state of affairs in Lebanon.

It is not our aim today to revisit the well documented record that the Lebanese state has been a sham ever since it was declared. Lebanon has not been able to fulfill the promise of acting as an independent and sovereign state and has never been able to build the required institutions for statehood. Yet the charade goes on.

President Suleiman, the symbolic head of the ruling pyramid declared a few days ago that the birth of the national unity cabinet should serve as a model to what we can do. He couldn't have been serious could he? A process that should have been accomplished within a week was hardly completed in 150 days and only after all sorts of pressures both external and internal should serve as a model? Yes it is a model of indecision, a model of divisiveness, a model of the inability to lead, a model of subservience. Sa'ad Hariri the prime minister designate was more sober in his assessment but not much more realistic. He did recognize the great potential for transforming the whole basis on which the Lebanese project rests into what it is not and so he tried to assure the worried public that the process that was just completed will not become a tradition. Many of us hope that the PM is right and that this will be a onetime deal but then reality sets in. What is there in the record of either MR. Hariri, the Al Mustaqbal party or March 14 that inspires confidence? Isn't he the embodiment of the same group that had the majority in both the previous Chamber of Deputies as well as the current one but yet have been unable to either pass or implement a single resolution without the support of Hezbollah in the opposition.

Let me, at this stage; make it crystal clear that I am not bemoaning the previous system, its social inequities, sectarian preferences or its corruption. I am though very concerned when we are about to throw away the baby with the dirty water. The previous system was ineffective, corrupt and unjust not as a result of the hollow democratic institutions that we had but because of the individuals that were permitted to ride rough shod with these institutions. We have a duty to preserve these institutions and replace their hollowness with vibrancy and accountability.

The opposition, led by Hezbollah has had a master plan that they have been implementing a step at a time for almost 5 years. The country is practically ruled by the opposition while the parliamentary majority sits licking its wounds. When would Sa'ad Hariri realize that the Prime Ministerial job that he has agreed to has no powers attached to it. He couldn't allocate the portfolios or even name the ministers. What is even worse the PM will even be prevented from adopting his vision even in the almost worthless ministerial declaration. The Prime Ministers 'office has been diminished tremendously under the new arrangement and so has the concept of transparency and democracy. Lewis Carroll would have gotten a great kick out of the ongoing Lebanese tragedy where nothing is what it appears to be. Lebanon has fallen down the rabbit hole and it will be a miracle if anything resembling what went into the whole will be able to eventually come out.

Sunday, November 22, 2009

66th Anniversary of Lebanese Independence?

The 22rd of November, 1943 is a bitter sweet occasion for all Lebanese or at least it ought to be. It was 66 years ago today that Lebanon won officially its independence. Lebanon was the first Arab country to gain its independence from the French mandate. Such a glorious occasion is to be reserved for celebrations and reflections. Celebrations for the great opportunity to act as a sovereign power, as an independent one and as a power that takes decisions based on common good. It is an occasion to reflect on what has been accomplished and what is yet to come. It is an occasion to express thanks to the founding fathers as represented by the duo of Khoury-Solh for all their sacrifices and their deep belief that they could form a nation out of the area of land called Lebanon.

The first three decades after the birth of the nation were full of trials and tribulations, ups and downs that are to be expected as a new nation is growing up and trying to establish an identity of its own. These years witnessed many mistakes committed by all sides. Christians in general and Maronites in particular were more than glad to exploit their preferred status and rule as supremacists which led to deepened hatred , alienation and divisiveness. The Moslem Sunnis overcompensated by resisting the emergence of a Lebanese identity and thus throwing their lot with Nasserism and Pan Arabism. The Shiites on the other hand were the odd man out, exploited and not taken seriously by both sides.

Maronite Hegemony begot the 1958 conflict which ended only when the Marines landed in Beirut. The road to independence and nation building regrouped under President Fouad Shehab who was able to introduce some reforms and to keep the country together. But the regional effects of the 1967 defeat of the Arab armies which led to the rise of the PLO and Palestinian resistance was too much for the young, small and fragile country to handle. A civil war that lasted 15 years started in 1973 and did not end until destruction and exhaustion had forced all sides to seek a new constitution in Taif. The age of Syrian suzerainty had already started in 1975 as the Syrian army entered Lebanon on behest of some Lebanese political groups but that "temporary" presence became deeply entrenched after 1991 with the complicity of the United States. Then 2005 witnessed the passage of 1559 by the UN Security Council and the Syrian Accountability Act by the US Congress which led to the assassination of Premiere Rafic Hariri. This heinous act emboldened the Lebanese opposition to call for massive demonstrations which helped force Syria to withdraw from the country. Bashar Assad, the Syrian President, promised that Syria would be back. Well guess what. He has kept his word, thanks to Hezbollah, Amal, FPM in addition to a few other Lebanese factions and Lebanon's promise of independence and sovereignty was put on hold again. The dream of a Cedar Revolution ebbed and flowed for 4 years. Its official death notice was the formation of a "national unity cabinet" a fortnight ago.

This sweet bitter occasion, the 66th anniversary of the end of the French Mandate, should be a time to reflect on what we have done and what we want to become. The grand mistake that has haunted us for 66 years and that we had agreed to exorcize from our sick body politic in Taif has been political confessionalism. We are at a tipping point where this project will either go down as a historical mistake or it can be resurrected like the phoenix. It is all up to us as it has always been. We have to decide whether we truly want a vibrant modern democracy or whether we are going to be satisfied with the sham existence and hollow institutions that have so far been our trade mark. If it is the former that we desire then we have no choice but to renounce all aspects of sectarianism and confessionalism. Otherwise pity a nation where the state has no power and "Pity the nation that raises not its voice save when it walks in a funeral, boasts not except among its ruins" a nation that does not deserve the name.

Saturday, November 28, 2009

Elimination of Sectarianism: If Not Now, When?

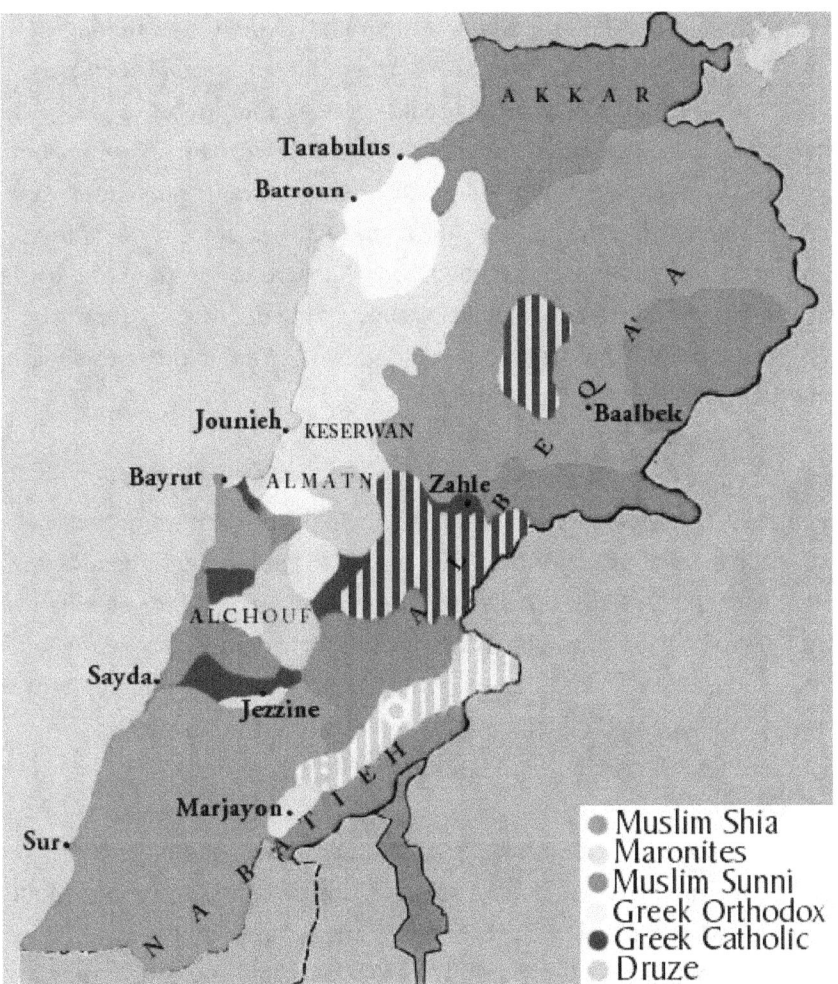

The current Lebanese political structure is built on two irrational and undemocratic principles: (1) Rigid Political Sectarianism for allocating posts and (2) equal distribution of parliamentary seats along a Christian- Moslem axis. In a country where political identity does not arise from citizenship but from cosmopolitan, regional, racial or religious identification the above is a recipe for disaster. If tends to perpetuate the divisiveness instead of the healing and it will emphasize the attributes that divide us rather than those that we hold in common. And the most egregious part of the above formula is that it treats some as being more equal than others by allocating to the Christians a proportionally higher level of representation than the raw numbers establish. It is as if each 4 Christian votes count for five, a 25 % premium.

Since it would be very difficult to rationalize such an inequitable and unjust system one finds that the Lebanese have repeatedly lent their vocal support to the need to abolish sectarianism provided no one ever does. This is precisely the reason for the maelstrom that has engulfed the Beri- Suleiman recent proposal to establish a committee that will recommend steps to be adopted in an effort to abolish "political sectarianism".

Politicians on both sides of the aisle, especially those that belong to the March14 political grouping, have always advocated the enactment of the Taif accords which recommends a bi cameral Lebanese Parliament in addition to abolishing sectarianism in elections and civil service appointments . Meritocracy is to become the only workable criteria both in elections and in appointments. It would not be farfetched to envisage such a meritocracy as being essentially secular. Recent events have been very revealing and quite informative. We now know that the support for a non sectarian system was offered, especially by the Maronites, but only with some strenuous preconditions. Patriarch Sfeir, the Kataeb, the Lebanese Force, The Free Patriotic Movement among others have already stated very clearly their opposition to the plan by speaker Beri to form a committee as demanded by the Taef in order to abolish political sectarianism on the ground that this is not the right time for it.

So how can they be for it and yet against it at the same time? All the parties mentioned above in addition to some independents such as Justice Minister Najjar and Labour Minister Harb claim that they are in principle for eliminating confessionalism but are opposed to the step at the moment because it might result in the underrepresentation of the Christians. Yes you heard it right. They are for eliminating confessionalism provided it does not diminish their privileged position. This logic demands a clear cut answer to two issues: (1) if the status quo is to be maintained then why bother and change the system in the first place? And (2) isn't the whole idea behind electing representatives on merit based on the principle that one's religious affiliation is not a factor in their identity?

Sectarian politics is the anathema to democracy, efficiency justice and equity. One cannot support it provided it results in favourable outcomes to her group. The benefits are to accrue to the common good and the results are known only after the fact. If we are to elect representatives based on their allegiance to the state and their commitment to its constitution then it shouldn't matter whether we elect only females, only Shiites or only short men. What matters is that the representatives are Lebanese.

The accusations against Speaker Beri for daring to suggest that it is time to tackle this thorny issue of eliminating "political sectarianism" ought to be dismissed as disingenuous protestations. The timing of the announcement by Mr. Beri might very well be intended to stifle the attempts of some to make an issue of the legitimacy of the arms of Hezbollah but that is not material. A serious and thorough national dialogue about how to de-sectarianize the political system in Lebanon is already 66 years overdue and must not be postponed again. Our future depends on it.

Monday, December 7, 2009

Elimination of Sectarianism Revisited

Those who persist in criticizing Speaker Berri and President Suleiman for their plan to implement the Taef accords ought to be reminded of the saying: "You can fool some of the people all of the time, and all of the people some of the time, but you cannot fool all of the people all of the time."

The well orchestrated attacks on the Berri-Suleiman plan can best be described as disingenuous, close minded and even bigoted. Political confessionalism is a misguided idea that has been gnawing at the Lebanese body politic ever since the establishment of the state 66 years ago. This idea of using the personal attribute of religion as the single factor for preventing a citizen from seeking a public office and many other civil service jobs is discriminatory, inefficient, harmful and egregious. One can even blame this single idea for most of the domestic tragedies that have consumed Lebanon in 1958, the 15 year civil war in addition to all the other social ills and inequities.

Speaker Berri ought to be commended for agreeing to spearhead the call by President Suleiman to take steps in order to implement the Taef accords that have stopped the Lebanese hemorrhaging over 15 years ago by demanding the creation of a bi cameral parliament and the total abolishing of political sectarianism all across the political sphere. Mr. Berris' call to establish a commission whose only charge is to study and recommend steps to phase out this most destructive of all practices in the Lebanese political system must be seen in its true historical context. It is simply a call to do what all the Lebanese parties have agreed to do 15 years ago but have always found an excuse to carry on business as usual. Unfortunately it is these same procrastinators who have risen to challenge Speaker Berri for daring to remind them of their duties and their commitments. Obviously one should not expect those that have benefited from an arrangement to go ahead and cheer on its demise but it is important to remember that when such institutions, organizations and individuals act as obstructionists and obfuscators they are doing so for very selfish reasons. Sure they would try to rationalize their demagoguery as if they are driven by love of country when in effect their only intention all throughout the decades has been preserving their preferred status. The logic and irrationality used by Patriarch Sfeir in order to prevent this hugely important and crucial step from becoming realized boggles the mind. How can we explain to our children that 35-40% of the population is entitled to 50% of the parliamentary seats or that a bright young educated Shiite woman cannot become a prime minister for no fault of her own besides the fact that she was born on the wrong side of the track so to speak.

It should not be too difficult to understand that any form of discrimination, racial, ethnic or religious is just as bad as any other form of discrimination based on gender, sexual preferences or the colour of one's eyes. Patriarch Sfeir makes an excellent point when he says that it is important to eliminate sectarianism from the inner soul of individuals. That would be a tremendous accomplishment but to use the need to create a perfect state made of saints sounds as an excuse to derail badly needed reform efforts is unconscionable. Society has a duty to set laws and regulations that would enhance the common good and citizens have the right to disagree with such laws but must obey them while they are in effect. Anti discrimination laws do not mean by any stretch that we have eliminated bigotry but it means that it would be illegal to act upon it.

President Suleiman and Speaker Berri need all our support in order to proceed with this project upon whose completion the future of the state rests. (Prior to this initiative the author has been a vocal critic and an opponent of both Mr. Berri and Mr. Suleiman).

Sunday, November 8, 2009

Cost of Indecisiveness

Many have often sang the praises of "going with the flow" and "putting off until tomorrow what you can do today". No doubt the great pull of such exhortations is very tempting. Why bother and take a stand or do a task when one can postpone the pain until another day? This is what utilitarianism is all about isn't it? Humans are supposed to be pleasure seekers and thus humans are acting rationally when they postpone the acquisition of a disutility as long as possible. No rational person will volunteer to pay say $10,000.00 one year before its due if for nothing else but to avoid the substantial opportunity coast that would be attached to such an irrational act.

Unfortunately there are circumstances when the above "logic" should be avoided at any cost. I am not suggesting that one should never postpone any task but I am simply saying that whether to postpone or not to postpone must ultimately be determined on the basis of a cost benefit analysis. Decisions may be profitably put off whenever the benefits derived from the delay are greater than the possible associated costs. Obviously if the reverse is true and the benefits derived from the equivocation are less than the potential cost of the indecision then a delay will be too costly.

The majority of the parliamentary bloc in Lebanon; March 14; has had to deal with such a situation. They could not resist the appeal of compromise; which was in reality appeasement in disguise; guided by the principle that no tough decisions need to be made today since time is on their side. That attitude was best exemplified on November 6, 2009 by Marwan Hamadeh who explained that "dialogue is preferable to arms". No one doubts this but Mr. Hamadeh and March 14 used a faulty logic to justify their inability to lead and take decisive action. Their seminal mistake was not in favouring dialogue over arms and destruction but in presenting the use of arms as being the only alternative to civilized dialogue. To them inaction was appropriate because it avoids the debilitating cost and sufferings associated with civil strife. But what if civil strife was to be avoided? Then all their calculations would turn out to be faulty.

It is crucially important to understand the dynamics of what transpired in Lebanon over the past five months in order to learn from this sad experience. An in depth analysis would make it abundantly clear that the plan of the opposition; led by Hezbollah and put into action by the FPM; was not to gain a specific portfolio or even a specific minister. The aim all along, since the occupation of downtown Beirut, the walk out of the opposition ministers from the cabinet and the demand for a veto power has been the transformation of the tradition that has been in use during the process of cabinet formation. The dye has been cast, thanks to the inability of March 14 in general and Sa'ad Hariri in particular to understand the real implications of this indecisiveness. From here on the Lebanese cabinets are to be formed according to the newly established principle; each parliamentary bloc will be represented in the executive branch of government according to its share of parliamentary seats. Goodbye democracy and welcome to the unworkable hybrid where many will be and not be at the same time. They will function as opposition and yet change their fedoras, whenever it suits them to become part of the government that they oppose. Thank you March 14, for driving in the final nail into the coffin of the Cedar revolution and the aspirations that it gave rise to.

Sunday, December 27, 2009

Resistance as Vigilantism

Every so often MP Ra'ad of Hezbollah, leaders in Amal and Sheikh Tawook, the Hezbollah Commander of the South, regale us with the argument that resistance is a natural right that is not negotiable. The logic behind such declarations is impeccable and the strength of the presentation rests on solid philosophical foundations that are centuries old. Belief in natural rights is often associated with the writings of John Locke whose ideas found their clearest and most popular presentation in the United States Declaration of Independence as written by Thomas Jefferson. The part of the Declaration that states: "We hold these truths to be self evident, that all men are created equal, that they are endowed by their creator of certain unalienable rights, that among these are life, liberty and the pursuit of happiness" has become known as the most widely recognized statement in the English language.

Had the spokespersons for the "resistance" confined their discourse to the above then it would have been difficult for anyone to raise major objections to their claims save for an attack on the very nature of whether natural rights exist. But that is not the case. Hezbollah and its supporters, however, commit a fatal logical flaw by combining the above mentioned natural right to resist with the right to bear arms and form a militia that functions above the law of the land that it professes to support. What the "resistance" becomes, once it advocates such a stand is more similar to a vigilante organization rather than a resistance movement. A vigilante has the right to life liberty and the pursuit of happiness , just like all other citizens, but when a vigilante individual or organization take the law into their own hands by punishing offenders illegally then they would have forsaken the rule of law and would have become transgressors themselves. Vigilante groups operate according to their own interpretation of the law and their actions become extralegal. The "Death Squads" of Latin America and "The Minutemen" of the US Southwest are good examples of these groups. Vigilantes confuse their inalienable right to protection with their perceived duty to right a wrong through illegal means.

Members of Hezbollah and all other citizens have the right and even the duty to resist occupation by an aggressor state as well as the right to rebel against rulers who governance violates the social contract. But what they do not have a right to is be a part of the government and yet flaunt its laws and regulations. They do not have the right to become vigilantes. Hezbollah can argue that the right to resist is a natural right that cannot be taken away but it cannot use that as a basis to form its own private militia and to establish its semi autonomous fiefdom.

Then there is always the option of rejecting the whole idea of natural rights as Jeremy Bentham did when he called it "nonsense on stilts" and when David Hume and Edmund Burke rejected the whole notion. Natural rights cannot and must not be used as a substitute for legislation voted upon by the community.

Arguably, Hezbollah does take note of the weakness of its current position as a member of the government and yet as the main unauthorized militia in the land. That is why Hezbollah has been working feverishly to reconcile the contradictions by "forcing" the Lebanese government to legalize the resistance and thus to make the need to use logic of natural rights unnecessary. That was the whole logic behind the fight over the Ministerial Statement. It's only logical to expect Hezbollah to force the Lebanese cabinet to annul unilaterally UNSCR 1559.

Wednesday, December 30, 2009

Lebanese Decadence?

It has often been said that the clearest image of the values and mores of a country can best be seen in the way that it treats its poor. What better time of the year to take a look at the level of poverty, income distribution and the resultant inequality than on the eve of a new year and a new decade for that.

No one likes to pay taxes and especially so if you are a wealthy Lebanese. The sum of all taxes collected by the Lebanese government , excluding customs duties, are estimated to amount to less than 15% of the GDP which is quite low for a country at this stage of development. Even this low level of taxation would be 50% lower had it not been for VAT, essentially a regressive tax. The other major source of revenue for the government is customs duties which amount to 20% of its revenues or about 6% of the GDP and must decline if Lebanon is to join the WTO. So where is the revenue from the progressive personal income tax as well as the corporate income tax? Unfortunately they only amount; in the aggregate; to a sum that is essentially equal to what is collected from VAT and that is a shame. And that is a shame. Total taxes paid by all business entities in addition to the income taxes paid by all wage earners in Lebanon are only equal to what is collected from a sales tax. It does appear that the burden of taxation is exactly the reverse of what it should be.

Like most developing countries Lebanon does not have a good reliable record of macroeconomic data that could be used to develop meaningful policies to target the most pressing economic problems such as poverty and inequality. Yet, there is a recent study about poverty in Lebanon which was released during the month of January of 2008. This study done by the UNDP highlighted the plight of many Lebanese and the need to implement post haste an anti poverty program across the country. The following is a summary of the major findings:

(a) 28% of the Lebanese are poor and 8% are in extreme poverty.

(b) Extreme poverty is measured as $2.4 per day i.e. under $900 per annum per person.

(c) 20 % of the Lebanese live in between the poverty lines.

(d) Both extreme poverty and even total poverty are rather evenly distributed.

(e) The Gini coefficient ; a measure of economic equality; was estimated to be around 0.37 which is the average Gini for MENA (Middle East & North Africa)

(f) All Lebanese could be lifted out of extreme poverty at the relatively small cost of $12 per Lebanese per annum; less than $50 million.

(g) The top 20% of the Lebanese consume over 6 times what the bottom 20% consumes. (43% vs. 7%)

(h) Regionally the residents of the North were the poorest followed by the South, Bekaa, Mount Lebanon and then Beirut.

(i) The median per capita annual level of consumption for the year 2004-5 was estimated to be $2067.

Fast forward to the New Year celebration planned to take place on New Year's Eve 2009 at Solidere in Beirut. The price of admission to have a seat by the dancing floor, a 3 course dinner and an open bar will set one back by $5500.00. (Yes the price of joining the festivities is five thousand five hundred dollars in case you thought that was a misprint). Now go back and take a look at item (i) in the list above and cry.

Yes I know, we live in a free market economy and individuals should have the right to spend their wealth any way they choose. That is true provided they recognize that their wealth was not generated in a vacuum and that they have a moral obligation and an ethical responsibility to carry their fair share of the costs of running the society that they are members of. That means that they should act responsibly by shouldering more than a token income tax while the majority of government revenues are collected through a regressive taxing structure. It means that it is decadent and totally irresponsible when a country whose level of welfare is dependent on grants and gifts from the Saudis, French, Norwegians, Americans, Russians ;just to name a few of the donor countries; is capable of throwing such expensive private New Year celebrations for the pure hedonistic pleasure of the few. The privileged reap most of the benefits from the government expenditures while the poor carry the national debt burden. This is pure debauchery.

Sunday, January 10, 2010

Is Lebanon to be the Sacrificial Lamb for Qom?

United Nations Security Council Resolution 1559 called clearly on Sept 2004 for the "'disbanding and disarmament of all Lebanese and non-Lebanese militias". This resolution was passed in an effort to help the Lebanese government establish its authority over all Lebanese territory as is the case in any modern independent and sovereign nation state. But unfortunately almost six years have gone by and the Lebanese authorities have failed to disarm the Palestinian people both within and outside the Palestinian refugee camps as well as their failure to get Hezbollah to comply by 1559.

Any follower of the Lebanese current events will tell you that during that period of almost six years, Hezbollah has not only refused to comply with the demands of the international community as well as the requests of the official Lebanese government to do so but has actually amassed a larger cache of arms. Hezbollah has taken advantage of its "military" superiority as to defy the local authorities and to establish undubiously a state within a state. Hezbollah has made a mockery of the idea that the central government has a monopoly over arms and the ability to enforce the laws of the land.

The leadership of Hezbollah passed along to Sayed Hassan Nasrallah who does not hide the fact that he is a strong believer in the concept of Wilayat Al Faqih as promulgated originally by Ayatollah Khomeini and currently by the Grand Ayatollah Khomenei. This is a concept that preaches a special kind of nationalism that demands total allegiance to the spiritual leader (Marja) in Shiism that happens to reside in Qom, Iran.

So it is important to keep in mind that despite the protestations of Hezbollah the primary allegiance of the group and its illegal militia is not to the state of Lebanon and the welfare of its citizens. Instead of a belief in the abstract notion of paying homage to the idea of a state Hezbollah has shown its readiness and willingness to take stands detrimental to the welfare of the state but in accordance to its interpretations of what God has commanded them to do. What better example to illustrate its misguided policies and beliefs than the destructive war of 2006 that Hezbollah initiated against the will of the state and is proud of having done so. It is instructive in this regard to recall the statement attributed to Ambrose Bierce "God and Country are an unbeatable team, they break all records for oppression and bloodshed".

It is clear that Hezbollah has spread its hegemony over Lebanon and has managed through a combination of deft political maneuvering and "military" intimidation to turn its failure at the ballot box into an actual victory. In addition to all the above abnormalities Hezbollah has even attempted to force the government of Lebanon to declare UNSCR 1559 null and void , in total disregard to the ideas of international jurisprudence.

Iran, the only Marjaia that Hezbollah accepts is in its own way defying the international community over the issue of constructing the ability to build nuclear weapons. This issue has preoccupied the international community for years and appears to be more or less at a deadlock. The level of hatred and animosity between the Iranian regime and the state of Israel is at a feverish level and most observers in the world have come to the conclusion that if the negotiations between Iran and the group of six fails to establish assurances that Iran will not be in a position to build nuclear weapons then the state of Israel will find itself in a position where it must initiate military action.

If such a military confrontation is to take place, then it would be rather costly for the region and the world but I am afraid that a significant burden will be carries by the innocent Lebanese who should be at best by standers in this conflict. Many analysts estimate that Hezbollah has upward of 40,000 missiles and some of these are capable of reaching Tel Aviv. Israel has been working hard to establish an anti missile shield which might be able to offer some protection but odds are against an effective deterrent. Hezbollah has hinted in the past that it will not hesitate to defend Qom in case of an Israeli initiated aggression so it is to be expected that as soon as Mosad determines that Iran is about ready to produce its first nuclear bomb and that the group of six will not prevent that from happening then Israel will initiate a strike that can delay the Iranian plans by a few years.

Let us assume that all of the above is to take place then the real question is whether Hezbollah will add to all its transgressions another one. Will it sacrifice the wellbeing of the Lebanese people in order to act as a loyal soldier of Qom? If it does then this observer feels that Lebanon will be hit very hard and the level of death, suffering and destruction that will have to be carried by the Lebanese people will be impossible to rationalize and explain. If that is to happen then Lebanon will be sacrificed for nothing. The Lebanese people and their representatives should demand answers about Hezbollah's' intentions before it is too late. Let us not become the victims of a Hezbollah nationalism, a "nationalism that makes you drunk, then it makes you blind then it kills you". Some believe that an Israeli action is to be expected within nine months.

PS: For those who do not read Arabic: Lebanon is written on the tree and Hassan Nasrallah is saying "We are standing at the side of the cliff and we intend to go forward.

Tuesday, January 12, 2010

Hezbollah: Creative Destruction?

Joseph Schumpeter's idea of creative destruction has attained world wide use over the past quarter of a century as economists, sociologist's businessmen and others try to explain the rapidity of change that seemed to have taken hold of most areas of the world. This phenomenal rate of technological innovation appears to be increasing at an exponential rate of growth. Ray Kurzweil who wrote the classic "The Singularity Is Near" projects that our knowledge will increase over the next 20 years by as much as it had increased over the past 200 years.

It is not enough to introduce a new product or a new way of producing an old one and at times the new innovation does not have to be superior to its direct competitors to dominate and prosper. Does anyone remember the Beta max vs. the VHS? Most observers admit that the Beta max was the superior product but it had to bite the dust. Why? Simply because it could not convince enough end users to adopt its technology. Apple computer on the other hand has been moving from one innovation to another, all successful beyond any expectations and all have left an indelible mark on the way that some functions are done. (Obviously the reference in this case is to the ubiquitous iPod, iPhone and many expect the same to be true of the iTablet). So why did Apple succeed in this field as well as Google and many others in different fields? They managed to somehow create a demand for their new products. Once the demand was there the products sold in great quantities, dominated their fields and forced everyone else to adapt if they wished to survive.

But what is true of physical products is also true of ideas. What would have been the influence of Karl Marx had his dialectical approach to explain the way the world works had not found enough adherents? He would have been another Beta max if you will9. Marx seemed to have the ability to attract followers and to appeal to some powerful intellectuals who took his ideas and almost precipitated a global revolution. But any study of history will demonstrate that many a time better ideas do not always win. Paradigm shifts are very difficult to achieve as Thomas Kuhn has explained in his Theories of a Scientific Revolution. That is precisely why in one field after another one person rises to prominence although that individual has basically revived ideas that someone else had introduced sometime in the past.

So what does all of this have to do with a column essentially devoted to Lebanese affairs? Quite a lot. Allow me to use one more real world example prior to my showing my cards9. General Motors decided to produce city buses in large quantities, in the early half of the 20th century, but it did not want to take any chances about whether the expected demand would materialize. General Motors used its financial strength to buy many of the city transit tramlines through a subsidiary. Then it proceeded to declare these entire rail based public transport companies bankrupt. Naturally the cities then had no choice but to adopt the technology of the new comers and buses became adopted in large numbers. The effect of that "conspiracy" can be felt decades later all across the metropolitan areas in the United States.

As you can see from the above there is a fool proof way of making an idea spread or a new product take hold. Create a demand for it, by force and through a conspiracy and illegal means if you have to. Once the demand is there then the idea becomes established.

Hezbollah had a product with a limited appeal to some Lebanese as a result of their sacrifices to force the Israelis out of Lebanon. But once Israel pulled out and all other militias disarmed the Hezbollah leadership had second thoughts about relinquishing the power that they had become accustomed to. Hezbollah did exactly what GM had done. They went all the way out to create a demand for their arms cache as illegal as it might have been. To convince the Lebanese of the imminent Israeli threat they had to make sure that the borders were always ground for conflict and so they cooperated with some radical Palestinian groups based in Syria, pledged allegiance to the Iranian Mullahs and kept on increasing the level of rhetorical threats. When all of that was not enough Hezbollah kidnapped two Israeli soldiers knowing full well that the consequences would be war.

Our intention is not to argue whether the Israeli threat to Lebanon is as real as Hezbollah portrays it, partially as strong or even nonexistent which it might be. Remember that the borders between Lebanon and Israel were very quiet for the first quarter of a century and that the brutal Israeli assault on Beirut was to a large extent in response to Fatah land provocations. Yet the question must be raised: What is the extent of the true Israeli threat to Lebanon and how much of the current emotional position about the threat is a result of a diabolical plot to create a demand for the military capabilities of Hezbollah. Let me conclude by raising another question; if the purpose of Hezbollah and the constant demand for an effective Lebanese Army is the ability to meet this perceived threat then why doesn't Lebanon defuse this potential problem in the same way that its larger and more powerful Arab brothers, Egypt and Jordan have done? Or how about agreeing to a mutual defense treaty with a large and credible foreign power whether it is Russia, NATO, the Arab league or even Iran is immaterial. If the purpose is to neutralize the Israeli threat then it is incumbent on us to choose the most effective and least costly way. That would be real creative destruction.

Saturday, January 16, 2010

The Webs We Weave

The campaign to portray the Lebanese Finance Minister as a person who has taken charge of the Lebanese economy is an ongoing one. Hardly a day goes by without a news story about what she is doing and her tremendous accomplishments. Normally a new minister would still be getting used to the lay of the land after such a short period of time in office. But that is perfectly legitimate since Ms. Hassan would make a very good spokesperson for this cabinet and especially the views of the Hariri camp that she represents. The fact that she is one of the few females with a high profile in the Lebanese government does not hurt either.

What is disturbing however are the meaningless stories that accompany the items related to Ms. Hassan. They are not outright lies but the choice of items to highlight is very deceptive on purpose. It is frustrating when such stories are published in the press without generating any outrage from the press, other government officials or the public (The only possible exception, as far as I know, has been the staff at The Executive magazine).

A good example to illustrate the deliberate efforts at misrepresentation of the facts by carefully worded news announcements and placing them in a prominent position where they do not belong is the January 16 issue of Al Mustaqbal. A boxed news item on the left hand side of the leading headline on page one proclaims the tremendous demand for the Lebanese sovereign debt as can be seen by the change in prices paid for such debt at the end of last week when compared to the earlier week. The prices of the 5 year bonds went up to 103.25 from 102.19 while the yield dropped from 5.37 to 5.13 There is nothing that is factually incorrect about this but the prices for such instruments are volatile and depend on a variety of factors besides faith in the issuing economy. The most important other factor for sophisticated investors is the size of the Credit Default Swap (CDS). A CDS is in essence the insurance premium that protects the holder of these bonds against default. The simplest way to manage risk would be to buy the bond and buy also a CDS. In the case of the Lebanese 5 year bond that is highlighted in the Al Mustaqbal article the bonds are selling to yield just over 5%. A smart investor could cover the risk of default by buying a CDS for about 2.5 % for the Lebanese 5 year Eurobond. Note that this investor has now a 2.5% net yield that is 100% secure. If the Lebanese government defaults then the CDS will make the investment whole and if the Lebanese authorities honour their obligations then this model investment will net over 2.5%. Another factor that could play a role in the price of the Lebanese Eurobonds is the fact that they are priced in dollars and the dollar has strengthened slightly against other currencies.

But the most egregious part of the story is the boast that the CDS premium for Lebanese debt has fallen to 250 from 285 basis points the week before. Again the figures are true but the boast is misplaced. Lebanese debt still carries one of the highest CDS spreads in the world. Even Greece still has a CDS (211 bp) that is below that of Lebanon. The few countries that have a higher cost of insurance premiums are Venezuela, Iceland and the Ukraine. But that is nothing to be proud of. Yes the news items was correct in saying that Dubai still has a higher CDS but keep in mind they Dubai has in essence declared a moratorium on part of its debt and that Venezuela has devalued its currency by 50% and threatens to do another devaluation round.

I am also sure that observant readers have noted why Lebanese national debt will have to carry such exorbitantly high interest rates. Potential buyers will have to spend a large share of that interest income on the purchase of insurance if they wish to manage their risk exposure; half of the yield goes to purchase insurance.

Sunday, January 17, 2010

Nabih Beri 1, Sfeir et al 0.

Patriarch Sfeir, General Aoun, Sa'ad Hariri and most of the other non Shi'ite political luminaries in Lebanon have been on the receiving end Beri jabs and swift combinations that they cannot seem to duck or avoid. They have not been able to as much as touch Mr. Beri. They have been outclassed and I am glad that they have been made to look like the disingenuous people that they are on this all important issue of removing sectarian allocation of parliamentary seats, the post of the Presidency, the post of the Speaker, the Premiership as well as many civil service jobs.

The case against sectarian allocation of jobs and political posts is so strong and convincing that no one has dared be associated with supporting it outright. It is more likely that all political leaders have condemned the system as a relic of the past that is holding Lebanon down and that is the cause of most of its problems. Unfortunately these same leaders who extol Taef on a daily basis had to circle the wagons when they were finally challenged to implement one of the most important features of Taef, ban political sectarianism by de confessionalizing the political structure of Lebanon.

Let us be clear about what the Speaker is proposing. He wants to finally start the process that the Lebanese were mandated to implement by the Taef agreement of 1995. He is suggesting that the Parliament must form a committee to study the process of abandoning sectarianism and make suggestions about implementation. Once this committee studies and analyses all aspects of the problem by holding hearings and talking to all sides it will issue its recommendations to the Parliament which would proceed to accept, reject or modify the suggested legislation. That is a straight forward process that should not have generated any opposition but should have been welcomed with open arms by all. It was not though and for a very simple reason. The traditional leadership never wanted to change the system. They are happy with a system that has given them power and prestige; equity, efficiency, justice, democracy be damned. That is also why all these leaders are scrambling to find a legitimate argument against the Beri proposal. They have not found any and allow me to predict that they will not find any.

The best that they could come up with are various explanations of the need to eliminate political sectarianism in Lebanon but the time is not right. They claim that they do not object to the idea but they are opposed to the timing. If fifteen years is not enough time then what is? Logically the weakest of the specific arguments to counter what has become known as the Beri plan; when actually the first person to call for the commission was President Suleiman; is that of Patriarch Sfeir. Prior to eliminating sectarianism from the laws let us eliminate it from the soul he said. How does one test that an idea has been eliminated from the mind? Isn't it true that once something is eliminated from the inner self then there is no need for a law to address that problem? Maybe Patriarch Sfeir should oppose all criminal laws and wait until the idea to steal, rob, deceive and maybe murder is eliminated from the soul? That is rubbish and I expect that all the supporters of this idea know it. All what can be said about this weakest of defenses is that I am glad that no one suggested eliminating slavery from the mind prior to passing laws against it or that Martin Luther King Jr. had the courage to demand Civil Rights legislation instead of waiting for people to eliminate it from their hearts.

Inner beliefs cannot be legislated but we sure can legislate what is acceptable behavior and what is not. It is high time that the accusations that Mr. Beri has an ulterior motive for making the suggestion when he did to stop and it is time for everyone in the whole nation to lend this most noble of efforts the support that it deserves. Our future as human beings and as a state rest on this commission. Nothing else is as important as how we treat our fellow citizens. I look forward to the day when a Lebanese Moslem woman is elected President; a Lebanese Greek Orthodox is nominated as Premier and a Lebanese Armenian as a Speaker. Obviously I would expect half of the Parliamentary seats to be occupied by females and each of the occupants to be driven by their commitment to the national welfare of the citizens irrespective of their gender, race, religious beliefs or sexual orientation.

Saturday, January 23, 2010

Sectarianism, Municipal Elections And The Voting Age

It is paradoxical when the response to an effort to eliminate sectarianism is voiced in sectarian terms. That would be similar to countering an argument for integration in purely bigoted segregationist terms. Unfortunately that is the level or should I say the low level to which the standards of deconfessionalism discourse has fallen in Lebanon.

The major fault line, on which the shaky Lebanese system is built, as we have discussed many times before, is the discriminatory sectarian structure. Speaker Beri has finally decided that it is time to appoint a commission, as called for by the Taef agreement, to study the process that is needed in order to eliminate sectarianism from the state. It should be obvious that it would be difficult to find fault with such a democratic call. Such a call has created oppositions from all across the political spectrum, as is to be expected, because if implemented then it will shake the current system of political leadership to its core; as it should. The opposition was to be expected and the bankruptcy of their arguments was to be expected as well. It has been very entertaining watching one leader after another walk down the plank by adopting nonsensical positions in an attempt to critique the Speaker's plan. Ms. Mouawad even had the audacity to state with a straight face that eliminating sectarianism is similar to eliminating democracy. Does she really expect anyone whose IQ is above 60 to take such a position seriously? Apparently she did and it looks like she had the blessings of Patriarch Sfeir since she made her declarations after a meeting with him in Bkirki. That should serve as a strong argument, if there ever was a need for any, why people of the cloth should confine their uttering to that which they know best, myths of creation and intelligent design.

It appears that many of the same politicians who have opposed the Beri plan were not content with the level of derision that their counter plans have produced and so they proceeded to look for newer areas to show their ignorance and farcical powers of analysis. Low and behold they did find a new area to add to their ludicrous arguments in another Beri initiative which calls upon the legislature to put the finishing touches on the plan to lower the voting age in Lebanon from 21 to 18. And what do you think is the reason for their opposition? You guessed it, a purely sectarian mindset. The estimates by the Ministry of the interior is that if the voting age is to be lowered to 18 then the potential number of voters will increase by about 280,000; three quarters of whom are Moslems and the other one quarter are Christians. So one more time what do these Christian geniuses come up with to counter this other very democratic proposal? Why they come up with their own conditions to approve the lowering of the voting age. They will agree to vote for the new law provided that Lebanon adopts simultaneously a plan that grants everyone who is of a Lebanese descent the Lebanese citizenship and the right to vote.

Do they really want to offer the 12-15 million Lebanese scattered around the world the right to vote in both national and municipal elections? Do they really want individuals who have never been to the country, who cannot speak its language and who do not understand any of its problems to have the final say in what policies to adopt and what to reject? Of course not. This is another purely selfish and cynical stand calculated to disenfranchise 280,000 Lebanese the majority of whom belong to a different sect. Someone should remind these politicians to be careful what they wish for, their wishes might come true and the votes from their diabolical plan might come back to haunt them.

Monday, February 1, 2010

Expats, Immigrants,Descendants, Sectarianism and the Vote

It is very rare to witness as much confusion, and attention paid to the superficial as has characterized the dialogue regarding who is to be given the right to vote in Lebanese elections. And that is unfortunate. One would have expected the discourse to be serious and well informed since the issue deals with the fundamental democratic institution of extending the suffrage to many that have been denied the right unjustly and unfairly.

Universal unrestricted suffrage does not exist anywhere in the world and is unlikely to become the law of the land anywhere in the foreseeable future. There appears to be a universal restriction on the right to vote for anyone under 18 years of age in addition to the restrictions against extending the right to those that are mentally ill, felons, unregistered or that do not meet the requirement to vote from outside the country in question. External voting exists in one form or another in 115 countries out of more than the 200 states in the world and even when external voting exists it does so in a big variety of ways.

Let us make it absolutely clear from the outset that giving the right to vote is not the same as making sure that the affected individuals have the proper access to the facilities that would enable them to cast that cherished vote. To offer the right and withhold the access is cruel; in effect it is equivalent to not having offered the right in the first place. But what is arguably more important, in the Lebanese case, is the need to distinguish between expatriates, first generation immigrants and all other individuals that claim to be of Lebanese descendancy.

No one could argue against offering the right to vote to civil servants who are stationed overseas, businesspeople whose work demands make it difficult to be in the country during election times, students who are completing their education overseas in addition to those that are seeking medical services abroad. Obviously the expatriates, those that work overseas on either temporary or permanent bases also deserve the right to vote because they do contribute to the welfare of the state and have a strong connection to it. But the right of the long term immigrants is not so obvious. When would a Lebanese descendant lose the right to vote? I should hope that the answer is not never. Suffrage is a privilege so that those that inhabit a place can have a say in how it is run. The vote is not an inalienable right given to all irrespective of where they live and without any regard to how long they have not resided in the country.

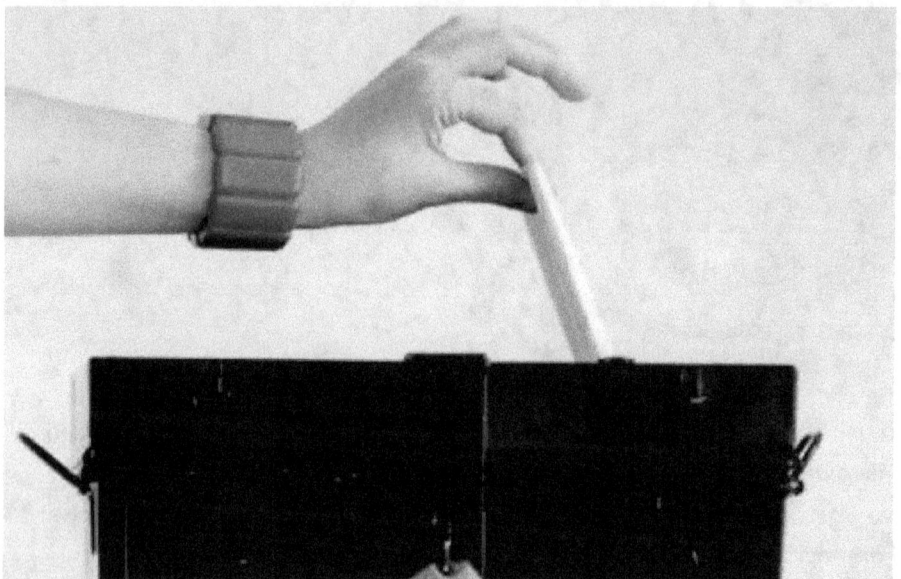

No country gives its citizens an unrestricted right to vote from overseas especially if the number of potential voters from abroad is larger than those at home. Armenia, who is in a similar demographic situation as Lebanon; 2.5 million Armenians live at home and 8 million are scattered all over the world, adopted a law in 2006 that does not allow any external voting. Even other countries that do not have to worry about disproportionate external voting place some rather strict limits about residency. In many cases a citizen loses the right to vote if she has been outside the country for fifteen years and in some cases the right to vote requires that the voter must have been outside the country for six years or less. Does it make any sense to offer a person whose parents left Lebanon say a hundred years ago the right to decide how I am to live and under what laws? Why should a rational person offer to give an outsider the right to veto anything and everything that is of importance to the community? Are we serious when we say that we want to give say, the grandchildren of Danny Thomas, Jamie Farr, John Sununu, Selma Hayek, Paul Anka and Shakira the right to vote in Lebanese elections? What do they now about what is good for Lebanon and why should they have a say in how we choose to conduct our affairs?

I am afraid that the demands by some Lebanese leaders to offer the Lebanese citizenship to 11-15 million people, who live overseas, who do not speak the language in most case and who have nothing but an emotional attachment to some aspects of Lebanese culture is a well orchestrated ploy to resist deconfessionalism. They are the same leaders who have declared allegiance to the Taef accords but opposed implementing them. The veil has fallen and the true colour of these political leaders is revealed for all to see. They are nothing but bigoted leaders whose backward sectarian ideology is built on grabbing power and discriminating against the other. To claim that their position is legitimate as a result of the geopolitical developments is pure rubbish. It is nothing but a sick excuse from a sick mind.

Friday, February 12, 2010

March 14 Has Not Stepped Up To The Plate

One of the most common definitions of a state is the one given by the great sociologist Max Weber: "it is that organization that has monopoly on the legitimate use of physical force within a given territory". Obviously not all states in the world meet the simple conditions set in that functional definition. A sovereign state is obviously the one that combines the de facto and the de jure aspects of that definition by exercising total control over its territory. Unfortunately there are some "quasi" states in the world where the governmental institutions pretend to have power when in effect they do not. Unfortunately there are many such cases in the world of government setups similar to those in Afghanistan where the official government enjoys international recognition but is not capable of either promoting its policies or even of governing its territory. The Taliban's present such a formidable threat to the government in all aspects that they might as well be viewed as the real power in the land.

Lebanon is even in a worse shape. Hezbollah is the real power behind the throne. Not much, if anything, can be accomplished in Lebanon if Hezbollah's' approval is not forthcoming, not even the privatization of the cellular telephone network that is falling behind the technological developments in the world and in the region as we speak. Nothing gets done in Lebanon if Hezbollah does not permit it. But the power of Hezbollah on the Lebanese scene goes far beyond that of the Taliban in Afghanistan. In Lebanon Hezbollah is part of the official cabinet that it openly opposes.

Most would agree to describe the official Afghanistan government of Mr. Karzai as a de jure state while that of the Taliban as a defacto one. But in Lebanon it is worst than this. Hezbollah and its allies are the defacto government and they are the ones that practically dictate all what passes as a dejure government.

The official Prime Minister, Sa'ad Hariri, who for some unknown reason thinks of himself as the leader of a dejure government has even admitted a few days ago that if the Israel-Hezbollah conflict is to manifest itself in a war then the Lebanese government will be on the side of Hezbollah and Iran.

Yes you heard it right. The Lebanese Prime Minister who has already acquiesced , maybe under duress, to a governmental power sharing with the political group behind the illegal militia that spearheaded savage attacks on peaceful Lebanese has declared that the Lebanese government will come to the rescue of Hezbollah if the later comes under attack or even if it initiates them. In effect Hezbollah has been transformed from a power behind the scenes into one that is hegemonic. Sa'ad Hariri has abdicated all his responsibilities as a Prime Minister of a sovereign state and is acting like a helpless agent bent on executing orders emanating abroad.

And if such an inglorious shameful record is not enough Sa'ad Hariri went even further. He mobilized all of the power at his disposal to stifle free thought at an academic institution of higher learning that dared use a quote questioning the level of corruption in the Lebanese state when his father was the Prime Minister. Mr. Hariri, the record is very clear, corruption is an endemic affair in both the past and the current Lebanese state and that level of corruption is gnawing at the very fabric of whatever is left of civil society in Lebanon. It is your duty to stop the posturing and to start executing a policy that would revive sovereignty, self respect and independence. To foster a tradition of cult personality and to pretend that the Hezbollah militia is not a threat to whatever is left of a country once called Lebanon is the biggest injustice and travesty that you can bestow on the Lebanese people.

Saturday, March 6, 2010

The Lebanese Government and the UNDP: An Unholy Alliance?

It is not very often that the object of a not-for-profit organization is a major party in funding the effort to help it overcome its challenges. That is simply like taking money from the poor in order to fund programmes that target the eradication of poverty. It just does not seem to be the right thing to do.
I wonder whether many Lebanese tax payers realize that the almost $40 million in expenditures spent by the UNDP during 2008 in various fields and numerous regions in Lebanon were partially funded by the Lebanese government. I bet not many are aware of this relationship that is full of conflicts of interest. What is the rationale to fund the charity that is supposedly delivering the needed work? If an organization is comfortable enough as to fund those that are providing it with aid and assistance then maybe that organization does not need the aid in the first place.
The following is a scanned page from the web site of UNDP Lebanon:

Delivery Rates
Starting 2004 UNDP Progamme Financial Delivery has been expanding from an average USD 7million delivery rate in the early 2000's to an USD 8.5 million programme in 2004 and USD 11.3 million in 2005. The steady increase continued in 2006 and was complemented with the launching of UNDP Recovery Programme following the unfortunate impact of the July 2006 war. 2008 reached an unprecedented Delivery level of more than USD 38 million expected to be sustained over the coming two years.

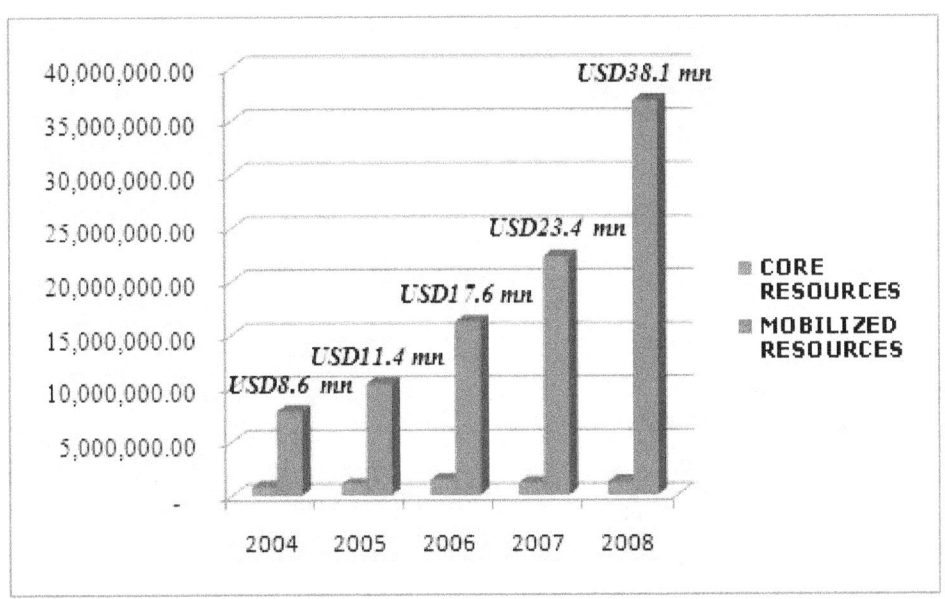

Funding Sources

As represented in the graph above UNDP programme Delivery for the 2004-2007 cycle is financed substantially by mobilized resources from Donors and the Government of Lebanon through contributions to UNDP programme and projects activities; as per the below summary table:

.............(USD ....2004........2005.......2006 ....2007........2008
Government of Lebanon..3.7million...3.3million..4.1million...3.3million...9.4million
International Donors......4.0million...7.1million.11.6million..18.7million..27.4million
UNDP core...................789,000....1.0million..1.4million...1.5million...1.3million
Grand Total................8.5 million.11.4million.17.1million..23.5million..38.1million

As per the above charts the Lebanese government provided 25 % the annual expenditures by the UNDP in Lebanon during 2008 and had funded as much as 42 % of the total UNDP expenditures in Lebanon during 2004.

There ought to be no doubt in the mind of anyone about the dedication, genuine interest and professionalism of the UNDP staff all over the world. But yet when the UNDP agrees to be funded by those that it professes to help then that is a sure sign that corruption and conflict of interest have found their way into the operation of one of our best and most dedicated organizations. The UNDP, in this case, should not have allowed the Lebanese government to skirt the Lebanese governments' own constraints on wages and salaries and expenditures in general. The UNDP has allowed itself to be used as an instrument to flaunt local regulations by in essence acting as both an employment agency and a high cost consultancy to Lebanese officialdom that is loathe letting the public know how it is wasting the treasury's scarce funds.

Tuesday, March 30, 2010

Lebanese Democracy: It Just Ain't What It Is Supposed To Be.

Whenever the subject of democracy, modernity , equality or liberty come up,; which is almost in every conversation; the Lebanese invariably advance the argument that the Lebanese society is the most liberal in the Middle East and is the most advanced and the most democratic. Some will even imply that the Lebanese are the smartest, the best educated and the most capable. Well guess what; narcissism and hubris are arguably the worst of sins. Misplaced arrogance is nothing short of self deception. But those who suffer of grandiose self deception will not usually listen to reason. This time, however, there is a factual study that presents as solid of an argument and as objective and scientific of an opinion as one can possibly ask for that can conclusively point to the errors brought about by hubris.

The process of healing whether it is for an individual, an institution or a state cannot begin until the offending entity admits to its mistakes and acknowledges that a different path is needed. The Second Annual State of Reform in The Arab World impressive study that calculates an Arab Democracy Index has just been released. The study is the culmination of an annual effort by a large number of Arab Think Tanks from Egypt, Morocco, Jordan, Saudi Arabia, Lebanon, Syria and Kuwait in conjunction with a number of European institutions.

The report for 2009 covered 10 Arab countries and concluded that democracy is not well entrenched in any of them. That in itself is a judgment that is worthwhile since it is in essence the result of Arabs who are looking at their own societies analytically. But what is of even greater concern for us in Lebanon is the fact that when all is said and done Lebanon ranks as the 4th country out of the ten in the study which is an improvement on our rank of being the sixth out of the 8 countries studied during 2008. Thank goodness for the improvements.

What the study shows conclusively is what many of us have known for a long time but unfortunately the politicians have consistently refused to admit. Lebanon is a hollow democracy with many ineffective institutions, legislation that is never implemented, social injustices that are dealt with through lip service and the most egregious of all a backward. Undemocratic even feudal electoral system based on the most discriminatory idea of sectarian belief.

This comprehensive study goes on to highlight some very relevant facts about other Arab countries. The two countries that have the most influence in Lebanon and the two that in essence shape many of its decisions and policies; Saudi Arabia and Syria; have the lowest Democracy Index rank among the ten countries covered by the study and the third lowest respectively.

Syria: 461
Yemen: 457
Saudi Arabia: 402

Can you imagine seeking instructions from a tutor who is more badly in need of remedial work than the client? That in a nutshell is our sad state of affairs. If we do not reverse these trends and introduce political, social and economic reforms then our chances of ever becoming a vibrant, modern and liberal state will just fade away. Will we ever realize that a wish is not a plan?

Saturday, April 10, 2010

<u>Mutant Democracy</u>

Democratic forms of government have essentially evolved, over the millennia, to follow one of two forms. There are the presidential systems similar to that in the US or parliamentarian systems exemplified by the German political structure. As is often the case there are a number of other systemic combinations that are characterized by elements of both.

Presidential systems have usually been established to enshrine the principle of the separation of powers between the three branches on which democratic governance rests. The Executive branch in these circumstances is lead by a President who nominates a cabinet to run the daily affairs of governments and to propose laws and policies. These proposals must be approved and voted upon by the legislative branch, the elected represented of the people. It is this separation that acts as to prevent one branch of government from running rough shod over its opposition. The resulting healthy tension between the executive and the legislative tends to lead to compromise and positions based more on the individual merit of the case rather than it pure ideological basis. Obviously an independent and well qualified judiciary makes sure that the constitutional principles and the basic laws of the land are adhered it and that no violations of these principles is allowed to take place.

This principle of separation of powers evolves into a fusion of power under parliamentary systems of governance. The cabinet is headed by a Prime Minister who is usually chosen from among the members of parliament and a cabinet is formed from among the members of the chamber of people's representatives. In this case the president's role is rather ceremonial and the ultimate arbiter is the legislative. Although the cabinet is chosen from among the elected members yet it always strives to have the blessings of the majority of the members on its side. The legislative in this case plays just as crucial of a role, through robust debates, as its counterpart in a presidential system. Again the judicial will be impartial and objective in order to ascertain that no branch is abusing its power.

In Lebanon, as is often the case, our system of governance does not belong to any of the forms although it pays lip service to elements of both. The most obvious shortcoming of the Lebanese system is its failure over its more than 65 years of existence to establish a respected, well qualified and independent judiciary. The constitutional rights of citizens will never be protected from various assaults on their integrity without the presence of a powerful and independent judicial branch. As if it is not enough to take away what is arguably the most important guarantee that individuals have Lebanon has managed to come up with another hybrid or should I say mutant. The efforts over the past couple of years have culminated in creating the principle of "national unity" government which is a cover to give the minority

110

the right to veto any and all plans by the majority. That in it would have been a strong enough blow for effective government but that was not enough to satisfy the ambitions of the "opposition". Diffusion in the current Lebanese system does not end with forming a government chosen from the elected members of the parliament but has even managed in creating a cabinet that is for all intents and purposes a "shrunken parliament". This new cabinet has in effect emasculated the legislature to such an extent that it does not ever get its approval but it even dictates to it. Decisions arrived at by the cabinet are so sacrosanct that no one in the parliament dares question. Our present iteration of diffusion has resulted in the effective annulment of the legislative branch. A mutant Democracy.

So what has the democratically based Lebanese political structure evolved into? A tower of Babel where the judiciary has no important role to play, an unconstitutionally elected president and a legislature that has willingly abdicated its responsibilities. Welcome to democracy, Lebanese style.

Tuesday, April 13, 2010

<u>Was The Lebanese Civil War A Total Waste?</u>

Civil conflicts are not exactly uncommon in this world. There is hardly a nation state that has not had to overcome a major civil conflict as it was becoming established. In a sense, it appears that civil strife is a rite of passage of some sort. Although there is no need to elaborate on this point as it is rather obvious and the historical facts speak eloquently for themselves let me remind the skeptics of the British civil war, the French Revolution, The American Revolution, the Russian Revolution and the Chinese revolution just to name a few.

In most cases, and certainly in each of the above mentioned ones, the bloody, destructive and painful civil wars dealt a decisive blow to the ancient regime and thus replaced the tension that dominated civil discord with a new synthesis that went on to serve these societies rather well. The deep scars have healed, relationships are harmonious, and a new identity was forged for all members of society. This laid the ground work needed for peaceful development of the human potential and for tremendous economic progress as well.

Unfortunately in Lebanon, this has not been the case, at least not yet. Besides the large number of Lebanese, most innocent civilians, who had lost their lives in this conflict, many more were maimed both physically and emotionally. The wretched war forced a large number to become displaced and an equally large number to immigrate to other more peaceful environments in all sorts of countries all over the world. But where is the meaningful change that we have the right to expect for all the misery and squalor that has been inflicted on us? Where is the grand synthesis of what separated us? Is it to be found in essentially the same political leaders that caused the catastrophe in the first place? How can the ones who created the problem be responsible for its resolution? Had they had the wisdom and know how to avoid the conflict then it would not have arisen in the first place.

Political feudalism, sectarian politics, corrupt representatives and not much concern for the common good were essential ingredients for the troubles that devastated the Lebanese social, economic and political structure. Regrettably, if we glance around the current landscape we will sadly discover that not much has changed. In a sense things have gotten worse. Corruption has become part and parcel of the system, traditional political leaders and families are still there yielding personal power guided by selfish motives, sectarianism is even stronger than ever, poverty and income inequality are on the rise and sovereignty is still a concept that is alien to most of our political representatives.

It is clear that we have paid a huge price during the civil war but our only reward thus far has been a forceful hijacking of democracy, personal rights, rule of law and economic prosperity. Yes we have paid a heavy price but so far we have been denied to collect any rate of returns on that investment. To make things even worse, the Lebanese are one of the very few people in the world who are economically worse off currently compared to where they were over 35 years ago. The most recent estimates for the 2009 GDP per capita in PPP terms is under $12,000.00 when a WHO study suggests that the Lebanese GDP per capita in PPP terms amounted to over $13,000.00 during 1973.

It is a shame isn't it when all the pain, suffering and hurt fails to result in any kind of a payback in any field whatsoever, not even the economic one.

Friday, April 16, 2010

Should anyone Listen To Walid Jumblatt?

Walid Jumblatt cannot be taken seriously any longer. You just cannot tell whether he means any of the things that he speaks about or whether he is just trying to please who is on top. Once one becomes that unprincipled then it is time for him to just fade away from the public sphere. He has lost all credibility once he decided to become a chameleon. That trait of adapting to ones environment is a great survival attribute but that is all what can be said in its favour. At times survival is not a great accomplishment and definitely it is not a leadership criterion. A chameleon manages to survive by blending in, being a yes person and hiding behind others whose colours he is always willing to raise provided they throw his way some scraps.

Does Mr. Jumblatt really expect others to listen to his meaningless utterances when the best that he can come up with is an echo of the demands of a regional dictator? Who does Walid Jumblatt think is being deceived by his silly empty utterances about the need to discuss only the strategic defense plan and not the illegal weapons of Hezbollah? Individuals paint their own portraits and write their own history through their acts and utterances over time. Measured by such an exacting metric Walid Jumblat turns out to be an amateur who does not deserve to be listened to not because one might disagree with him but simply because he is not worth it. There are more important things in life than to take semi seriously the pronouncements of a dilettante who is a spoiled brat, one that inherited a feudal position of leadership when in reality he would not have been able to rise to the level of any responsible position on his own. Who wants to spend time and effort listening to the blathering of a corrupt and unprincipled individual who is willing to change positions twice a day?

Walid Jumblatt ought to be ashamed of himself and should just wither away. I am not a fan of either sectarian structures or feudalistic regimes but since that is the order of the day in the current Lebanon then the Druze community will be served so much better by going with a known quantity such as Talal Areslan with whose ideology and mores I am in total disagreement, but who is willing to take a stand for what he believes in. Heck even Mr. Wahab, who I consider to be a Syrian agent, will be an improvement on Walid Bey.

An individual ought to be free to take any stand and support any cause that he/she likes and that is fine but to claim a mantle of leadership when the best that one can do is to adapt to the ideology of who is on top is utterly despicable. That is a far cry from the idea of "give me liberty or give me death". It is in essence a cry to allow own to survive even in a hole as long as one is spared. The" good life" as seen by Plato ought to be more valuable than this; he turned down the offer to spare his life if he would accept to tell a lie. I wish that Walid Jumblatt can live by such standards. But since he obviously cannot then the best thing that he can do for his clan, for his country and for socialism is just to fade away. He has earned a retirement in a far away island where no one would have to be subjected to his daily hallucinations.

Tuesday, April 20, 2010

Analyze This

Please poke me, wake me up and tell me that this is all a dream. A nightmare is more like it. Are we really living in the 21st century or is this a cruel joke, a charade. We are really living in the 14th century and adhering to all its values.

How else can one explain that a prominent political leader is proud of the fact that the state, the legitimate state should not even discuss with vigilante groups the methods for disarming them of their illegal weapons because the state, according to him, is not yet ready for that. He goes on to say that there will come a time when we will ask them, the illegally armed militia, to merge with the armed forces. Now please tell me is there a more blatant way of submitting to blackmail? To paraphrase the statements of Mr. Jumblatt, what he is essentially saying is that let us not worry whether the Hezbollah militia is legal or not, it makes no difference that it is against the law and that it is financed and trained my non Lebanese. What matters is that the group is too strong and so we have to submit to its will. Yes I almost forgot that this is Lebanon, a Hobbesian society where the rule of law does not mean a thing. This is a land of tribes and the tribe that manages to smuggle the most weapons gets to dictate its rules.

As if the above statements that belong to a feudalistic society of the 14th century are not enough Mr. Jumblatt goes on to regale us with his plans for the Municipal elections. He spells out for us who he is going to anoint and who he will prevent from standing for office. He speaks as if he owns all of these towns and villages lock stock and barrel. Is this what we are proudly calling an election? Traditional leaders, a handful of them, wind up in appointing people to municipal councils just in the same way that they appointed them to the parliament. Yes folks you heard it right, Mr. Arslan and Mr. Jumblatt met and determined to "preserve family privileges" according to a spokesperson for the Lebanese Democratic Party. What about the rights of the citizens and what about democracy, a word that is used in the name of each of the two parties in question. It becomes even more ironic, those who are shaping the fate of "democratic elections "by exercising their suzerainty over the "serfs" in their dominion never feel the absurdity of always referring to themselves as progressive socialists.

And then there is the chief of newspeak. He told his Spanish audience the same thing that he has been fond of repeating at all occasions. He stated that he had no quarrels with the resistance since "it was established to liberate the land and not to commit acts of terror". Why is it so difficult for Mr. Aoun to understand that no one is opposed to the concept of resistance but what is problematic in the case of the Hezbollah militia is the process? A process that creates a state within a state, one that uses its illegal cache to blackmail others, one that is above the law. There is no place for vigilantism in a democratic society. A process that glorifies those that oppose the established government is a process that is misguided and that needs be harshly criticized and totally rejected.

And alas, a man of the cloth, Grand Mufti Ahmad Qabalan declared that the weapons of the resistance are "our glory and we shall hold to these weapons" never mind that they are smuggled, illegal and sow discord. And the above are only a small part of statements and declarations in favour of "democracy and freedom" in only one day in Lebanon.

Thursday, April 29, 2010

Vigilante and Mob "Justice" in Lebanon.

The murderous events that took place at the village of Ktirmaya in Lebanon were an abomination that must be condemned by all. It is true that a gruesome crime was committed against the peaceful Mr. and Mrs. Abu Merei and their two grandchildren. But it is equally true that a suspect for this heinous crime was in police custody. As is usual in these cases the perpetrator is asked to show how the crime was committed. While the suspect was "acting the crime" a mob from the village attacked the suspect, while in police custody; and proceeded to deliver a physical beating that was stopped in the nick of time by the authorities who then transported Mr. Mohammad Mosalam to a local hospital at the town of Siblin. Unfortunately the mob was not satisfied with the results of its handy work and so it reorganized and this time managed to storm the hospital and deliver the final blows to the suspect.

The suspect has become the villain, thanks to mob rule and vigilante justice. But this was not enough for the mob, its sense of revenge and thirst for blood was not over. The mob tied Mr. Nosalam to the back of a car which was driven all the way back to the village square. And thus the criminal becomes the victim while the rule of law becomes trampled upon by a mob intent on taking the law into its own hands.

But this is not the end of the gore and mayhem that ruled over the village, the mob would not be satisfied until the cloths were taken off the victim and then he was hung half naked from a pole at the village square so that the whole world can witness the savagery and "bravery" of a mob gone wild. This was an infamous day for civil society, for law and order and for the authorities themselves. The PSP needs to be commended for issuing a statement in which it condemns these dastardly events.

I am sure enough still photos and maybe even video clips were taken of the happenings on this bloody afternoon. These must be put to good use, to identify the perpetrators and apprehend them in order to send a very clear message that there is no room for vigilante activities because vigilante justice is the biggest injustice of them all. Once each of us takes the law into his/her hands then that is the moment that none of us will ever be safe again.

But should we feign surprise when individuals merely copy and ape the behviour of some of the most powerful and major institutions? Is it fair to suggest that individuals learn from their institutions? Our most influential players, sfterall, have made a practice out of taking the law into their own hands and of

118

insisting that the law of the land applies only to the meek. The strong defy civil law by establishing militias that act on behalf of foreign powers but the same militias are partners of the government that they spare no effort in demonizing. When vigilantism becomes the guiding principle of our political structure then do we have the right to act surprised when a lowly mob attempts to take on the trappings of the big boys? You reap what you sow Vigilantism will beget lawlessness and an eye for an eye and a tooth for a tooth will make us all blind and toothless.

Sunday, May 2, 2010

Municipal Elections, What Elections?

Many of my fellow Lebanese are proud of the fact that Lebanon is finally, after a 35 year hiatus holding its municipal elections for the third time, arguably the most important exercise in democratic rule. But should they? It is an incontrovertible fact that although democracy is not the same as free and fair elections that there can be no democracy without the universal right to suffrage. Yes we should be glad that we are holding elections at the most basic level of society so that different cities, towns and villages will get to determine who is to run their day to day affairs and how to help improve the quality of life for these constituents.

The paradoxical thing however, is that as soon as we determined to hold these elections the major political bosses started their efforts to short circuit the democratic system and attempted to arrange for deals behind smoke filled rooms that result in coalitions and candidates whose choice is designed to achieve one goal only: rob from the citizens their right to vote. If the vote is sacred, and it is, then why do these feudal political lords wish to take away from us the chance to have our say? The answer is very clear; they do not want to diminish their total control over the political system. If we are given the chance to form our own lists of candidates then we would realize that we do not need them to run our lives.

Even in the places that are "allowed" to hold electoral contests the mistrust in the ability of the average citizen to behave responsibly during the elections is actually demeaning. A country of only 4.5 million people cannot hold municipal elections without the need to spread the process over a month and without the need to bring most aspects of civilian life to a standstill during the time set for elections. What is so dangerous about having restaurants and bars doing their regular business when some citizens are casting their votes in favour of one candidate or another? Why shouldn't I be able to cast my vote either on my way to work or on my way back from my job? The whole exercise should not take more than 10-15 minutes.

I am at a loss why is it that we cannot hold these elections all across the country on the same day without having the army and the ISF forces deploy all their armoured vehicles and most of their cache of weapons. Who are these security forces protecting, or are they just their in order to intimidate and make us think that we cannot be trusted to cast a vote without the protection of big brother. Maybe someone should remind the authorities that the UK, a country of 61 million citizens declared on April 6, 2010 that a general election is to be held in exactly one month, May 6, 2010 without the need for any disruption of any kind to civilian life and without emptying the barracks of all soldiers in order to set up

120

check points around polling places.

I am afraid that these municipal elections, like all other elections in Lebanon are a farce. They are an exercise in futility that was designed by the feudal lords, who wrote the rules of engagement, proceeded to prevent the average citizen from having the right to choose through their deals in smoke filled rooms and when no agreement was possible decided to treat us as if we were irresponsible immature children who cannot be trusted to cast a democratic vote for local officials. The message is that we should be grateful that sham elections are being held.

Democracy cannot thrive if the citizens do not take their awesome responsibility seriously. Elections are a crucial part of what democratic rule is all about. But democracy cannot work unless we ; the citizens; have the courage to act responsibly and to cast our votes for our genuine representatives and not for those that act as subservients of political bosses, the feudal lords determined to keep us from having a say in how to govern ourselves.

Thursday, May 20, 2010

Oligarchy Is Democracy, Vigilantism Is Honorable

The Middle East is a tough neighbourhood. That is incontrovertible. But to use that as an excuse not to call things by their real name is a travesty. Lebanese society is a good example of the dangers that reside inside such dismissive attitudes. Rampant corruption, misguided policies, human rights violations, social injustice, economic inequities and ecological degradations are excused, brushed aside and even justified by always comparing them to the records of other neighbours and constantly concluding that since conditions in Lebanon are less illiberal then they are to be tolerated and even promoted.

Current Municipal elections are an excellent illustration of the above permissive attitude and the tendency not to hold any party or political leader accountable. Elections in a democracy are expected to be an automatic process that takes place according to a time table that is predetermined by the law of the land. Both potential candidates and registered voters know in advance of a date certain when these seminal acts are to occur. But not in Lebanon. Our political oligarchs feel the need to reinvent the wheel, at every turn, in an effort to demonstrate their magnanimity to the ruled. The whole Lebanese government, including the President spent months discussing whether the elections are to be held, when they are to be held and how are they to be held. I always thought that responsive democracies, we never tire of proclaiming Lebanon a leader in democratic affairs, hold elections whenever the calendar triggers the process. Well such behavior can be excused because our oligarchs have nothing else to do and so they feel compelled to create pretense of work in order to fill their time.

So what was the outcome of all this hullaballoo in the three largest Lebanese cities? Sham election in Beirut, no elections in Tripoli and potentially quasi elections in Sidon. In Beirut, March 14, pulled all the stops in order to avoid an election by popular vote and cobbled together a coalition that satisfied most of the traditional political leaders. A renegade group dared to insist on challenging the status quo and so nominated its own slate of candidates that offered less than token competition. The oligarchs rule was not to be challenged. Tripoli on the other hand promises to be even more of a shady process. Mr. Samir Al Jissr, a Mustaqbal MP, told Voice of Lebanon radio that "an agreement has been reached as to who is to head the Tripoli Municipality and there is no problem in specifying the other members on the list…" Who is it that forged this agreement and what was the input of the residents of Tripoli? Is that what we call elections; oligarchs choosing who is to do their bidding. In Sidon on the other hand, Al Mustaqbal worked hard to prevent an actual election from taking place and almost pulled it off except that at the last minute a relatively credible opposition decided that if Municipal elections are to be held then voters must have a choice. This was reluctantly accepted by MP Bahia Hariri and MP Fouad Saniora. They are bemoaning the fact that Sidon is to have a real election when it could have anointed oligarch representatives.

Another illustration of the tendency not to call things by their name are the almost daily statements by Sheikh Naim Qassem in which he declares that "It is our right as a resistance to own arms that we see appropriate to carry out our obligations … "What the Hezbollah deputy secretary-general neglects to say is that the militia/resistance in question is above the law, exists in spite of the law and is trained and financed by foreign interests in order to do their bidding. Now that is representative democracy isn't it? What is the difference between the rationale of the Hezbollah militia and the egregious acts of many residents of Ketrmaya?

The current Lebanese oligarchs can teach George Orwell a thing or two about newspeak. Corruption is efficiency, social injustice is equitable, labour exploitation is progressive , environmental degradation is eco friendly, unbearable sovereign debt coupled with a real estate bubble is a sign of economic strength, daily electric power rationing is a sign of prosperity, private "public" beaches speaks of equality of access, poverty is a sign of economic growth, expensive private education implies equal opportunity , sectarianism and oligarchical structure is vibrant democracy and yes pigs do fly.

Wednesday, May 26, 2010

The Big Lie

"The truth is the greatest enemy of the state" wrote the Nazi propagandist, Joseph Goebbels. In the same article he went on to say that "If you tell a big enough lie and keep repeating it, people will eventually come to believe it". Oh how proud he would be of Hezbollah and their supporters for, alas, they have put this Goebbels doctrine to the test with an overwhelming record of success. The unending multifaceted daily praise for the accomplishments of the "resistance" has managed to obfuscate the unnatural state of affairs in Lebanon. Unnatural because some principles just do not coexist no matter how hard we pretend that things are otherwise. Democracy and authoritarianism are opposites just as much as freedom and civil liberties are the antithesis of enslavement and discrimination. To pretend that it is otherwise is to shield the lie from its mortal enemy the truth.

The truth is an absolute standard that is not open to negotiation and compromise. It has its organic whole whose integrity cannot be violated. "No one can serve two masters. For you will hate one and love the other; you will be devoted to one and despise the other" is the way that Mathew explains it. Unfortunately this is a lesson that Prime Minister Hariri has not learned yet. He travels the world to praise Lebanon as an exceptional place, a place based on democratic principles and the rule of law but then he neglects to say that in Lebanon an unauthorized militia leads a privileged existence as a paramilitary group in possession of sophisticated arms that are smuggled into the country, each rocket and bullet, not to speak of foreign training and foreign financing. Democracy cannot thrive in the presence of illegal activities in all facets of life and to pretend that there are no contradictions is either to be ignorant of these elementary facts, which obviously is not true, or a practitioner of the big lie principle.

The fact that history has inflicted upon the Palestinian people a gross injustice and the fact that Israel continues its aggression cannot be used as a justification for the unnatural contradictions that are being actively promoted as harmonious forces. It is crucially important that one does not confuse the political rights for a group such as Hezbollah to hold to any set of ideas that it chooses as long as these ideas do not infringe on the rights of others. That is what democracy is about. I will defend their rights to assemble and promote their beliefs, even though I disagree with them, with every single fiber of my being. But to argue that the rights , guaranteed by the Lebanese constitution, to assemble associate and run for political office allows them to maintain an illegal militia that does not answer to the state is unconscionable. It simply is an accommodation for a vigilante group obtained under duress, it is an oxymoron to preach democracy, practice oligarchy, settle for less than a perfect state monopoly on violence and yet proclaim independence.

No we cannot pray to two Gods. The state either exists or it does not. There is no such thing as a state and a no state at the same time in the same way that one cannot claim to protect a constitution by violating it. This government is not illegitimate, but it is neither democratic nor constitutional. It is not democratic because it has willingly accepted an illegal and an illiberal group to dictate domestic as well as foreign policies. As for the titular head of the Lebanese Republic, President Suleiman, he was illegally elected to a post that the constitution specifically prohibits him from occupying. The constitution is a sacred document in any and all states. To show such disregard for the constitution by accepting a position that one is prohibited from occupying is contemptuous of the constitution to say the least.

The Big Lie will ultimately fail since facts and the truth cannot remain as an inconvenience for ever.

Friday, May 28, 2010

Lebanon Needs A Truth Commission

"If It ain't broke don't fix it" is an expression that has spread globally in a relatively short period of time, 33 years if one is to accept that its first popular use was in 1977. The message implied by this idiom is not to be dismissed as being only a superficial statement that is attractively constructed. No siree. This is a pithy expression that can explain succinctly the forces behind the dynamic for change in any field of endeavour.

When things are working and delivering what is expected of them then usually no one devotes any substantial capital, time or effort to reengineer or change the procedure that has successfully delivered a good or service on time and as per specifications. The time for research and development becomes apparent as soon as expectations are no longer met or as soon as there is an obvious flaw in the traditional process. The Valdez led to double hull tankers, Chernobyl and Three Mile Island led to a total review of how to build and run a nuclear power plant, the global financial meltdown of two years ago is leading to all kinds of new regulations and obviously the current two crisis will lead to an overhaul in how to drill for oil at great depths and what kind of metrics are acceptable in sovereign debt.

If it ain't broke don't fix it but if it is broke then you better find a different and superior way of resolving the problem. Restoring the old order is not an acceptable solution because if it broke once then it will break again. What we have to do is to recognize the forces that led to the anomaly and thus adopt a resolution that is capable of moving the state of affairs forward. But this forward evolution is not possible unless those individuals or institutions that have created the problem are held liable for their misdeeds. It is crucially important to realize that those that were part of the problem cannot be part of the solution. Had they been able to be part of the solution then the problem would not have taken place to start with.

What is true of nuclear power plants, tankers, and financial systems is also true of political structures. A young state such as Lebanon has been moving from one crisis to the next ever since its inception over sixty years ago. It has yet to find a stable government that is responsive to the needs of its citizens and that has the power to extend its rule over all its regions, as small as they might be. One simple explanation for all of these persistent failures in governance is the refusal to admit that the problem is systemic and therefore the solution cannot retain the privileges and power of those that have created the current dysfunctional state.

At times change does not take place because those that have failed do not recognize their failure and so they cling to power at any cost. But, and I say this in all seriousness, it looks that our revolutionary job in Lebanon might not be as hard as many project. Take a listen to the attached video and you might be shocked to hear one of our most eloquent and charismatic political feudal lords confess to the costly, barbaric and grotesque crimes that he and all the other political leaders in Lebanon have committed. He even goes as far as to ask that all of them should be put on trial for the egregious acts that they (political feudal lords) have precipitated. Lebanon will not know peace and tranquility until all the traditional leaders are removed from office and prohibited from dealing with politics for the rest of their lives. Nothing short of a total change in the cast of characters and the architecture of the system will do.

Thank you Mr. Jumblatt for your confession and for implicating all the rest (Gemayels, Beri, Geagea, Aoun, Frangieh…)

Friday, June 4, 2010

<u>What Ails The Lebanese Political System</u>

The modern concept of sovereignty of a nation state and all its implications to the inviolability of borders, the sacredness of its territorial integrity and the supremacy of the state are traced to the treaties that ended the thirty year war through the Peace of Westphalia. I mention this only to highlight that this took place almost 400 years ago.

A young nation state can be excused, during its first few formative years, for its inability to exercise its sovereignty immediately at its inception despite the fact that independence for a nation state is usually based on the idea of sovereignty. Realistically no society can be expected to make the transition from dependence to independence overnight. Institutions have to be created, elections held, laws promulgated and citizens informed and educated. But a learning curve of 65 years that fails to make any progress whatsoever is only a sign of total failure in the effort to establish a viable independent sovereign state. Under such circumstances one must wonder whether the experiment that has so far gone awry is worth continuing or whether it would be more advisable to just stop the pretense and dissolve the state.

As you might have already guessed, the above scenario is not fictitious. It is a perfect description of what passes for political leadership in the nation state of Lebanon and for either the inability or the refusal of its citizens to act responsibly by demanding accountability from their so called leaders.

There is no doubt that the present is the sum total of our past decisions and choices. We are what we have become because of our history. But it is wrong to even suggest that the past shapes our future. The only time that the future becomes an identical image of the past is when we keep making the same decisions and choices over and over again. The future doesn't have to be an extension of the past since its most significant feature is that it embodies immense possibilities. Whether these possibilities are actualized or not is a function of the decisions that we undertake in the present. Our present is the history of the future moment.

So it is not enough to dream about equality, dynamism, individual freedom, economic prosperity, responsible government or a sovereign state. We need to take action that is commensurate with our objective if that goal is to ever stand a chance of being fulfilled. But we can never set our sights high and yet proceed to act as we always have when we were greatly displeased with the outcome. The same input will result in the same output irrespective of our hopes. For our hopes to be fulfilled, we must have the courage to reject business as usual. It will always fail to deliver on our dreams and aspirations because if we cannot change our actions then our goal would be only a wish. Lipstick on a pig.

If we are dissatisfied with the performance of the political regime and with all the politicians in Lebanon, as we should be then we have no right to complain if we do not have the courage to show our outrage at their incompetence, exploitation and feudalism. Note that the 4.5 million Lebanese sheeple find it easier to put up with the inconvenience of having one of the most outdated unreliable and expensive public electric power system in the world by installing private generators, at a great expense, rather than demand a solution to a problem that is simple to solve but that has persisted for over a decade. Why did we reelect the same rascals who created the problem in the first place? We complain about the lack of law and order but when the politicians elect a president by violating a very clear constitutional clause no one questions the decision. How can we expect a person to respect the sacred constitution when the same person accepted to be elected under unconstitutional grounds? The message is simple. Laws, including the constitution were made for the convenience of the Lebanese oligarchy. Their disregard to the constitution and the rights of the citizens is all around us. Its best manifestation is the unworkable new interpretation of a national unity government whereby the executive branch is a tower of Babel, the legislative branch has for all practical purposes been subsumed by the cabinet and the judicial branch has been abrogated. I ask you, have you seen any demonstrations against the above?

Then we have our "Progressive Socialist Party" that is everything but progressive or socialist. It is run by a feudal lord and its leadership is passed along as part of the inheritance. Actually the ever charismatic head of the party regaled us on a recent popular TV show by the analysis that part of the current Lebanese political problem is that PM Hariri represents the Sunni while President Suleiman does not have the support of the Maronites. And that from a progressive socialist. Somebody should remind Mr. Jumblatt of the high regard that Karl Marx had for religion. He went on to say that he; Jumblatt; will not accept an invitation to visit Iran unless King Abdullah of Saudi Arabia gives him his blessings. And that from a progressive socialist in Lebanon. (What is true of the incongruity of the positions of Mr. Jumblatt is endemic of all other parties bare none.

Given the above few examples, and they hardly scratch the surface, it should be clear to any observer that Lebanon is neither independent, nor sovereign. Its inhabitants talk the talk but never walk the walk. If freedom, democracy and sovereignty are important then let us act as if they are by vowing to hold all the current politicians accountable. We need to remind them that they work for us and we should make it sure not to reelect any of them again. The problem of Lebanon is not its politicians. It is its voters. Unless we learn to act upon our convictions then we deserve the government that we get.

Thursday, June 24, 2010

Why Does Lebanon Pretend To Have a Presidential System?

Quick, can you name the presidents of the following countries: Germany, Italy, Turkey, Iraq, Israel and Lebanon? Don't feel bad if you could not name any, besides Suleiman of Lebanon, since very few people know who these individuals are and for a good reason. In parliamentary systems the head of state, a president in republics, is merely a figure head. Presidents are symbols who perform ceremonial functions but play no role in the actual decision making of the government.

Lebanon has been effectively transformed from a Presidential system, similar to that of the US, Russia and France, into a parliamentary system but someone has forgotten to tell the Lebanese about that. The daily news media, both print and TV, insist on showing the comings and goings of the president and cover his every move and utterance when in fact he has no executive or legislative power of any capacity.

Obviously the legislative power resides in the 128 members of the Chamber of Deputies and the Prime Minister heads the council of Ministers where the executive power lies. Although the president names a Prime Minister to form the cabinet he is bound by the results of the consultations that he holds with the MP's. The cabinet once formed needs to gain the support of the Chamber of Deputies otherwise it will have to be dissolved. The president cannot on his own initiative dissolve the cabinet neither can he object to or veto the decision by the Chamber of Deputies.

If the President has no executive power, cannot appoint his Prime Minister, is not allowed to dissolve the cabinet or to introduce laws then what can he do? The Presidential prerogatives are limited to 3 areas:

(1) He is the commander in chief which could at times of national emergencies be an important function but not when private militias are stronger than the official armed forces.

(2) Foreign ambassadors present their credentials to the president

(3) The president is allowed to issue pardons by Decree

There is nothing wrong in having a parliamentary system of governance but what is strange is when both the public and the government officials insist on pretending that this is not the case. It is difficult to believe that MP's and cabinet members are not aware of the constitutional limitations on the power of the presidency which then begs the question why the pretense? The only possible answer to this question rests on the sectarian divide that the country uses for the allocation of its political offices. Technically the Shia community gets to control the legislative branch through the position of the speaker, the Sunni community takes control of the executive side through the Prime Minister and the Maronites get a figurehead although no one wants to call it that.

Well, the emperor has no clothes. Lebanon has a parliamentarian system of government and the president performs only ceremonial functions. Let's get used to that and stop treating this office as being what it is not. Enough meaningless stories about what president Suleiman did or did not do. Let us tell it like it is. A dynamic democracy can thrive and do well under parliamentary governance. What is egregiously wrong with the Lebanese system is the sectarian allocation of governmental positions in a totally unconstitutional manner.

Friday, July 23, 2010

Nasrallah: Why The Bluster? What Is He Hiding?

"The Sayed doth protest too much, methinks" ; with apologies to Shakespeare; is possibly the most appropriate way of describing part one of Hezbollah's two act play to explain why they were not involved in the assassination of Rafic Hariri although the five year investigation by the STL is expected to indict high ranking party members.

International investigators starting with Fitzgerald moving through Mehles, Brammertz and Bellmare in addition to the local investigations have unanimously demonstrated beyond the shadow of a doubt a very sophisticated plan of execution accompanied by well organized efforts to cover up evidence and mislead the investigation through made up claims and amateurish videos. What is clear is that however pulled the trigger was merely a foot soldier in an operation that could not have been conceived and carried out without the knowledge and cooperation of the Lebanese and Syrian Mukhabarat who were at the time in total control of all aspects of security in Lebanon.

The possibility of a Syrian involvement in this sordid affair at the highest levels was removed from consideration a few years ago upon the insistence of Russia that heads of state are immune from the STL investigations. The waters were muddied further by the "suicide" of Brigadier General Ghazi Kanan who was one of Syria's top men in Lebanon for two decades. Many observers do not believe that Mr. Kanan committed suicide but believe that he was liquidated either to protect others or as a punishment for acting as a "rogue" element.

Syed Hassan Nasrallah never wavered in his support of the Syrians. Who can forget his speech on March 8, 2005 in which he thanked Syria for its sacrifices in Lebanon? It provided the trigger to organize the

132

outpouring of support in a counter demonstration on March14 of over a million strong demonstrators. Such loyalty is to be expected since it was Syria that permitted Hezbollah to keep its weapons after Taef and it was through Syrian cooperation that Iranian missiles were delivered to Hezbollah.

If the STL is to issue indictments of individuals strongly connected to Hezbollah through a strongly documented case then this might be the "tipping point" against the Hezbollah as a political party in general and its illegal military wing in particular. An indictment does not need bring about either civil war or unrest. The Lebanese people have been patiently waiting for five years to learn what the investigation s has uncovered and they are anxious to move on. Unfortunately, it appears that Hassan Nasrallah is determined to make sure that no decisions critical of anyone connected to him are to be condoned. He will stop at nothing to protect his fiefdom in Lebanon even if that implies the use of force. And that is shameful.

It is hoped that the STL decisions will be accepted by all parties, as they should be and furthermore it is hoped that Al Mustaqbal will put an end to its misguided efforts of sanctifying Rafic Hariri. Let the man rest in peace and let history be the final arbiter as it should.

Sunday, July 25, 2010

Sedition: Nasrallah, Yes; Hariri, No.

In a democracy very few things, if any, justify sedition. Disagreements and dissatisfaction with policies can be opposed vigorously and dealt with through the ballot box during the next electoral cycle. That is the role of the loyal opposition.

Unfortunately this has never been the case in any Arab country including Lebanon since practically each of the countries is ruled either by an absolute monarchy or a one party dictatorship. Change under such circumstances does not take place without a violent revolution. Lebanon is an exception among the Arab countries. It is an almost democracy but not quite, at least in the sense that numerous political ideologies are represented in the Chamber of Deputies and even in the makeup of its government. Lebanon has managed to escape the strong one man dictatorship that has characterized Egypt, Syria, Yemen, Libya and Tunis just to name a few.

This very special delicate balance between the illiberal Lebanese political parties has led to a relatively liberal state, a state that recognizes more political and social individual rights than any other Arab state. Actually the latest Freedom Index, a sophisticated survey that has been conducted for over sixty years shows that the only two Arab countries that earn the Partially Free label are Lebanon and Kuwait. All the others are grouped under Not Free countries.

This tradition is in danger of suffering a major setback. Hezbollah and its allies have resorted periodically to measures that border on outside rebellion by occupying major public areas of Beirut for months at a time, instigating periodic road blocks and disrupting civilian life through the burning of rubber tires, occupying by force parts of Beirut and the mountains and even instigating a devastating war that has cost the country a heavy price in blood and treasure. As if all of that is not enough, Sayed Hassan Nasrallah has recently given two speeches and promises at least another one in the near future in which he has thrown the gauntlet to challenge the legitimacy of the Special tribunal for Lebanon, STL.

The STL was set up in 2007 under the auspices of the United Nations and due to a request by the Lebanese government for help in investigating the assassination of Rafic Hariri and others. Hezbollah was part of the Lebanese government that approved the establishment of the STL. Rulings by judicial systems rarely please everyone; actually they never do since judicial pronouncements on substantive issues are bound to be subjective to some extent. That has always been the case and always will, all over the globe. What promises to be unique in the current Lebanese case is not the possibility that one party or the other will find fault with the STL ruling once it is pronounced, it is that Sayed Nasrallah is busy laying the ground work for civil strife if the STL indictment goes against his party members. Compare this totally irresponsible behavior that is the product of a non democratic mind set with the calm, mature, statesman like behavior of Sa'ad Hariri. Mr. Hariri has been working hard to ascertain that irrespective of what the STL rules Al Mustaqbal and its allies are willing to accept such rulings. Mr. Hariri is guided by the national interest, the rule of law and democratic institutions when Hezbollah and its allies are driven by personal agendas and motivations that are bent on demonizing the other and that are based in authoritarian thinking.

The sordid affair that took the life of Rafic Hariri five years ago has to end. The only respectable and democratic way to accomplish that is to accept the STL ruling no matter what it turns out to be. The position of Hezbollah through its General Secretary, Hassan Nasrallah, to damage the legitimacy of the institution prior to an indictment and a ruling is preposterous. It is nothing but a cynical effort to reject any outcome that is not favourable to the party; Hezbollah will fight a ruling against its members but will accept a ruling that is favourable to them. What if all parties are to adopt such a position? Then no matter what the ruling turns out to be one group or another would give itself the right to use force and call for destructive behavior. Such attitudes and practices cannot be tolerated in a democratic setting. What we ought to do is follow the sensible democratic path being championed by Saad Hariri. That is democracy and responsible behaviour.

Sunday, August 1, 2010

Forecast for Lebanon: Cloudy Days Ahead.

The Arab world was abuzz with the news about the "historic" summit that took place in Lebanon last week featuring King Abdullah of Saudi Arabia, President Assad of Syria and President Suleiman of Lebanon. Many news outlets, especially the state controlled ones in Syria and Saudi Arabia, trumpeted the achievement of this meeting in the most glorious terms imaginable: "We have only dreamt about this day, thank God that we are alive to witness this moment" and Lebanon is "a strong model of the Phoenix" the bird in Egyptian mythology that rose from the ashes.

Such heroic words and great expectations described a 4 hour summit of dubious accomplishments at best. This was more of a public relations effort than an urgent summit. The only item on the agenda, if one can call it that, was for the visitors to send messages to their supporters in Lebanon that the expected indictments from the Special Tribunal for Lebanon (STL) need not cause the feared civil strife in the country.

It is rather bizarre when the only way to avoid social tension among various groups in a state is to accept to host a hurriedly put together visit of leaders of other states who are expected to influence the competing local parties to deescalate the potential confrontation over what is essentially a domestic issue. That does not speak very highly of allegiance, independence or even the quality of domestic leadership.

So what was the burning issue behind this summit? Ultimately the host and the two visitors were being asked to make their positions clear regarding the concept of the rule of law. And this is the rub. Lebanon, a state that has been moving from one crisis of governance to another ever since its modern establishment as a state more than sixty years ago has always had democratic aspirations that have never been allowed to take hold as a result of its discriminatory confessional political structure that rests on political feudalism. As a result the democratic institutions have been confined to the shallow, weak and ineffective. Simply put, an independent, strong and respected judiciary has not been allowed to flourish.

Paradoxically, the two visiting summiteers were not well qualified to give guidance about what is essentially a rule of law issue. Saudi Arabia is arguably one of the 3-4 absolute monarchies in the world while Syria has been governed for over forty years by one of the world's strongest authoritarian family rulers. As the above makes clear, in the same way that one does not have the right to expect effective advice on how to fix an internal combustion engine by seeking the help of, say, a carpenter or a physician no one should be surprised if the visiting summiteers in Lebanon failed to offer meaningful advice on how to handle a judicial matter.

It would be instructive to be reminded of a popular description of the rule of law and the role of an independent judiciary stated by Plato more than 2500 years ago:

"Where the law is subject to some other authority and has none of its own, the collapse of the state, in my view, is not far off; but if law is the master of the government and the government is its slave, then the situation is full of promise and men enjoy all the blessings that the gods shower on a state."

Only a society that is structured to operate as "a government of law and not a government of men" can offer the required foundation for democracy, personal freedom and respect for human rights. Obviously, none of these are attributes of absolute monarchies and one man rule. It is also helpful to recall that the onset of limits on absolute monarchs began almost 800 years ago with the Magna Carta.

King Abdullah and President Assad have come and gone, but the problem that they intended to address still festers. Actually, the positions of the two opposing groups in Lebanon are now as far away as they have always been, thanks to the uncoordinated messages sent by the two visitors. The Syrian president emphasized the need to discredit the STL while the king promised that he would try to delay the release of the indictment. They were able to divert, momentarily, the attention of the major parties for a day or two but now the domestic situation is back to where it was prior to the visit; and that, sadly, is to be expected. None of the principals; the king of Saudi Arabia, the president of Syria and the Lebanese president; is in a position to act as what they are not: leaders of regimes that are based on the principle of the rule of law.

Lebanon formally asked the United Nations to help investigate soon after the horrific explosion of 2005 in which former Prime Minister Rafic Hariri and 22 other people perished. This was later followed by a Lebanese request to establish a Special Tribunal to carry on the investigation and hold trials of the accused. The United Nations, in cooperation with Lebanese officials; established the STL in 2007 under a chapter 7 resolution of the Security Council. The chief investigator under the United Nations International Independent Investigation Commission (UNIIIC) became the prosecutor of the STL that is now headquartered in the Netherlands. It has adopted a voluminous set of documents that deal with all aspects needed for the smooth functioning of a judicial system. The STL has detailed descriptions of the rights of the accused, how the defense is to operate, the functions of the prosecutor and the type of trial.

Ever since it became known (but never officially confirmed) that the STL might be issuing its first indictments within the next few months against individuals closely connected to Hezbollah, all hell broke loose in Lebanon. Sayed Hassan Nasrallah of Hezbollah has already devoted two speeches to this matter and will be giving a third on August 3, 2010. No doubt Sayed Nasrallah has the right to object to the potential indictments by waging a fierce legal defense of his party. But that is not what he is doing. He has set the stage for civil strife by suggesting clearly that the court is an "Israeli" court and that the indictments are fabricated to discredit the resistance.

That is the reason for the current conundrum. Hezbollah happens to have a very well trained and equipped armed wing that is much stronger than the Lebanese army and its Internal Security Forces combined. The level of rhetoric by Sayed Nasrallh is very strident. He will accept nothing less than the complete rejection of the indictment; he threatens that if the Prosecutor is to issue the indictments, then Hezbollah will have no choice but to fight for its survival. This can only mean that Hezbollah will resort to force to make its point. Since they are by far the strongest military force in the country this action amounts to blackmail and the hijacking of the country. If Hezbollah is to use force, then many of the other political groups will feel justified in resisting such force which could drag the country back into the throes of a civil war.

It seems very clear that the logical theoretical solution to the pending Lebanese crisis is for all parties to deescalate the rhetoric, await the STL indictments, carry out a trial and rule on the culpability of the accused. All parties in a civilized society would be expected to accept the final judicial rulings and then to move on.

Alas, the problem confronting Lebanon rests on whether there is a commitment to the rule of law. If Hezbollah is right that some of its members are to be indicted and if the party is certain that these members are not guilty, then armed intervention is not the solution, legal defense is. However, Hezbollah cannot be expected to behave as it is not. It is a political movement based on a strong, theocratic interpretation with no room for secular law. Hezbollah must be made to understand that to defend its position through the use of force instead of the judicial system is actually counterproductive. There is no doubt that Hezbollah would win the immediate military battle but it would lose the war. There is only one fair, just and honorable way out: let the judicial system have its say.

(written for and posted at the site of Middle East Political Institute)

Wednesday, August 11, 2010

Yes, The Special Tribunal Can Accomodate Both Sides.

It has been obvious for a while that the case against the perpetrators in the case of former Prime Minister Hariri's assassination lacks the proverbial "smoking gun" ,which is not surprising for a very well organized and sophisticated operation that took place more than five years ago. Many of the news leaks however, have suggested that when the indictments by the office of the prosecutor of the Special Tribunal for Lebanon , STL, are to be issued in September that the indictments will name some Hezbollah party members on the basis of circumstantial evidence.

Hezbollah seems to take these allegations very seriously otherwise Sayed Nasrallah , its Secretary General, would not have threatened civil strife but then softened his position to suggest that he is only presenting evidence that has not been considered by the prosecutor of the STL. The bulk of the Hezbollah evidence is circumstantial. It suggests that Israel could have organized the hit against Mr. Hariri. Mr. Nasrallah showed video of the intercepted feed from Israeli Unmanned Vehicles that criss crossed the sky of Beirut and Lebanon but seemed to show that the UMV had a specific interest in the routes usually used by Mr. Hariri. This was the explicit material evidence presented by Mr. Nasrallah in addition to the important implicit evidence that made it clear though that the reason for all the Hezbollah related cell phone traffic in the immediate area of the explosion on February 14, 2005 was due to the fact that Hezbollah operatives were at that stage in pursuit of Ghassan Al Jid who is an Israeli collaborator and who has managed to flee the country to Israel. As you can see the strength of the Sayed Nasrallh presentation rested on showing a potential interest in the exact movements of the former prime minister in addition to providing a rationale for the presence of Hezbollah operatives in the immediate vicinity of the scene of the crime.

Mr. Nasrallah has the right and even the obligation to defend his party and its members against all and any accusations. No one should cast any doubts on the validity of such a claim. Defense though should be within the accepted judicial institutions and only after the indictments are made. Hezbollah and its many supporters however claim that they have earned the right for a preemptive defense, if you will, since the STL record is full of wrong accusations based on false witnesses. They thus claim that the STL is therefore politicized and is actually an "Israeli court" whose only aim is to discredit Hezbollah. That is a weak position since it fails to distinguish between the United Nations International Independent Investigation Commission (UNIIIC) and the STL. Most of the complaints by Hezbollah and its allies tend to be related to the Mehlis era of the UNIIIC when the STL had not been created yet.

So what is to be done at this point? Should the claims by Nasrallah be totally dismissed or should they be taken into consideration. I believe that under different circumstances these accusations could be dismissed but it would be a grave error to do so under the current set of circumstances that is prevalent in Lebanon. This does not mean that the STL should be discredited but neither does it mean that a major proportion of Lebanese society should be allowed to feel slighted and treated unfairly. There is an elegant solution which rests on the formation of a special Lebanese Judicial commission to study all the details that Mr. Nasrallh has voiced and then refer its conclusions to the STL.

المحكمة الخاصة بلبنان

Such a move will be within the current statutes of the STL in general and Article 4 in particular which does not preclude such investigations provided that the results of these inquiries are referred to the STL. Under such circumstances the rule of law would have been preserved, sides would have had their say, the Lebanese factions will accept the final rulings of the STL and then we will have this sordid affair behind us. What is crucial is to preserve the principal that the evidence leads to a determination and that in the field of law there is no place for deciding on an outcome first and then look for evidence to support that hypothesis. There is no place for reverse engineering in the judicial system.

Wednesday, August 18, 2010

Why All The STL Critics Are Wrong.

Let us be clear, from the outset, that there is no institution, official or person anywhere in the world that is to be held immune from criticism especially when the subject has betrayed and/or violated the principles with which they have been charged. But to be accused of having committed an act that the subject has not done is the epitome of injustice and demagoguery.

It seems to have become fashionable among Lebanese individuals, politicians, the media and political parties to never let an opportunity go by without making a statement about how biased, politicized and Israeli the Special Tribunal for Lebanon,STL, has become. Usually the only supporting documents for such accusations are often limited to a rehash of the undocumented charges that the STL has leveled accusations that are based on false witnesses.

Any investigation of the record would reveal that there is no justification whatsoever for the above position. There is no basis in fact for any of these accusations. After the horrid planned explosion that killed Rafic Hariri, the former Prime Minister of Lebanon and 22 other individuals a one month (Feb. 25 – March 24, 2005) fact finding mission was set up by the United Nation and headed by Peter Fitzgerald. This was later followed by the creation of the United Nations Independent International Investigation Commission, UNIIIC, whose function was to help the Lebanese authorities investigate the deadly explosion of February 14, 2005. The UNIIIC was established on Apr. 7, 2005 through Security Council resolution 1595. Mr. Detlev Mehlis was put in charge of this Commission that proceeded to issue two reports under his tenure ship that ended at the end of 2005. The first report by the UNIIIC, released on October 20, 2005, summarized the progress on the investigation by stating the belief that such a sophisticated operation was a few months in the planning and that it could not have conceivably been carried out without the knowledge of both the Syrian and the Lebanese security services who were known for their almost total and complete control on Lebanon at the time. Yet it is crucial to note that the report ended by stressing that all parties are entitled to the presumption of innocence until proven guilty. The UNIIIC did not indict anyone but merely reported what its investigations have uncovered. A second progress report was issued by the UNIIC ,still under the leadership of Mr. Mehlis on Dec. 20 2005 in which the commission stressed that it is continuing its line of inquiry and that it is also reassessing in order to "close out any lines of inquiry which no longer have a direct bearing on the case". This was the last report by Mr. Mehlis who resigned and was replaced by Serge Brammertz who issued the third progress report of the UNIIIC on March 16, 2006 in which he made it clear that the commission was investigating those who have deliberately misled the investigation.

The UNIIIC continued to issue its periodic reports under the leadership of Mr. Brammertz until he resigned effective January 1, 2008 when Daniel Bellemare was appointed as a replacement until the expiration of the UNIIIC mandate at the end of 2007.

Meanwhile the United Nations Security Council had established the Special Tribunal for Lebanon upon the request of the Lebanese state. The Security Council did so under chapter 7 of the United Nations Charter. The negotiations between Lebanon and the United Nations determined the structure that would become the STL: a Registry, Chamber with a pretrial judge, and a Prosecutor. The selection committee had recommended that Mr. Bellemare be appointed as the prosecutor for his familiarity with the details of the investigations that had been carried so far both by the Lebanese authorities and by the now defunct UNIIIC. But it is important to note that when the STL was established the UNIIIC had ceased to exist.

The STL became operational on March 2009 and that was when the Pretrial judge, an independent international jurist who is not a member of the Chamber, exercised his authority to review the evidence upon which the Lebanese authorities had held individuals in this case in custody. The Pre trial judge determined, at the earliest period possible, that the 4 generals held in custody should be released for the lack of evidence against them. Up until this moment the STL has not issued any indictments of anyone and has not made any accusations or issued any other rulings on this matter.

Based on the above, admittedly condensed and brief reading of the developments it is clear that:

1. There is a clear and distinct separation between the UNIIIC and the STL.
2. The Lebanese public and the media have failed to make that distinction.
3. UNIIIC was established to help investigate. It could not and did not issue indictments.
4. The Prosecutor of the STL happens to be the same individual who led the UNIIIC as its mandate expired. This, however, does not make the UNIIIC an organ of the STL.
5. The STL has developed a sophisticated set of rules under which to operate including a detailed account of the rights of the accused, and an independent Pretrial judge to review and approve indictments.

It should be obvious, based on the above that the barrage of daily accusations notwithstanding, there are no legal, rational or logical grounds to besmirch the integrity of an organization by constantly making allegations to which it is not even peripherally connected. The common complaint that the STL anchored its case to the testimony of false witnesses is patently false as the STL did not exist when the issue of false witnesses surfaced and since it must be also emphasized that the UNIIIC was aware of the false witnesses and said so in its reports. The UNIIIC, just like any credible investigator had a duty to weigh the evidence as it appeared and consequently to decide whether to use the evidence or not.

In an effort to get as much clarity as possible on this case a question was submitted to the STL spokesperson, Ms. Issawi, whose response is very informative and revealing:

"With regard to the relationship between the United Nations Independent Investigation Commission (UNIIIC) and the Special Tribunal for Lebanon (Tribunal), you are right to treat them as two distinct institutions. UNIIIC is separate from the Tribunal, which only began operating on 1 March 2009. UNIIIC's mandate, according to United Nations Security Council Resolution 1595 of 7 April, 2005, was to assist the Lebanese authorities in their investigations in collecting information and evidence, but not to conduct prosecutions. Conversely, pursuant to Article 10 of the Tribunal's Statute, the Prosecutor is responsible for the investigation and prosecution of persons responsible for the crimes falling within the jurisdiction of the Tribunal. Following the Pre-Trial Judge's deferral order of 27 March 2009, the Tribunal now has primacy over the case and thus the legal framework is completely different, since the Prosecutor now has lead over the investigation. As such, the Prosecutor can use information and evidence collected by UNIIIC, in accordance with the Rules of Procedure and Evidence of the Tribunal."

Friday, October 1, 2010

STL Indictments: The Begining of the End of Hezbollah?

Hezbollah might eventually be described by the adage "The faster they rise the harder they fall". This popular adage is applicable to individuals as well as institutions that are thrust into the limelight as a result of some favourable developments but then the same institutions implode because they were not ready for prime time.

Hezbollah is such an institution that rose to prominence as a result of its ability to resist Israeli occupation and to continuously act as a thorn in the side of the Israelis who overstayed their welcome in Lebanon. But Hezbollah was not satisfied with these important gains in its stature since its real goal was not to only help drive the Israeli army from Lebanon. It can be argued, rather convincingly, that the ultimate aim of Hezbollah was to act as an Iranian vanguard by spreading the power of the Qom Grand Ayatollah to the Mediterranean. That goal of establishing a state run by the faqih was never totally abandoned but instead its full implementation was put on hold for purely strategic reasons.

History, in general, unfolds by moving forward in such a way as to create new visions and new realities that expand the concept of rights and ethics. It is note worthy to point to the continuous expansion in the circle of ethics all throughout history. This concept started with the self and then expanded to the family, the tribe, the nation and nature but will not end until it covers the whole cosmos, as suggested by Chardin. Those that cannot accept the challenges of the new realities but insist on solving all problems by going back to an imaginary mythical past will do so at their own peril. This has been the problem of Hezbollah right from its inception. It refused to act democratically and still insists on a very strict and fundamental religious dogma that is based on undemocratic values, rejection of diversity, the right to dissent and above all its ferocious stand to protect its right to stand above the law.

These destructive attitudes have contributed to the creation of an imaginary world where Hezbollah can do no wrong. Hezbollah demanded and won the right to be part of a cabinet that it does not recognize and started what turned out to be a devastating war with huge losses in Lebanese blood and treasure but declared the result a divine victory. Things were never what they seemed.

All of the above though, pales when placed next to its present dilemma. As if it is not enough to be an illegal militia that has no regard to the rule of law and the institutions of the state, a body politic that operates on Lebanese land but pledges allegiance to foreign powers it is currently acting as a guilty party in the case of the assassination of the former prime minister Rafic Hariri. The Special Tribunal for Lebanon ,STL, was set up by the United Nations at the behest of the Lebanese government to investigate the egregious events of the 2005 explosion that killed Mr. Hariri and 21 others.

Hezbollah has gone on the offensive to counter what is allegedly expected to be indictment of many of its members in the Hariri case. Sayed Hassan Nasrallah has made a number of appearances to declare to the world that the STL is illegitimate and that it is ultimately an Israeli/American court. We are also inundated with daily proclamations by all sorts of party officials that no one should accept the legitimacy of the STL and those that do are to be considered traitors and Israeli collaborators. Many have even hinted rather bluntly at sedition once the party members are indicted.

This desperate behavior seems to corroborate the validity of the alleged accusations. The honorable and rational thing to do would have been to await the indictments and then respond to the charges. But how can we expect a party whose power rests with its illegal militia to act democratically and within the dictates of the law? It's a party that rejects the legitimacy of the power of the state that it wants to be a part off and instead is threatening street demonstrations and hinting at pulling out of a cabinet that it would not have been invited to join had it not been for all its threats and machinations.

There is no doubt that Hezbollah can withdraw its members from the cabinet and maybe even force the cabinet to resign. That would actually be a good thing since Hezbollah would have started actions that will end up in marginalizing it. They might force a reshuffle of the government but they will not be able to form one under their leadership. Hezbollah's reaction to the potential indictment of some of its members in the explosion that killed Rafic Hariri and many of his entourage; if the case is strong; could set in motion a chain of events that will usher in the beginning of the end of this chapter of Lebanese history. Could Hezbollah be the frog that keeps on inhaling to get bigger until it explodes?

Monday, October 25, 2010

Is War the Only Choice?

It has been almost a century of tension, conflict, war, death and destruction in the Middle East. The conflict that has preoccupied the UN world leaders, Arab regimes and Zionists appears as far from a comprehensive resolution as it ever was. That is unacceptable since the killing, destruction, misery and mayhem must stop. This single conflict has resulted so far in the wars of 1948, 1958, 1967, 1973, 1982, 2006, 2008 in addition to the two Intifadas, Black September in Jordan, Damour, Sabra-Shatilla, Palestinian –Amal and Naher El Bared in Lebanon. Since tragedies, all tragedies have to eventually come to an end; it behooves us to ask whether this imbroglio is so exceptional and so unique that it will go on forever. History teaches us though that no conflict, between any two peoples, goes unresolved. If we know that at some point there will have to be a resolution then wouldn't the sensible thing be to lessen the uncertainty, decrease the misery and seek an honest and equitable synthesis of what separates the two sides.

Egypt and Jordan have signed separate peace treaties with Israel. These treaties have failed to live up to the expectations of the optimists but at least they have stooped the periodic devastating wars and allowed the governments to concentrate on civilian projects rather than wasteful expenditures on arms and killing machines. It would be difficult to argue that these two peace agreements have not served the countries well. Each of the two Arab states was able to negotiate an honourable agreement that respects its borders, sovereignty and ability to concentrate on its primary duty, improvement of the level of welfare of its citizens. I am sure that thousands of mothers have been spared the pain of losing their children to the war machine and an equally large number of fathers grateful for the opportunity to experience the joys of grand fatherhood that might have been stolen from them otherwise. And of course many young brides and good friends have been spared the ravages of war. If all of that is good for the Egyptians and the Jordanians then why isn't it acceptable for the Lebanese to do the same? Where is it written that Lebanon is not allowed to pursue its own aspirations to prosper and avoid war? Are we condemned to fight on just because the Iranian Grand Ayatollah believes that the state of Israel should not exist? If that is so then why is it that Iran is willing to fight Israel to the last Lebanese and possibly the last Gaza resident?

All activities, be they of individuals, institutions or states must have a purpose and a well defined mean to attain it. No state should chose constant war when it can seek peace. The ultimate responsibility of a state is to protect its borders against incursions and to provide conditions within its borders that are conducive to the betterment of life for its citizens. The first goal, protection of the borders, is best accomplished through negotiations and peaceful means provide the outcome does not infringe on the

148

rights and sovereignty of the parties. When such an option is available then it would be criminal to reject it and chose the attainment of the same exact goals but by paying a higher price in blood and treasure. Only irrational people will opt for the more costly and more painful solution. Unfortunately that is what Lebanon appears to be doing. Our political leaders, our businessmen and women and our civil society owe the country in general and the youth in particular an answer to the question of why must the option of suffering, death and destruction is the only choice? What if we can get back all the land and have safe borders without war? Why are we standing by as Hezbollah takes us to the abyss?

Sunday, November 21, 2010

67th Lebanese Independence: A Cruel Joke

Sovereignty and independence, you cannot have one without the other. These two ideas form the basis upon which states are formed. Unfortunately there is no international standard that requires a state to demonstrate that it meets the prerequisites of statehood if it wishes international recognition and if it wishes to be entitled to the privileges that accrue with such recognition.

Lebanon, within its current borders, was created by the French mandate in 1926 and was ultimately declared an independent nation on November 22, 1943 upon the release of the Lebanese detainees from Rashia. Yes Lebanon is 67 years young today and deserves to recognize this day if for nothing else but managing to survive through the past 67 tumultuous years. But survive is barely what it has done.

Right from the first moment of its inception as an independent state Lebanon found a way to institutionalize, implicitly, its sectarian structure. What looked at the time as a wise and accommodative decision on the part of the President Beshara Al Khoury and the PM Riad Al Solh has evolved to be a great historical error that has prevented Lebanon from ever attaining any of its potential. It is a sad occasion indeed when a country celebrates its 67th anniversary of independence while it has no independence, no sovereignty and no state to show for its efforts.

Where have the last 67 years gone? They have been wasted in squabbles, conflicts, civil wars and in paying fealty to political feudal lords and religious leaders. Lebanon has spent every second of its existence so far trying to maintain the illusion that there is a state when in reality what we have become is nothing more than a sectarian federation of residents with no allegiances to a state.

150

Lebanon has failed to grow the idea of citizenship among its residents who are willing and anxious to do the bidding of any state as long as it is not Lebanese under the mistaken and deadly rationale of sectarian balance. Yes we have managed to keep a sectarian balance of sorts but we have failed to create a state. "No one can serve two masters. Either he will hate the one and love the other, or he will be devoted to the one and despise the other." You cannot devote your life to the promotion of a sect at the expense of the state. Religion, faith, sectarian wellbeing should be a private affair and must never be allowed to dictate national policy. When we let that happen, which is exactly what we have done for 67 years, then we become what we are, a nation of pretenders. We pretend to be free, we pretend to be independent, we pretend to be sovereign we pretend to have a state.

All is not lost. We can still redeem ourselves but our first act must be to take an oath of allegiance to an idea, to freedom, democracy, human rights and total unquestioning allegiance to a state that is not based on sectarian principles and discriminatory practices. We can still actualize our dream of establishing a state worthy of the name but in order to do that we have no choice but to relegate religious leaders to their spiritual roles only. We have to forge an identity that is not primarily defined by our religious faith but by our civil rights. We have to shout it from the roof tops that the emperor has no clothes.

If we are to save the Lebanese experiment then we have no choice but to establish the power of the state all over the land and to elect the best and the brightest to positions of power no matter what god they pray to or even whether they pray at all. The last thing that we need to hear tomorrow (today) is an empty rhetoric from a president who was unconstitutionally elected praising accommodations with a party that acts as a state within a state and whose major concern is the appeasement of our neighbourly dictator or absolute monarch.

The Lebanese experiment is still alive after 67 years but barely so. We are on life support, in all fields. Unless we come back to our senses in order to renounce all the traditional leaders and reject sectarianism then we should not complain once this essentially noble experiment comes crashing down. It is not too late to save the day but such drastic action requires more than wishful thinking. Are we up to it? Time will tell but don't forget that time is running out.

Sunday, December 12, 2010

National Unity Cabinet: A Disaster

The current Lebanese make up of the cabinet; the so called national unity government; has been nothing short of an abject failure in every single respect. The Lebanese experience should be used as a poster child for the inefficacy and absurdity of a multicoloured government. The real victims of this unworkable mixture of two ideologies that have diametrically opposing aims and that have totally opposing visions of what should guide the policies of the state are the Lebanese citizens whose aspirations , dreams and hopes have been dealt one blow after another.

Lebanon needs to go back to a single colour government. It does not matter which party forms the cabinet as long as the party in question can put together a cabinet whose ministers are committed to a single vision to which they agree to devote all their energies and powers of persuasion.

The past two cabinets have amply demonstrated the inadvisability of a cabinet whose membership is not homogenous. How can we expect ministers, who have nothing in common, not even their allegiance to the state, to function as a team. There are certain things that do not mix no matter how hard one tries or wishes for them to operate as a team. Whenever the members of the same team do not pull in the same direction then their efforts will at best neutralize each other at the expense of the citizen who is left waiting for Godot.

Both major camps are equally to blame for not having the courage to level up with the Lebanese people to tell them that the current cabinet has been just as ineffective as the previous one. In a sense one can even make the case that both cabinets have even been counterproductive when measured by the total lack of accomplishments on any front. The previous cabinet spent most of the time arguing about whether the cabinet lost its legitimacy as soon as the HA cabinet members and their allies stopped attending cabinet meetings. Many in the March 14 alliance blamed the HA cabinet coalition for taking the government hostage by paralyzing the ability of the cabinet to meet and adopt meaningful policies that the Lebanese were eagerly awaiting in all areas, political, social and economic.

What is unfortunate but not unexpected is that March 14 seems to have switched positions with the Hezbollah cabinet members. March 14, led by Sa'ad Hariri the prime minister has done everything possible but call a cabinet meeting in months. But what is even more tragic is that the cabinet meetings are superfluous anyway. The public has become accustomed to the lack of ability to govern and to lead by both sides.

Hezbollah and its associates carry a larger part of the blame for the current standoff since this novel but silly idea of forming a cabinet from all sides is their idea. What this national unity government has effectively done is subvert the Lebanese democratic system that is built on the idea of separation between the executive and the legislative. In the current makeup the Chamber of Deputies plays no important role besides rubber stamping what the opposing parties agree to in the cabinet, which has not been much lately.

Lebanon needs to restore to the Chamber its role to hold the cabinet responsible for the progress or lack of it. But when the cabinet represents all of the factions in the Chamber then who is going to hold whom responsible for what? There is a solution and an effective one for that matter; let the party with the most votes in the Chamber form a one colour cabinet that will have no excuse not to meet and perform the people's business. These ministers and MP's do not come cheap anyway. Actually they are some of the best paying jobs in the country and the poor Lebanese citizen can hardly afford these expenses especially when the recipients fail to perform their assigned task. Let the majority govern and let the minority oppose so that the public will be able to hold the parties accountable. A one colour cabinet will have no excuse not to meet and not to perform because as soon as it fails to meet or perform then the other party could call for a vote of confidence. No one can do that under the current unworkable system of unaccountability.

Wednesday, December 29, 2010

<u>Save Lebanon: Sack the political Class.</u>

A major academic work about International Systems defines sovereign state to be:" any nation or people, whatever may be the form of its internal constitution, which governs itself independently of foreign powers"; and furthermore, The New Oxford American Dictionary defines sovereign as an "adjective (of a state that is) fully independent in determining its own affairs".

Lebanon in its current form does not even come close to meeting the basic qualifications of independence and sovereignty. Whenever there is a seminal question that needs to be dealt with it appears that the solution of choice is to abdicate our responsibility and to ask our neighbours to decide for us.

Whether it is the issue of Palestinian arms, the problem of how to deal with a state within a state, the question of cabinet formation, the terms for ending a civil war or even the potential ramifications of an international indictment by a judicial tribunal set up by the United Nations on our behest, the Lebanese have shown their preference for always dealing with the superficial by never having the courage to address the root cause of what ails them. The tendency to live in denial and to ask outsiders to decide on our behalf is best described as a reflection of immaturity, incompetence and inadequacy.

How can we be up to the task when most of the politicians do not believe in the Lebanese project? They do, after all, spend most of their time competing for the grace of regional dictators and monarchs when they should be looking after the welfare of their citizens and the affairs of the state. Lebanon is threatened, again, with political instability and a total ineffectual cabinet but yet the PM, Sa'ad Hariri, has spent more than 50% of his time in office traveling on either peripheral missions, such as a visit to the Sultan of Oman, or a personal visit to Saudi Arabia or France every other week, a s if the current political standoff is not dire enough for him. I do not doubt the sincerity of the PM but what counts are actions much more than words. I see no difference between his busy personal travel schedule and Marie Antoinette's "Let them eat cake". His behavior is at best insensitive and comes across as a non chalant attitude. If he is not willing to immerse himself in governing then he would do us all a favour by resigning.

The criticism of Mr. Hariri is not to be taken as an endorsement of the opposition. Far from it, Hezbollah does not bother to hide the sources of its funding, illegal arms and spiritual and worldly devotion to Qom and its concept of Wilayat Al Faqih. The head of the FPM, on the other hand, has proven himself to be a megalomaniac who will side with whoever promises to aid him attain his only goal of becoming a president. The FPM, as Wiki leaks has demonstrated, have been very handsomely rewarded financial for their positions; $50 million from Qatar for OTV. As for many of the other s such as Beri, Frangieh and Jumblatt they will do anything to win the favour of Damascus, Lebanese affairs be damned. Then there are the second and third tier parties and leaders such as Mr. Gemayel and Mr. Geagea who carry so much baggage that it will be difficult to give them the time of the day.

Then there is the President, Michael Suleiman. He wants to be taken seriously but forgets that he has made a deal with the devil to be elected. How can he possibly defend a constitution that he shredded when he accepted to run for an office that the constitution prohibits him, explicitly from seeking? There isn't a shred of difference between him and Assad of Syria, Mubarak of Egypt, Bin Ali of Tunisia or Sale of Yemen not to mention the absolute monarchs of Saudi Arabia, Morocco, Bahrain or the inherited leaderships of Kuwait, the UAE and Jordan.

The only logic that can justify the creation of a state is to empower its population to elect representatives that will act on their behalf and in such a way as to promote their welfare. When the politicians fail in exercising their duties, as they have amply demonstrated in the Lebanese case, then the good citizens have the obligation to retire every one of those that have failed them. If we choose not to exercise our natural right, to rule ourselves and to have representatives up to the task then we have no one to blame except ourselves. It is ironic that many of the Lebanese are constantly complaining about the total and utter failure of the political class, as they should, and their tendency not to act to right the ship of state.

Monday, February 7, 2011

Lebanon: Single Colour Cabinet and a Constitutional President

A team must be cohesive if it wishes to succeed. Its members must all share an understanding and a commitment to the goal so that they can execute the plays flawlessly. Unless they can communicate and cooperate selflessly then their efforts will not be in harmony and will result in missed plays and a record of bad calls.

Government cabinets are not any different. A cabinet must be composed of members that share a vision of what needs to be accomplished so that all ministries would align their policies and efforts in order to reinforce each other. Furthermore as challenges arise the discussions will be collegial and not antagonistic. These matters are elementary and are used as a guide in cabinet formations all over the world. Unfortunately, this very simple and obvious idea is not being heeded in Lebanon and the results have been simply disastrous. The last two Lebanese governments have failed to have any meaningful accomplishments in any field and have resulted in nothing else but governing paralysis and dogmatic infighting. These results were to be expected since the structure of the last two cabinets has been anything but homogenous; in a sense the members did not even speak the same language. The cabinets have resembled the biblical story about confusion, lack of effectiveness and disarray told about the Tower of Babel.

It has often been said that one must experience pain in order to appreciate happiness and chaos in order to seek coordination and cooperation. Although we can assume experience is the best teacher, some slow learners will get their fingers burnt repeatedly by touching the same hot service again and again. The best that can be said about the current crop of Lebanese politicians is that they appear to

157

suffer of a serious learning disability that is preventing them from internalizing the lessons from the recent past two attempts at forming cabinets that are designed to fail.

March 14 had fought unsuccessfully the idea of sharing the cabinet with March 8 under PM Saniora and then repeated the mistake, under pressure, with PM Sa'ad Hariri. In both of these cases March 8, a group that is the antithesis of March 14, cannot be blamed for insisting to be included in the cabinet and be given veto powers. This brilliant policy transformed the parliamentary minority into the effective group whose approval is required for any and all government acts and it allowed the minority to demonstrate the inability of the majority to govern by preventing the majority from any accomplishments.

One would have hoped that this experience of ineffectiveness would make the idea of incongruous cabinet something to be shunned by all. Not so. A few of the March 8 allies are willing to form a cabinet that accommodates their adversaries and what is even more astonishing is that many in March 14 are also open to the idea of joining the Mr. Mikati cabinet as the blocking minority with a veto power.

Responsible governance should be the only guide and whoever is to form the cabinet must avoid at all costs the mistakes of the past. Mr. Mikati can demonstrate his ability to govern by assembling a group of either politicians or technocrats or possibly a combination of both provided that all the members share the same vision of what is good for the country and also share the vision of how to get there. Let the cabinet govern, let it be homogeneous and let it be held accountable to the parliament and to the public. It is time that we stop playing the silly unconstitutional games of allocating ministries to groups and political offices. A cabinet must be one colour and must not award the veto power to any group or even offer the president a group of ministries. That would be a gross violation of the constitution and will introduce another governing tradition that is misguided. A country is to be ruled by a set of laws embodied in its constitution. If these laws do not offer the president any meaningful executive power then we have no choice but to obey these laws as long as they are in effect.

Lebanon needs to demonstrate its ability to respect its constitution by forming a government guided by and based on laws. This implies that those who have the most votes form a single colour cabinet and that whenever the constitution is violated then these alleged violations must be addressed. Lebanon would be doing itself, legitimacy and democracy a disservice if it does not clear up the issue of whether its current president, Michel Suleiman, has been constitutionally elected or not.

Wednesday, March 16, 2011

Lebanon needs Deconfessionalism and a Bill of rights

We all belong to tribes. Some well defined by such obvious physical criteria such as race or national origin others are based on metaphysical ideas such as environmentalism, democracy, liberalism or religious affiliation. Tribal loyalties are a significant factor in determining allegiances especially during events that require decision making abilities such as elections.

It has been said time and again that the biggest challenge of modern Lebanon is its political sectarian system, a system originally conceived as a creative solution to a young state made up of different groups that do not share a strong sense of belonging to a nation. The problem that faced our "founding fathers" in 1943 was to find a formula that will bring about stability and cohesion. Thus was born the "National Pact" which allocated the top four national elected offices to various tribes/ religious sects. The President of the Republic was to be a Maronite, The Prime Minister a Sunni, the Speaker of the Chamber of Deputies a Shiite while his Vice President was to be a Greek Orthodox. I wonder whether the National Pact will accept a convert to a sect or whether ones religious views are important at all beyond what the official records show as the new born's religious affiliation.

Sociologists will go on to explain the need to belong to a group of like minded people especially when civil society is not well developed. In that case the individual does not feel secure and protected from the arbitrary and often unjust application of rules. In such circumstances various individuals will find that by offering their allegiance to the group the tribe will reciprocate by defending the individual and will always come to her aid.

Based on the above, it is clear that tribal allegiances are based on rational thinking. And so is sectarianism. As a result a predominantly Moslem community will not elect a Christian as its representative nor would a Christian village vote for a non Christian. Voting for a person from a different faith is almost similar to voting to an enemy. One does not feel comfortable that the members of different tribes have the same interests and concerns. There isn't enough trust between the different tribes. Partisanship carries the day.

Being confronted with such traditions that have been well established a society has to find a way to break away from this archaic model. One way is to just proceed and eliminate the current system that allocates elective offices on confessional basis. Whenever this solution is mentioned it is met with a lot of mistrust on all sides. Each tribe feels that the others are waiting to pounce on it and take advantage of its members. As a result no tribe is willing to take the first step and agree to the new method of thinking. The basic obstacle, besides the clergy, appears to be personal concern about personal rights.

That is a legitimate concern but there is an easy way of eliminating it totally. The present government could pass a strong "Lebanese Bill of Rights" that spells out clearly the intrinsic rights of each Lebanese citizen to freedom of speech, expression, assembly, marriage, property etc... The Bill of Rights must also be accompanied with strict transparent enforcements at all levels. Once such measures are enshrined in the Lebanese constitution then the Lebanese citizen will no longer feel the need for protection by pledging allegiance to a religious faith and will be liberated to act as a responsible citizen.

It is important to recognize the rationale that has led to a wide adoption of a feeling that tribalism is essential. We can take two simultaneous steps towards ending this ineffective, unconstitutional and discriminatory system by adopting a personal bill of rights, eliminating political confessionalism and erecting strong walls that separate government from religious practice.

It is important to remind some that article 12 of the Lebanese constitution speaks of merit as being the only requirement for an elective office. It says nothing about religion or lack of it. Isn't it time that we judge people by their expertise rather than how they pray or even whether they pray at all.

Friday, April 29, 2011

Hezbollah' Contradictions

Ideas espoused by an individual, an institution or a political organization must be clear, unambiguous and consistent if they are to be taken seriously. It is not unknown or unacceptable for a change of heart regarding any position but that is different than holding contradictory positions regarding the same issue. Lord Maynard Keynes might have provided the best explanation for changing loyalties when he quipped "I do change my mind when new facts become available, don't you sir? ". The above might be acceptable even in explaining the constant flip flops in the positions of Walid Jumblat, who is always holding his finger in an attempt to find which way the wind is blowing.

That however is a far cry from the pickle in which Hezbollah and its allies have placed themselves. They must think that the Lebanese public in general or at least their constituents cannot see through the light fog of their machinations. It is time that someone reminds these political leaders and all the talking heads that favour their positions, of the teachings of Aristotle: ""One cannot say of something that it is and that it is not in the same respect and at the same time." This simply means that one cannot be for liberation and yet for oppression at the same time.

But that is exactly what Hezbollah, Amal and the FPM have been promoting without any fear of appearing inconsistent, irrational and unprincipled. Hezbollah and its allies lent their full support to the Egyptian uprising and were instrumental in the vote of Lebanon at the Security Council in support of a Western led and enforced no fly zone in Libya. That vote argued that the Libyan government was to cease and desist from shooting at its own unarmed people who should have the right to demonstrate and express themselves without the fear of brutal reprisals from Libyan authorities. If you thought that taking such a position in Libya would mean that Hezbollah and its allies would then offer support for the Syrian demonstrators then you would be wrong. Nabih Beri, Hezbollah MPs plus many an FPM spokesperson never let a day go by without offering full support to the Assad regime in its efforts to subdue by force the peaceful and brave Syrian demonstrators of Dara'a, Banias, Homs and other cities.

Whether by accident or by design the mask is off and the real intensions and motivations of this group, the so called "new majority", are clear for all to see. They view Colonel Qaddafi as a dictator, as they should, but the equally brutal, undemocratic and arguably more authoritarian Syrian regime of Bashar Assad and his circle of acquaintances as worthy of support. How is it possible to value innocent Libyan civilian blood but support and even encourage acts of brutality against Syrian innocent and unarmed civilians? The answer to this conundrum is simple enough: Hezbollah and its supporters are acting as a

162

bunch of unprincipled thugs who se stand in Libya is not so much in support of those seeking liberation as much as it is taking revenge on Colonel Qaddafi for having participated in the disappearance of Moussa Al Sadr. Yes the message to the Syrian people is loud and clear, Hezbollah and its allies are wards of the illegitimate Syrian state and they will spare no effort to show their support to those that oppress, discriminate and shoot at innocent civilians provided that they keep the illegal flow of arms to the Hezbollah forces flowing, in total disregard to resolutions by the United Nations and in contradiction to the sovereignty of a neighbouring state.

Unfortunately the contradictions do not stop at condemning in the strongest means possible the Libyan oppressors while exonerating the Syrian brutal crackdown on demonstrators. The political stands of the Lebanese "noble resistance" and its supporters become even more inconsistent, more incongruous and even more incoherent. Hezbollah has condemned the judicial verdicts issue in Bahrain against Bahraini demonstrators, again as they should, but they have not offered even a word of support or shed a tear on the more than 450 murdered civilians in cold blood by the Syrian dictator, their friend, protector and arms supplier.

Then there is the most bewildering position of all. Hezbollah, Amal and all their allies never allow an opportunity to go by without praising the concept of resistance, as if anyone is opposed to it. They continue the charade of obfuscation, the charade to prevent the distinction between the concept of resistance and the implementation of that concept in a monopolistic, undemocratic, authoritarian and even theocratic style.

Yes the mask is off and the ugly truth behind the pretenders is clear for everyone to see. Hezbollah's has just about run out of deceptions and the truth shall set the people of Lebanon and the region free.

Wednesday, May 18, 2011

Mikati Must Form a Cabinet of Technocrats Now.

When the coalition forces of March 8 agreed to bring down the Lebanese Cabinet of Sa'ad Hariri by asking their 11 representatives to resign they started a process that no one at the time would have ever thought to be possible. What has unfolded since then, almost 4 months and counting, would have been comical had it not been so tragic.

The complaints by some that the previous cabinet was brought down by what borders on an illegitimate coup should be dismissed as rationales of frustration by those who lost power. The tactics employed by March 8 were perfectly legal, democratic and proper. My complaint is not about how the cabinet was forced out of office but about the total lack of a plan about what to do next.

Every move taken by the "new majority", since then, has been nothing short of amateurish improvisation. The major reason that many were at a loss to explain the reason for the move by the coalition of March 8 to force the Cabinet out of office was the clear lack of an alternative PM. That is why initially it appeared that Sa'ad Hariri will be designated one more time to form a slightly different cabinet. Obviously that line of thinking proved to be wrong as the FPM and others declared that they will not nominate Hariri again. So who would they nominate? It turned out that they had no nominee outside of Mr. Karami whose consideration as a viable PM designate was short lived.

The coalition of the hapless was rescued from its own bungling my no less of a respected politician than Najib Mikati, an ex Premiere himself. Mr. Mikati offered himself as an alternative and muddied the waters. He had been elected to Parliament on a ticket backed up by March 14 and could not commit to the Hezbollah demands of distancing Lebanon from the STL investigating the assassination of Rafic Hariri , the most dominant Sunni political leader in Lebanon. But due to the lack of another viable alternative March 8 forces backed up the nomination of Mr. Mikati and had to apply all their political muscle to get him officially nominated.

If you think that once he was nominated and once March 14 made it clear that they will not join the cabinet then the formation of a cabinet will be accomplished in a matter of days then you would have been wrong. A delay in forming a cabinet made up of many different divergent groups is reasonable but not to be able to agree on a cabinet composition for a cabinet made up of one coalition; that has precipitated the whole governmental crisis; is ludicrous.

Mr. Mikati who is not in a position to alienate his Sunni constituency; that will be sure political suicide; and who never made any public pledges to enact the Hezbollah agenda has had a clear choice right from day one. He has to act as a Premiere for all the Lebanese and must form a cabinet that is effective, capable and that is guided by the welfare of the country. Under the current circumstances this can only mean a cabinet of technocrats who +understand the demands of their respective ministries. This is the time for effective professionals and not the time to train all of these political candidates whose only qualification at times is kinship to a political leader.

Lebanon cannot afford any more amateurish and ideologically driven behavior similar to the calls to eliminate gasoline taxes and to withhold from the government its own funds. That behavior is reminiscent of the childish acts of cutting ones nose to spite ones face.

Mr. Mikati has formed a cabinet of technocrats before and that cabinet of 14 members performed extremely well. He owes it to the Lebanese, to the constitution and to his own conscience to form another cabinet of capable responsible and well experienced ministers. That is what Mr. Mikati should have done four months ago; it's never too late to do the right thing. Better late than never.

Tuesday, May 24, 2011

Can the Lebanese Politicians Save The Economy?

Whenever a country is subjected to some turbulence; social political, economic or natural; its economic performance is bound to suffer. This has always been the case, all throughout history and it still is. Just witness the economic pain that was inflicted on the United States and on Europe as a result of the subprime problem, the failure of regulations and the extended leveraging indulged in by most actors. This has also been the case in Japan that suffered from the twin natural disasters of an earth quake and a tsunami when it was barely out of the "lost decade" debacle.

The Arab uprisings have not been more merciful. It has left in its wake a weakened Tunisian economy, an Egyptian economy that is caught in a painful down spiral, a Libya that is in the midst of a civil war and economic decline and a Syria that would most likely be hit by a severe economic contraction due to the ongoing social strife and the ensuing economic insecurity that accompanies it.

Lebanon appears to have escaped, so far, the political upheavals plaguing the region not because it is not in need of reform but because its citizens have freely chosen the reigning corrupt system of government that they are free; at least in theory; to change if they choose to do so. But the Lebanese do not have much to gloat about. The economy is not in shambles yet but it is, at best, in an unenviable position. Unemployment is high, social spending is meager, capital inflows are decreasing, the central governmental budget deficit is growing, exports are diminishing, the tourist sector projections are rather gloomy and the sovereign debt is growing both in absolute terms and as a percentage of the GDP.

In spite of all the above very few of our politicians devote much of their time to a serious discussion of the economic policies and priorities that Lebanon needs to adopt in order not to avoid falling into the economic abyss that the country is hurtling towards. The hubris of the politicians led them to build castles on the sand. They are all proud of the relative economic performance of the country in the last 2-3 years although that success is illusory and rests on very weak fundamentals.

Obviously the ability to finance the national debt is arguably the single most important issue facing the country. The lessons from the problems of Greece, Portugal and Ireland amongst many have not been learned by the Lebanese politicians whose expectations to manage the national debt are based on nothing else besides wishful thinking.

The easiest way to look at the burden created by the national debt is to determine its relative size to the GDP. Lebanon has the disadvantage of having an extremely high debt/GDP ratio which has increased recently. How difficult is it to project the size of this burden over the next decade? A detailed projection would require building a complicated macroeconomic model. But one can get a feel for what is likely to happen by simply looking at two variables, the average interest rate paid on financing the current debt and the average expected nominal rate of growth in the economy.

I have worked out for you three different scenarios. All what you have to do is choose the scenario that you think is most likely to occur.

My projections are based on a ten year cycle. This means that the following figures are projections for the year 2020 based on 2010. Another very conservative assumption is that the rate of interest paid on the debt will average only 7%. Most probably it will be much higher. Another starting assumption is that at the end of 2010 the GDP was 60,240 billion LL while the national debt amounted to 79295 billion LL. We will also assume that the Lebanese government will not be in a position to reduce the principal outstanding but will not borrow except to pay for the interest.

Sovereign Debt 2010:LL 79295 billion
Sovereign Debt 2020: LL 155,807 billion
GDP 2010:....LL 60,240 billion
GDP 2020.....LL142,500 billion (assumes annual average growth rate of 9%)
GDP 2020.....LL118,500 billion(assumes annual average growth rate of 7%)
GDP2020.....LL98,000 billion (assumes an annual average growth rate of 5%)

As you can see from the above it is crucially important for the economy to experience a nominal growth rate that is larger than the average rate of interest paid on the national debt. Any growth rate that falls short of the rate of interest is simply disastrous. Note that the 2010 Debt/GDP =132 and the rate will decrease to 109 if the economy can achieve an average rate of growth of 9% per annum but 159 if the average rate of growth is to be only 5% per annum. Obviously at an average rate of growth of 7% the ratio will not change.

For those that think that 9% or more is likely I have lovely plots of land for sale in the center of Beirut.

STL Indictments

The Lebanese public life has been held captive to all sorts of speculations regarding whether the STL will ever conclude its investigations and issue indictments in the case of the assassination of Rafic Hariri, a former Lebanese Prime Minister. Over the years there have been leaks, false witnesses, some more leaks, numerous speeches by Hassan Nasrallah , the secretary general of Hezbollah, accusing the STL of being a Zionist conspiracy, an American plot hatched by the CIA, some other assassinations and obviously some more leaks. Even the UN appointed chief investigator prosecutor has changed three times.

Well finally, just as Le Figaro and Der Spiegel had predicted years ago, the 130 page indictment has been handed over to the Lebanese Prosecutor General along with the request to arrest 4 allegedly Hezbollah operatives. It is tempting to say that over the years many have written and speculated about practically every possible conceivable scenario and so it is time to just wait and see what is going to happen. Alas doing so would be similar to avoiding the proverbial elephant in the room since the STL has been the only topic of conversation in Lebanon as well as many other world capitals.

To avoid the topic until the judicial process has had enough time to issue indictments, hold trials and then pass judgments on the accused would have been the order of business in any country that is informed by the concept of "the rule of law" but sadly not in Lebanon where this all important concept is alien.

So what is next and what is the expected time frame? It is very likely that as you are reading this column the STL would be handing its Syrian indictments in Damascus and releasing the names of the Syrian indictees. It is widely believed that the plot to assassinate Rafic Hariri had to have at least high level clearance from the Syrian authorities who were exercised tight control over all aspects of life in Lebanon. Some would even claim that the Syrian role was that of instigator of this sordid affair. The actual planning was carried through by the four individuals already named and indicted in Lebanon. It is also expected that there will be also a long list of foot soldiers/grunts who actually implemented the plan. This means that you should expect the final number of indicted people to be quite large, say over 25.

The Lebanese government was the one who requested the formation of the STL and is the one that had pledged its full support and cooperation with the STL. Actually most of the law used by the STL is based on Lebanese law although the court itself is in The Hague. Hezbollah was part of the cabinet that had initially asked for the establishment of the STL and the previous cabinet that had promised total cooperation with it. But when it became clear that the investigation is moving towards an indictment of individuals connected to Hezbollah the party embarked on a scorched earth policy of vilifying the STL at every possible moment.

Hezbollah has seldom acted as if laws mattered, whether it was the call to disband its military wing, hand over its illegal communication network or allow the Lebanese authorities into its geographic areas. Hezbollah has not shied away from flexing its military muscle to blackmail and intimidate. The latest such incident took place around six months ago when they forced the resignation of the cabinet headed by Sa'ad Hariri and were able to put together a thin majority to nominate Najib Mikati whose cabinet has not won the parliamentary vote of confidence yet. That is expected to take place within the next fortnight otherwise the cabinet will become a care taker one. I mention all of this since many believe that the major reason why the old cabinet was forced out of office; constitutionally; and why a new PM was designated but cabinet formation has not been facilitated is essentially the STL. The previous cabinet had a clear cut obligation to cooperate with the STL while the current cabinet does not have such an obligation so far. I would even suggest that the state of limbo serves HA rather well. It would be much easier for them and their allies to claim that since there is no government then no one is in a position to deliver on the promises of the previous Lebanese cabinet.

Things however could get out of hand and rather quickly. Lebanon has only 30 days to act upon the indictments. If the Lebanese government fails to live up to its international obligations under UNSCR 1757 which was passed under chapter VII then the international community will be in a position to force compliance through sanctions and other means.

It is my considered opinion that Hezbollah is playing a game of chicken that can only backfire on Lebanon if Hezbollah is allowed to proceed with its obfuscations and charades. Hezbollah is acting like a vigilante group who believes that they are always right and that they are above the law. That is a recipe for disaster potentially for Lebanon as a result of the uncertainty and political instability that could result. This misguided policy will also lead eventually to the weakening and even marginalization of the party. If that does occur then that would be the silver lining in this gathering storm.

Sunday, July 3, 2011

Totalitarianism in Lebanon

By most common metrics Lebanon is essentially a failed state. It is arguable whether it has ever been but a failed state ever since this experiment was established 66 years ago. The early formative years of practically all states promise to be uphill struggles. These are the years that are spent in establishing a national identity and allegiance to an idea instead of allegiance to tribes, feudal lords and religious orders. Lebanon is no exception and actually it has done better than some of its neighbours by preserving a modicum of liberty, freedom and human rights. But what is frustrating and even dismaying is the fact that as the state gets older its grasp on freedom, sovereignty and statehood becomes less certain. That is ironic when many other states in the region are moving in the opposite direction. An excellent illustration of the above point can be gleamed from the latest speech by Sayed Hassan Nasrallah.

As is often the case, SHN spent over an hour repudiating the legitimacy of the Special tribunal for Lebanon, the STL, by all sorts of attempts to make it appear that the whole set up is a sham, a conspiracy. SHN does not bother to tell the listener why is the conspiracy of the STL needed and what are its objectives. To him it is enough to accuse the STL of being an Israeli Western tool whose aim is to discredit Hezbollah and thus by association the resistance. He seems to intimate that all of the hundreds of workers at the STL have only one function in mind, create judicial structure and fabricate from nothing judicial evidence that would implicate certain Hezbollah operatives of being involved in the planning and the execution of the assassination of Rafic Hariri.

The STL structure is very transparent and is possibly far from being perfect. But SHN does not, ever, critique the "biased structure" or request a modification in the proscribed procedure so that it can become fairer to the accused. He simply lambasts the structure as being illegitimate. Well if it is biased and illegitimate then what does he suggest to make it more legitimate and less biased? He is numb on this front since it appears that he has chosen the tactic that the best defense is a strong offense. Again that is perfectly acceptable if Hezbollah was going to marshal its resources to mount a vigorous defense of its accused members.

But that is not what SHN opts for. He uses lies and half truths to paint an unflattering picture of the STL and its personnel but then proceeds to conclude in the most bombastic and even demonic manner by throwing a gauntlet for the opposition, the STL and the international community by stating flatly that he and his organization are above the law. He affirms the suspicion that he is the only master puppeteer in this proposed government that should never think in terms of executing its moral and legal obligations to serve warrants to the accused and to subsequently deliver them to justice.

The essential part of the whole speech is the final challenge. It makes no difference whether there is any truth to all his previous accusations leveled and fabricated against Cassese and other member. What is essential is that Hezbollah will never entertain the idea of submitting its members to the court irrespective of whether the proceedings are fair or not. Mr. Nasrallah has acted as judge, jury and executioner. He has determined that his people are not guilty and that no one should dream of arresting any of them, not in 30 days, 60 days, 30 years or even 300 years.

This is not the speech of a statesman but of a Don Nasraleone (the phrase coined by V on Qifa Nabki). This is the language of a vigilante, a bombast who views himself to be not only above the law but as being the state. It is unfortunate but true, Mr. Nasrallah is acting as the President, the PM and the Speaker. Lebanon has devolved into becoming nothing short of a perfect debased theocratic totalitarian state of Nasrallah land. And that is a shame.

Let me conclude one more time by stating that the future for Lebanese legitimacy needs not be gloomy. The power of Hezbollah is derived from their patrons. One of the patrons will most likely not survive and the other is facing tremendous domestic challenges. That is why I believe that since history does not unfold backward and that it is very highly likely for either both or at least one of Hezbollah patrons to be weakened that the anything outside the immediate future does not look rosy for Hezbollah. It just is not rational to expect the irrational to prevail for long.

Wednesday, July 6, 2011

Reflections on the Hezbollah March 14 divide.

Since we have been going around in circles for a few years, at best we are running on the spot, it is time to stress for the umpteenth time what appears to still be misunderstood by many.

Sayed Hassan Nasrallah, SHN, and all the Hezbollah, HA, allies have chosen to oppose the STL on some of the least logical grounds, they have primarily depended on an emotional appeal to the general concept of resistance without ever mentioning the specifics of the indictments. All ideas, no matter where and what they are about, will have supporters as well as opponents. That is the way it should be.

What is unique to the current Lebanese standoff, which has been in effect for about 6 years, is the fact that both sides enjoy practically equal popular support. Each side has a perfectly loyal base that will blindly follow its leadership without any questions asked. It makes no difference what SHN says, he can count on the support of all FPMers, Maraada, Arslan, Amal and probably 90% of the Shia. The other side will also follow, maybe slightly less enthusiastically but equally blindly, the decisions of Al Mustaqbal leaders and other March 14 politicians.

Since the sum of the supporters for both sides add up to represent practically all of society then none of these two parties ever feels the need to listen to the other, to reevaluate or to compromise. Why should they? They already have 45-50% of society on their side. What Lebanon seems to be lacking is a substantial independent swing group that can force each of the other two groups to seek its support. Such support can be sought only by widening the appeal of the respective parties which implies more flexibility and less rigidity. It means that no side can afford to dismiss the other, as they currently do. Had this been the case then the HA group would not have stuck to its policy of opposing STL and yet be for it at the same time. It's an untenable position but one that creates no problems for a leadership that feels comfortable with its large base of support. It's a position best represented by what Nawaf Al

173

Mousawi said on behalf of his HA colleagues" We invite the others to talk all they want but we will not listen". What a productive recipe for dialogue?

The same logic applies to March 14 who have spent the last six years preoccupied in creating a bigger than life image of Rafic Hariri. This is not to suggest that a thorough investigation of his assassination is not called for but this is to suggest that statesmen and stateswomen should be able to govern and yet carry on an investigation of a most heinous political crime. The public will chose to sanctify individuals that are important to it without the need for a well orchestrated campaign built around ubiquitous photographs of the deceased and constantly planned visits to his grave site.

I am one of the Lebanese how is totally dejected by the attempts by HA and their ally to paint everyone and everything that is not in agreement with them as an Israeli agent. Being sanctimonious is the height of hypocrisy. Their continuous veiled attempts to push their religious, totalitarian agenda is no longer that veiled when their chief spokesperson, SHN, declares to the world, that he would prevent the state and any of its operatives from enforcing an international warrant. That is nothing short of being bombastic and maybe even drunk by power to dictate. He acts as a combination of French royalty, d'état ce moi" and a grand ayatollah who staunchly supports the structure of a Wilayat Al Faqih.

But it is crucially important to understand clearly that as much as individuals as myself, object to the HA ideology and rhetoric this should never ever be taken as an endorsement of March 14 who , in my opinion, are marginally more acceptable but essentially just as much part of the problem as HA.

So what does it mean if one is opposed to both parties? It means a lot. The future of Lebanon, and paradoxically I still believe that there is one; is not represented by any of these two backward and incompetent alternatives. History moves forward, unfolds, through a dialectical process. I am very welcoming of the present day high tension between these two parties since I firmly believe that none of them can represent the future aspirations of the young Lebanese. These two alliances represent a thesis and an antithesis and the resulting conflict between then would result in a synthesis that will represent for a time to come a more just, a more democratic and a more viable future. The efforts to establish, in any form, a faqih led society have failed and those that look towards the 1960's for inspiration are equally at a loss of understanding that the root of our current dilemma is found in that which they are trying to resurrect. Our salvation lies in a movement that will liberate us of both.

Sunday, August 14, 2011

The Mikati Cabinet: More Incongruities

So the Lebanese politicians were not satisfied with the lack of accomplishments by the Sa'ad Hariri led cabinet. That is their privilege. A new majority was cobbled up in an effort to form a different cabinet. Alas the new coalition could not agree on the cabinet formation for over 5 months and then when the new cabinet was formed its composition turned out to be as unwieldy and as incongruous as the "national unity "cabinet that it was to replace. So it is logical to ask, isn't it, why bring down a cabinet in order to replace it with another one that is just as divided , incompetent and unable to rule as the first one? The answer to this question is regrettably easy and shallow at the same time.

The major factors that led to the "Lebanese coup" stem from essentially the same root problem, the Syrian Ba'ath dictatorship. The international investigation into the assassination of Rafic Hariri had to be distracted and the accused had to be protected even at the expense of civil strife. Obviously the coordinated effort to demonize the United Nations sponsored Special Tribunal for Lebanon, STL, would be easier to accomplish if the cabinet is beholden to the party to which the accused belonged. Hezbollah engineered the coup by reneging on its Doha commitments in order to call the shots more clearly and they did. As soon as the STL released its indictments, Sayed Hassan Nasrallah delivers a fiery speech in which he dares the world community to enforce its warrants. What makes this challenge especially galling is that the source of this challenge is the king maker in the Lebanese cabinet which insisted that it is bound to carry all its obligations to the world community. This bad cop good cop routine did not fool anyone since the real intension in this case was obfuscation. Pity Najib Mikati, a successful billionaire who might have truly believed at one point that he can make a difference for taking on the role of trying to explain the unexplainable: a cabinet cannot be for the STL but yet against it. All the protestations of

175

Najib Mikati and his confidants to the contrary, will not succeed in changing his image as a Hezbollah enabler.

As if this reason to protect the perpetrators was not enough the Syrian uprising that started in Mid March 2011 gained more popularity and spread across Syria as time went on. The initial response of the Syrian security forces was to dismiss the protestors as hooligans and foreign agents but that turned out to be a wrong policy. The Syrian Ba'ath has been forced to offer one reform after another and one compromise after another in an effort to subdue the uprising that is still gaining support domestically and internationally by the minute. This uncomfortable situation in which the Syrian masters of Hezbollah and its allies found themselves in became another major reason for forming a Lebanese cabinet controlled by Hezbollah and subservient to the Syrian regime that has very few friends left, if any. The Syrian foreign minister, Muallem, declared that he was willing to forget that Europe exists. I am sure that as a result of the most recent UNSC Presidential Statement he had to erase North America, as well as Russia, China and India from the world map. But his consolation prize is that Lebanon dissociated itself from the vote. What a farce.

The contradictions in the positions taken by the various members of the Lebanese cabinet headed by Mr. Mikati have never seized. Lebanon who has refused effective cooperation with a UN set body, STL, and has threatened to discontinue its share of the funding is calling on the UN to arbitrate in the maritime demarcation of the Lebanese Economic Exclusive Zone. If the UN is part of a Zionist conspiracy in setting the STL then why is it to be trusted in maritime demarcation? Again Hezbollah makes threats of war while Najib Mikati seeks UN conciliatory role.

The same contradiction reveals itself in regards to the role of UNIFIL, the UN sponsored force in South Lebanon. The Mikati government claims that it is crucial for Lebanon to support the UNIFIL in the south but yet the UNIFIL contingent is used often for target practice in an effort to send messages to the Western powers that their contingents in Lebanon are not safe unless Hezbollah says so.

Although it is not the intention of this brief column to document all the incongruities that have surfaced in the Mikati government let me add quickly another few examples. The FPM, through no less of a spokesman than GMA himself doubts the honesty and the transparency of the finance minister, Mr. Safadi, possibly the single most important ally of Najib Mikati. Add to the above the fiasco that occurred in the dahieh a couple of weeks ago when the Lebanese security forces had to seek permission from the HA elements to enter the area in addition to the way that the Estonian kidnapped were released. Some media outlets have even carried reports that PFLP had kidnapped these Estonian by mistake. When was the last time that George Habash dared oppose the demands of his Syrian masters? That is laughable.

Then there is the so called Electricity Plan that the FPM has presented as its own solution to a devastating Lebanese problem that has dragged on for over a decade. It turns out that the whole plan was prepared under the previous administration but was being presented by GMA as a personal accomplishment.

It has become very evident that Mr. Mikati has either willingly accepted the role of trying to explain the acts of Hezbollah or that he is a willing participant in this charade. In either case this cabinet is just another tower of Babel. It is ineffective, opaque and cannot govern. Lebanon deserves better. Mr. Mikati ought to resign and go back to his roots by forming a truly independent cabinet of technocrats. That was his appeal in the first place.

Sunday, September 11, 2011

Lebanon: Who Is In Control?

No institution and especially no cabinet can perform effectively if its members hold contradictory beliefs and are guided by incompatible ideas and paradigms. That is the reason why effective governments are usually formed by a majority party or a workable coalition of members that agree to keep their differences under control and to work essentially to further the public welfare.

Unfortunately Lebanon has departed from this almost universal standard over the past 6 years. Taif started this trend towards diffusion of power by keeping the President of the Republic as a symbolic figurehead who is basically entrusted with accepting ambassadorial credentials and other ceremonial functions such as meeting with cabinet ministers and even presiding over ministerial meetings if he chooses. The President however cannot cast a vote or even introduce an item on the agenda. There is nothing unique about this since that is the norm in all parliamentary democracies. The problem in Lebanon is that someone has forgotten to inform the public about this change and so many, especially among the Maronites, still believe that we have a Presidential system. FPM among others still maintains the belief that presidential powers can still be restored. Let them dream or maybe more appropriately keep them in their make belief reality!!!

But a Parliamentary system cannot function efficiently and productively when the powers of the Prime Minister have been abrogated to a large extent by the so called council of ministers. This set up suffers of two major flaws:

(1) The Prime Minister is not treated as a chief among Indians but as only another chief among many others. The PM cannot be held responsible for what transpires under his/her term in office since the PM is not in a position to shape the cabinet policy. When the power resides in the council of ministers then each minister acts as if he/she is a mini PM and thus the premiership becomes so diluted that it becomes totally ineffective.
(2) The trend to have either a so called "national unity government" or one that is composed of irreconcilable ideologies ends up in creating a cabinet that in essence robs the parliament of its function. The cabinet becomes a mini parliament and thus it ends up in usurping parliamentary authority.
The situation does not need to be hopeless. We have a moral obligation to wage a major educational campaign to inform the Lebanese public that ours is no longer a presidential system and that we have

opted for a parliamentary one. But that is not enough. We also have the duty to allow the PM to govern. That cannot be done under a system where the major power rests in the ministerial council. We have to make it clear that the bulk of the executive power rests in the Premiership and that the PM has the power to dictate eventually the beliefs and the policies of the office. If it so happens, as it is inevitable to occur, that certain members of the cabinet cannot go along with the vision of the PM then these ministers must submit their resignations. Once the policies of the PM can no longer get the required support from the chamber of deputies then the cabinet will have to resign and be replaced.

The current as well as the past 3 cabinets, presents an excellent example about the absolute necessity for a change in the way that cabinets are formed. Najib Mikati, the current PM, never tires of saying that the cabinet is fully committed to honour all of Lebanon's' international commitments under international law including UNSCR 1701, 1559 and financing the STL. Normally that should be enough of an indication about what official Lebanese is in these matters. But is it? Not when Hezbollah and its minions keep on stating that they will not favour financing the STL neither would they want to enforce 1559. In this regard it is fair to ask, isn't it? Who is it that speaks for Lebanon? Is it the PM or is it the ministerial council?

I strongly believe that it is time that we put an end to this unworkable cabinet composition. It is high time that we shout from the hill tops that Lebanon has become a parliamentary system and it is also time that we allow the PM to lead and govern if the premiership is to be held accountable for the successes or failures. To allow the cabinet to substitute for the parliament and to encourage individual ministers to subvert the role of the PM is eventually ineffective, unworkable and even undemocratic. The PM must head the cabinet and choose those that are willing to enact the plays that he calls.

Tuesday, October 4, 2011

Patriarch Rai: A Shephard Endorses A Wolf?

When viewed through the prism of citizenship; and that is the only view that counts; then no country has any minorities. All citizens irrespective of their gender, race, physical attributes, educational skills, sexual preferences of religious persuasion are treated equally. In the eyes of the law of the land they are to have equal rights and equal protection. The state is not allowed to differentiate between any of its citizens as long as they are law abiding.

In a modern democratic state, as the one described above, the fears expressed by minorities are unfounded. Actually when a religious leader such as the Maronite Patriarch Rai express concern about the destiny of minorities then that flawed sense of identity is a reflection of his narrow vision of what a sense of citizenship entails. Citizens of a nation cannot be minorities in their own countries whereby the constitution does not discriminate between its residents. Yes inhabitants can always be classified by a myriad of characteristics that will result inevitably with a minority and a majority. But such distinctions are meaningless in determining qualifications for a political office or the ability to perform a certain job. If ones girth is not grounds for state discrimination and thus for fear that overweight people will not have access to political posts or financial institutions among other things then why should the issue of prayer or non prayer be any different.

A state is composed of different people who have different beliefs and who belong to different sub categories. That is what natural diversity, a hugely important feature for healthy evolution and growth, is all about. All countries will have conservatives, liberals, progressives, libertarians, highly skilled, rich, poor, Moslems, Christians, atheists... but each member of any of these groups belongs to only one class of citizens. That is why the scare mongering about minorities and the equally meaningless boast of some that this nation or that one is composed of minorities is based on a flawed logic of what is muwatiniah. Citizenship has no minorities.

It is especially troubling when such discriminatory language is used by those that are expected to embody the highest of values of ethics and morality. Patriarch Rai, among others, is essentially a preacher and a servant of Jesus Christ the man who had the courage to never waver from his beliefs and who threw the money changers from the temple. He was also the one who said in the Sermon on the Mount "'Blessed are those who hunger and thirst to see right prevail; they shall be satisfied.'" It is with lots of trepidation that an atheist should be reminding the leader of a 1600 year old Catholic Church about the teachings of Jesus Christ whose message was about courage, love and forgiveness, not about political compromise and expediency. It was in the same sermon that Jesus went on to teach the multitude by saying:' "But if anyone strikes you on the right cheek, turn the other also." He did not say "If someone strikes you then support their oppression so that you may be protected ".

And finally I will let Billy Graham speak to the Patriarch about what the real historical message of Christianity has been about for over 2000 years: ""Christianity grew because its adherents were not silent. They said, 'We cannot but speak the things we have seen and heard.' ... They stormed against the evils of their day until the very foundations of decadent Rome began to crumble."

I sincerely and humbly think that Patriarch Rai ought to be reminded of the message that his church has stood for all throughout history but above all he must reconsider his stand of offer spiritual solace to those that represent moral decadence in the Middle East, those who have violated every shred of decency for over forty years, those who have used the full power of the military against unarmed civilians, the Ba'ath regime of Syria led by Bashar Assad. Unless Patriarch Rai finds a way to speak truth to power, to speak against dictatorship, oppression and violators of human rights he will have to endure the opprobrium of his stance on the dark side.

The above tale should also serve as a reminder about the dire need for secularism. Individuals should be free to practice their religious beliefs any way they choose but such beliefs must be banished from the public square. Let the Patriarch tend to his spiritual flock and have the imams and sheikhs do likewise to their followers but let civil society be a free place for all citizens to fulfill their earthly dreams and pursue their aspirations unhindered by a religion that is often bestowed upon them by birth.

Sunday, December 4, 2011

STL Funding and Lebanese Polity

And so Lebanon dodges another bullet. What was billed, by all sides, as being potentially an explosive event ended up being a whimper just like the Elliot had predicted in "The Hollow Men" :

This is the way the world ends
This is the way the world ends
This is the way the world ends
Not with a bang but a whimper.

But has the problem been solved or have we applied the traditional Lebanese formula that has been in control of the country for over fifty years. La Ghaleb wa la Maghloob. No winners no losers. What a crock. Why anyone should be obligated to act responsibly if the outcome never matters. It always ends with the La Ghaleb wa la Maghloob.

In the last round things are different. No matter what kind of a spin anyone wishes to apply to the outcome Mr. Mikati has scored a touchdown in the last seconds of the fourth quarter. As a result the big losers are both Hezbollah who promised that the STL will never be financed and then obviously the clAoun who never seems to know what he wants. It is as if he is always waiting for orders from Damascus.

But this apparent victory is hollow. It does not mean much. Lebanon is still waiting for the real independent Najib Mikati to stand up and make a statement that is based on nothing else but the Lebanese national interest. He has not done that yet and it is highly unlikely that he would. The FPM on the other hand is busy bending itself into a pretzel form to say that what they have always cared most about is the integrity of Lebanon more than the simple singular issue of STL finance. The only response to that is bunk!!! This fiasco has demonstrated again the lack of professionalism, the amateurism in decision making and the total incompetence of those in charge of the FPM. But don't blame them blame those that have voted for them without holding them responsible for anything and blame those that will vote for them again.

But the biggest looser by far is Hezbollah. A party that has threatened and cajoled a people on this very same issue that they had to eventually agree to. It will be next to impossible to explain rationally this flip flop of Hezbollah.

But Lebanon has not won except a small moral victory. HA still acts as a state within a state. Note the recent problem with electric generation at AlZahrani power generation plant. The official Lebanese authorities have not been allowed to enter that area because it is only a "ghost" part of Lebanon an incorporeal region. The South is ruled by HA and neither the Lebanese Army, nor the Lebanese PM nor the Lebanese President have much to say about that.

Unfortunately Lebanon's problems are not limited to those mentions, as seminal as they might be. The opposition; March 14; is not in a much more enviable shape. Sa'ad Hariri has demonstrated amply enough that he was not born to lead. He is neither charismatic, nor well read he is neither creative nor principled. He simply has no vision; if he does he has not articulated it. The others in his camp are at least equally as disadvantaged and even more so. Samir Geagea carries so much baggage from the civil war that he must never be given even the chance to lead while the Gemayels will never be able to escape from their self made image of religious and political dinosaurs. Mr. Jumblatt appears to be a liability to both sides.

Lebanon's salvation is in modernity, democracy and a clearly defined bill of rights, i.e. a truly secular society. But how can we have a secular society when the Patriarch, the head of the largest Church in Lebanon behaves on a daily basis as a political chieftain, a non elected one for that matter. What hubris and what chutzpah. Why does he think that he is qualified and/or entitled to act as a political feudal lord when he is at best a priest, a man of the cloth who is supposed to offer some guidance to his flock on strictly spiritual basis? The Maronite patriarch and all the other Christian church leaders must, in the name of Christianity, renounce all semblances of political power and simply encourage their flock to develop an identity that transcends religion. If they fail to do that then they fail the basics of the Judeo Christian ethics, the egalitarianism of St Francis of Assisi.

And in all fairness the same is true of the Moslem Sunni Mufti. He must emphasis to his followers that to be a good citizen of a state does not diminish one's ability to be a good observant Moslem. Religion is a personal matter and must not be brought into the public square. That is purely for the secular. And that is another fatal flaw in Hezbollah who have stated clearly their belief in Wilayat Al Faqih. It simply states that the head of the church is to dictate and rule. No one else is important. That is autocratic and dictatorial. That is the interpretation of Qom and not Najjaf.

Yet I will be willing to put at risk everything of value to me in order to protect the right of Hezbollah to the freedom of self expression and belief but not for the right to abuse this freedom by taking a whole country hostage. They can rationalize it any way that they want but no one has a monopoly on resistance and no one has a right to establish a state within a state through illegitimate force and foreign interference.

A democratic Lebanon shall rise from the ashes and the tyranny of hooliganism and vigilantes shall perish. Either the outright fall of the Syrian regime or the introduction of meaningful democratic changes ogre well for Lebanon. They would only mean the diminution of the HA power. But let us remember that that is not enough in itself for the establishment of a potentially vibrant democracy. We have to declaw the other clerics also, the Patriarch and the Mufti.

Saturday, December 17, 2011

The Bane of Lebanon: All Encompassing Sectarianism

There is a time for everything. A time to live and a time to die but there is never a time to be sectarian "a member of a sect or faction, especially one who is bigoted in his adherence to its doctrines or in his intolerance towards other sects, etc." To be sectarian is to be close minded, to be a bigot, to see the world through a very narrow angle that distorts reality and makes a mockery of diversity, pluralism and democracy. Paradoxically these are some of the most important themes that many in Lebanon pretend to be promoting when in effect they are doing the opposite by pledging their allegiance to the backward and reactionary visions of the men of the cloth of the clergy.

Lebanon is currently in the midst of dealing with such three schizophrenic issues, each of which demonstrates clearly the need for a law that prohibits the clergy from meddling in political affairs. Interestingly enough each of the three largest sects in Lebanon has to face reconciling the irreconcilable; political stands that are the exact opposite of what each sect wants to appear to be promoting.

Maronites and Democracy:
No one can ever seriously question the commitment of the Lebanese Maronite church to a sovereign and free Lebanon. The church has played a major role in the creation of Greater Lebanon, as it exists today, and has always taken positions that challenge the political hegemony of foreign powers in Lebanon. Unfortunately though, the church leadership has seen it fit to play a political role in Lebanon instead of concentrating on its spiritual one. By doing so the church has promoted a distorted vision of identity. It has claimed in the past and still maintains that all Lebanese are equal but some are more equal than others. That is at least one reason, why it insists that the Lebanese official institutions are not to be populated either by elected officials judged by the merit of their vision nor are appointed officials to show superior knowledge and expertise in their respective fields. The Maronite church has favoured in the past and continues to favour the fact that the "official" sectarian denomination of a specific number of both appointed and elected officials should be the only criterion taken into consideration in these elections or appointments. Merit can easily be trumped by religious practice. What seems to be crucially important to Bkirki is to have 50% of the Lebanese MP's be of the Christian faith and they are willing to lobby government for what they consider to be their fair share of political appointees whether these individuals are qualified or not to perform a certain job. Bkiriki and all Maronite MP's do not seem to see the irony , maybe one can call it even the hypocrisy, of claiming to be democratic but yet insisting on a quota. The recent discussions regarding a reformed electoral system have even magnified the antithesis between what they claim to espouse and what they actually support. Most of the major Maronite blocs are on record supporting the strange proposal by the Orthodox Church that would

mandate each sect should elect its own representatives. Isn't that the most antiinclusive measure that a society can take and isn't this a measure that defines personal political identity in terms of religious sect at birth? Is there any room in this vision for non believers or for those that make a profound distinction between the sacred and the secular? Whatever happened to personal qualification as being the only yardstick against which potential recruits are to be judges?

Sunnis, Civil Marriage and Women's Rights.

The Sunni Dar Al Fatwa does not fare any better than the Maronite church. They are just as schizophrenic if not even more so since what is at stake does not appear to be that fundamental. Yet the Sunni clerical hierarchy has seen fit to oppose, and rather strongly, the proposal that would offer Lebanese women some official protection against domestic violence and abuse. The strange reasoning by the Mufti is that protecting women against abuse by the male hierarchy would lead to the dissolution of the sacred family institution. Did they ever stop to think that if abuse is so crucial to this institution then maybe it does not deserve to survive? But the beat goes on. The Sunni mufti speaks of equality and individual rights but promotes domination and hierarchy by one gender over the other.

Shia and Independence

Yes not all Shiites in Lebanon are members of Hezbollah but HA acts as if it is the sole representative of Shiism in Lebanon, and to be fair it is the strongest of the Shia factions. Its leadership has never hidden their total commitment to the Wilayat Al Faqih, the relatively new interpretation that arose in Qom and was popularized by the Grand Ayatollah Khomeini. If the clergy are to be the rulers and if Islam is to be the answer then how does HA propose to bridge the vast chasm that would never accept non Shiites as equals? To claim a belief in the philosophy of Wilayat Al Faqih eliminates immediately any belief in the other, in nation states and in their sovereignty. To HA Lebanon as an independent state would be tolerated only because it cannot be conquered. As soon as it becomes feasible to transform society into a totally Shiite one then the individual rights of others will never act as a hindrance. That is not democracy or the rights of the down trodden masses. That is ultimate discrimination.

Salvation

Based on the above it should be obvious that each of these three sects has a major problem of credibility. Each advocates, for convenience only, an idea that it opposes vehemently in practice. These in compatible positions cannot persist for ever. Each of them will at one point or another be called upon to stand up and be counted. Inconsistent positions will ultimately cause the collapse of the edifice that is built of quick sand. Lebanon's salvation, for all its citizens, is to judge each of them on His/her merit and allegiance to the common good. It is time that men of the cloth should retire to their respective religious institutions and it is time for the Lebanese to define their political identity in terms of what is good for the state and not by whether various members prey, or how they pray. The clearest sign that Lebanon has joined modernity would be when voters cast their ballots on the basis of ideas and not sectarian affiliations. We should rejoice when the Lebanese elect a Shia woman for Presidency, a Protestant as a PM and a Druze as a speaker of the Chamber of Deputies. It is only then that we would have transcended the narrow politics of divisions and chosen real democracy.

LEBANON
ECONOMY
MATTERS

Friday, December 23, 2011

Are The Proposed Minimum Wages Too High?

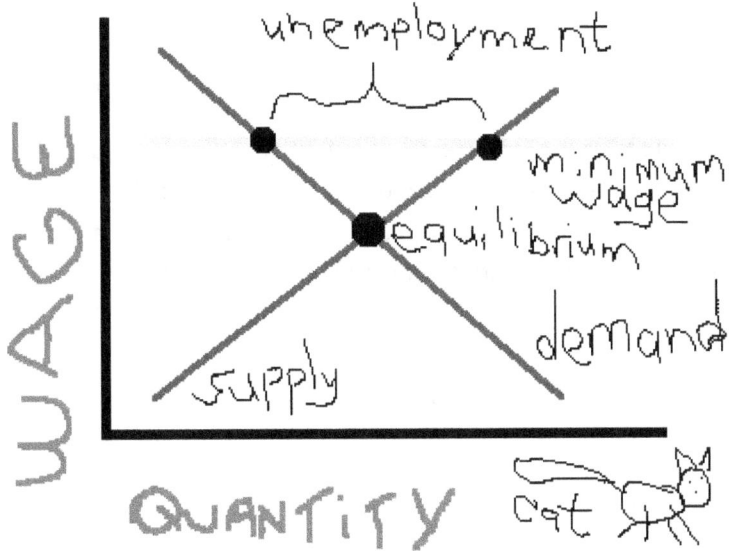

Minimum wages have always been very controversial and chances are that they will always be so. The idea is so contentious since it deals with one of the most sensitive ideas of a market economy, that of Laissez Faire. Is there room for government regulations and how much government interference is acceptable is at the heart of this issue?

One school of thought in mainstream economics, the positivists, refuses any kind of government regulation as being ultimately ineffective. They simply maintain that a society must accept what is, the market dictate. The opposing view, represented by the normative school, argues for what ought instead of what is. Members of this school of thought admit that a market economy faces many market failures and the only way to correct for these failures is for the Government to interfere and force the markets to change their behavior into what ought to be. It is clear that the second school is built on subjective thinking since what is, say, equitable to one might be inequitable to another. Let it be said though that market failures are not a theoretical construct since one can point to any number of such instants. In a sense all prices are not the real prices since the cost of externalities is never internalized fully by any supplier and thus the point of equilibrium is never the true efficient one. That is the whole idea that was initially advanced by Pigou and has become known as Pigouvian taxes.

As controversial as minimum wages are yet the arguments on both sides are rather simple and straight forward. Those that do not favour minimum wages argue that free markets are best at allocating resources and that government is not in a position to make such judgment. They argue that minimum wages end up in hurting those that they are planned to help; the poor. There are many studies that support this point of view by showing that job losses more than compensate for the increase in wages. The arguments on the other side are just at straight forward but in my opinion more convincing. They rest essentially on two pillars:

(1) Moral: No one should work when the rewards would not lift one from under the official poverty line. These are the ideas that have become called "living wage" and that are often supported by ones view of what ought to be considered as fair rewards.

(2) Economic: Labour markets are neither homogenous nor perfectly competitive. This means that the simple textbook model of supply and demand that the positivists depend on is not applicable. It is easy to show that in imperfectly competitive markets a higher wage could act as an impetus for greater productivity and thus even more employment. The great majority of labour case studies support this argument.

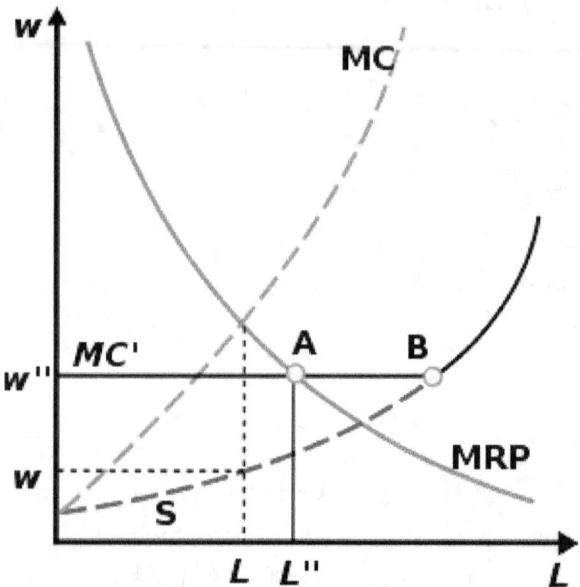

The above presentation is meant to show that almost all over the world governments have sided with the normative school of thought by mandating a minimum wage rate. This however does not imply that government has a carte blanche at setting any rate it chooses. Obviously if the minimum wage rate is to have any meaning then it should be above the minimum market rate but it should not be set at a level that would become counterproductive by choking off hiring and reducing the competitiveness of the affected industries. And so the real question is how high these rates should be? Unfortunately there is no set answer for this question although there is some rough evidence to where it normally is set. A quick review of the minimum wages all over the world reveals that they are usually related to the level of economic development of the countries in question. As a general rule the industrialized countries tend to have a higher cost of living ,a relatively high GDP per capita , a higher absolute minimum wage rate but that rate usually replaces a low proportion of the GDP per capita. In most of these major countries the minimum wage represents less than 50% of the GDP per capita: USA 33%; Germany None; France 53%; Japan 35%. Only the least developed and the poorest countries have adopted a wage rate that is either close to or even higher than the GDP per capita: Ethiopia 95%; Benin 108%; Burkina Faso 133%.

So where should the level in Lebanon be and what do the world levels say about the recent controversy that was set by the new minimum wage adopted by the council of ministers? The best judgment is to take a look at the group of countries that are in the same group of GDP per capita:

Country	$GDP/capita	Min..... Wage/GDP/capita
Hungary	13,000	34%
Poland	12,300	45%
Uruguay	12,000	23%
Chile	11,800	38%
Lithuania	11,000	35%
Libya	10,800	13%
Brazil	10,800	37%
Latvia	10,700	37%
Russia	10,400	19%
Turkey	10,300	57%
Venezuela	10,000	60%
Lebanon	**10,000**	**70%** (based on the new proposal of $576 per month)
Mexico	9,500	13%
Argentina	9,100	63%
Kazakhstan	9,000	12%
Gabon	8,800	27%
Costa Rica	7,700	36%
Saudi Arabia	7,600	33%

As the above table makes it abundantly clear the Lebanese proposal would make the Lebanese minimum wage represent the highest such wage rate in the world. Actually had it not been for Argentina, Venezuela and Turkey the Lebanese rate could easily be judged to be twice the global average for countries at its level of GDP per capita. So even if one is to be progressive but yet realistic it is abundantly clear that the Lebanese minimum wage rate should be scaled back to a maximum of $500 per month. That would still keep the Lebanese rate as the second highest in its group of countries, barely behind Argentina. Any rate higher than that would be irresponsible and will NOT help either the country or those that it is intended to favour. The government has many other tools that it can apply to improve the level of welfare of the poor besides a forced unrealistic minimum wage rate. It is one thing to be progressive and it is another thing to be suicidal.

Friday, May 7, 2010

Can Lebanon Avoid A "Greek Tragedy"?

"Those who cannot learn from history are doomed to repeat it" This George Santayana saying is as true as it ever was. How else to explain the current international financial debacle de jour? It is rather disturbing that after all the handwringing about the worst financial crisis that the world has encountered in over seventy years and after so many have questioned whether capitalism as a system can survive that we keep on repeating the same mistakes over and over again. Karl Marx's' popular quip about how "History repeats itself first as tragedy then as farce" also seems to be tailor made for these rough economic times had the farcical not been so tragic.

Almost everyone who follows the news knows by now that the 2007-2008 economic meltdown, whose cost was estimated to be around $30 trillion, began in the United States before it spread all over the world. There is also a consensus that irresponsible behavior by financial institutions, their regulators as well as individual actors have contributed to the strength and depth of what could have been a second Great Depression. Greed was the most common word that has been used to describe what led to the economic crisis. Greed of institutions for larger and larger profits, greed by managers for bigger bonuses and the greed by individuals to live beyond their means. The financial wizardry of the new "rocket scientists" on Wall Street made all of this possible and then some. They developed new fancy instruments out of common mortgages and then did the same thing for bank loans. Loans and or mortgages were bundled and sliced then diced into so many tranches and sold separately with different levels of risk to anxious buyers all over the world. No one could have enough; neither the originators of these synthetic derivatives nor the buyers. It looked that the "masters of the universe" have created the magic formula that will transform subprime mortgages into AAA securities.

But in order to securitize mortgages and satisfy the insatiable demand for these securities more homes had to be sold and more potential buyers found. As the number of eligible buyers dwindled, as it must, the standards were loosened until there were no standards at all. Home owners bought homes they cannot afford and as prices of real estate went up many home owners decided to participate in the melee by using their homes as ATM machines. The charade went on until the market started to run dry of buyers and home prices cracked. As the prices fell millions of these subprime loan holders defaulted since they cannot meet the monthly obligations neither could they sell. Many of those that took out second and third mortgages also found their holdings under water also. What started as a problem in one sector spread like wild fire all throughout the financial system since all players were interdependent and equally greedy to "dance while the music was playing?"

The crisis of two years ago made it apparent that both individuals and institutions had to deleverage their balance sheets which many have done. Regulators are still struggling with a solution to the "Too Big To Fail" but are making some progress in that regard. Unfortunately the lessons of the misbehavior, excessive risk and too much leverage were applied only selectively.

It turns out that the greed of governments was the most serious flaw in this system of international finance. Governments found a way to appease their populations through deficit finance. They offered benefits that they cannot afford and undertook expenditures on projects that are neither viable nor feasible. Actually these governments have mishandled so much of the borrowings that they had to find ways to keep the level of indebtedness off the books. Elected officials in many countries acted as if they have found the secret for wealth creation. Borrow the country into prosperity. For a while the scheme worked, just like subprime and the housing bubble did. But at some point the truth about the ability to repay the billions borrowed and squandered becomes known and the whole cycle of financial collapse gets started again.

That is what is becoming known as the Greek Tragedy or the Olympian Tsunami. Would the Greek Tragedy be confined to Greek soil? Don't bet on it. The Greek Tragedy is about to become a contagion and there is no reason for Lebanon to be spared.

The Lebanese sovereign debt is 146% of the GDP, debt service is over 40% of the government budget, wealthy Lebanese do not pay their fair share of taxes and corruption is endemic.

To Default or Not To Default...

December 11, 2011

There comes a point when an ever expanding level of debt and the ability to service it become unsustainable. It is my belief that the state of Lebanon has reached this stage. A Lebanese national debt of over $50 billion and rising is being fueled by a huge annual deficit that is also unsustainable in its own way. The urgency of the situation is put in sharp focus when the debt service of almost $5 billion annually is factored in. That sum is larger than the total of remittances by the Lebanese nationals who are working abroad and it is also greater than the estimated annual earnings from tourism. It must be ironic when all the revenue from the countries' most vibrant economic sector is essentially wiped out by interest payments on the national debt.

One common indicator of a country's ability to carry a debt burden is to express the debt service as a percent of its total earnings from exports. By that measure Lebanon already devotes close to half of these earnings to debt service which makes it the fourth such highest proportion in the world. For comparison, Egypt spends 10% Jordan 9% and Tunis 14%. **Furthermore, I estimate the Lebanese GDP to reach the $50 billion mark by 2020 and the Lebanese National debt to exceed $75 billion by then. These modest projections imply a debt service requirement of around $7 billion a year which is around 14 % of the GDP.** If the Lebanese Government budget is to be around 25% of the GDP then in a decade over half of the Lebanese budget will have to be earmarked to debt service.

The ability of an individual, institution or state to carry on the burden associated with a certain level of indebtedness rests on some rather strict parameters regarding the size of the debt relative to the estimated income in addition to the conditions under which the debt in question has been issued. The relative size of the Lebanese official debt as a percent of GDP is already one of the highest in the world. In addition the fiscal deficit, at over 10% of the GDP, is also one of the highest deficit gaps in the world. Both are judged to be unsustainable. How can they be sustainable when the estimated annual growth in the economy falls short of even meeting the annual interest obligations not to mention the need to finance every year the new fiscal deficit?

Lebanon has no choice but to stop the national hemorrhaging by taking preparatory steps to restructure its government obligations. A good place to start would be the Paris Club that specializes in debt restructuring. **The current Lebanese government should not shy away from considering either an outright default or at least a debt moratorium on all its obligations if a major restructuring agreement to wipe out at least 80 % of its current obligations is not arranged.**

Such major steps are not to be taken lightly but they are not to be unrealistically feared also. Argentina has defaulted 5 times over the past century or so and each time it regains its economic vigour and access to the international capital markets. The recent unilateral and sudden demand by Dubai World for restructuring most of its debt is another instructive case about the debilitating effects of an unsustainable debt burden and a possible mean for diminishing its severity.

Until such possibilities are studied seriously the Lebanese Finance Ministry must stop in due haste its misguided policies of seeking more risk. Minister Raya Hassan was very proud in announcing the recent ability of the Lebanese state to issue $750 million worth of Eurobonds. These efforts that have gone so far unchallenged both by the press and other government members should cease immediately. External debt adds a new dimension to the problem of Lebanese indebtedness, that of an annual outflow of scarce capital. Very few countries, if any, are in a position to seek proactively to increase the rate at which financial capital is drained from the state.

An equally serious risk, which a rational investor shirks, is the added exposure to foreign exchange risk that comes neatly packaged whenever a portion of the domestic debt is reissued in foreign currency denominations. It must also be emphasized that the Finance Ministry has been less than forthcoming when it boasts of its ability to obtain 5 year paper at 5.87% interest and 7 year paper at 7% interest. Ms. Hassan did not find it convenient to mention that the going market rates for the above maturities are 2.03% and 2.74% respectively. .

In conclusion it is clear that the Lebanese authorities must take meaningful action to reduce the annual fiscal deficit, restructure the hugely unsustainable Lebanese debt before it evolves into a major uncontrollable crisis. They need to embark immediately on a path of reducing the exposure to foreign currency and external ownership.

Saturday, March 14, 2009

Lebanese Banks: Profiteering?

Commercial banking in its simplest form is an institution whose primary function is to act as a financial intermediary .Attract funds from a variety of savers and then loan these funds to investors at a premium. This interest rate spread is often used as an indicator of how efficient is the banking system in performing its task of collecting funds and then making them available to entrepreneurs and investors. The size of the spread changes from one bank to another and from one region to another but in general it is an accepted principle that the wider the spread the more profitable are the banks and the more expensive it is to raise capital by the growing businesses whose need for financial resources is often indirectly related to the cost of funds. The lower the interest rates charged by banks then the greater is the demand for investment funds and the higher is the cost of capital then the lower is the demand for loanable funds.

The commercial banking sector in India is currently operating under an interest rate spread of 3.75% and that is considered to be the second highest in Asia. But such a spread would be considered low by many of the Lebanese banks who have become used to spreads that at times go above 5.5%. No wonder that the Lebanese banking sector has shown relatively high and stable rates of increase in its profitability. They have become accustomed to high and relatively safe rates of return by gorging themselves at the expense of the poor Lebanese citizen.

What is unfortunate about all of this is that it is done with the explicit knowledge of the Lebanese state. The Lebanese finance minister, Mr. Shatah, is proud of the fact that his cabinet was able to arrange to roll over around $2.25billion of Lebanese national debt denominated mainly in US dollars but partially in Euros. The debt was reissued to carry an interest rate of 7.5 % for the three year bonds and 9.0% for the

8 year bonds. The comparable rates on US treasuries were 1.36 % and 2.45% while those on both the British debt and the German debt sold at a slightly higher yield of around 1.4% and 2.6% respectively. It is true that Lebanon does not enjoy the high credit ratings of these countries but even the UAE issued its $20 billion 5 year bonds two weeks ago at 4%.

The announcement by Mr. Shatah did not specify who were the buyers of these newly issued Lebanese sovereign debts. Yet it is not difficult to conclude that the majority of such debt is usually held by Lebanese banks. Actually if one was to deduct the interest income earned by the Lebanese banks from their Lebanese treasury holdings then most would not have shown a profit. If the average interest rate that is being paid on three year dollar denominated savings account is around 2.5-3% then these banks are operating with an interest rate spread of almost 5 percent.

Let me be clear about this, the banking sector is not doing anything illegal by taking advantage of an investment opportunity. It is the combination of a the lack of transparency in government finance, the failure of the elected representatives to ask the right questions, the total inability of the press to perform its only function of investigating inefficiencies and reporting on them and the banking system to act willingly as an accomplice in fleecing the poor Lebanese citizen.

Friday, December 4, 2009

Finance Ministry needs to Come Clean

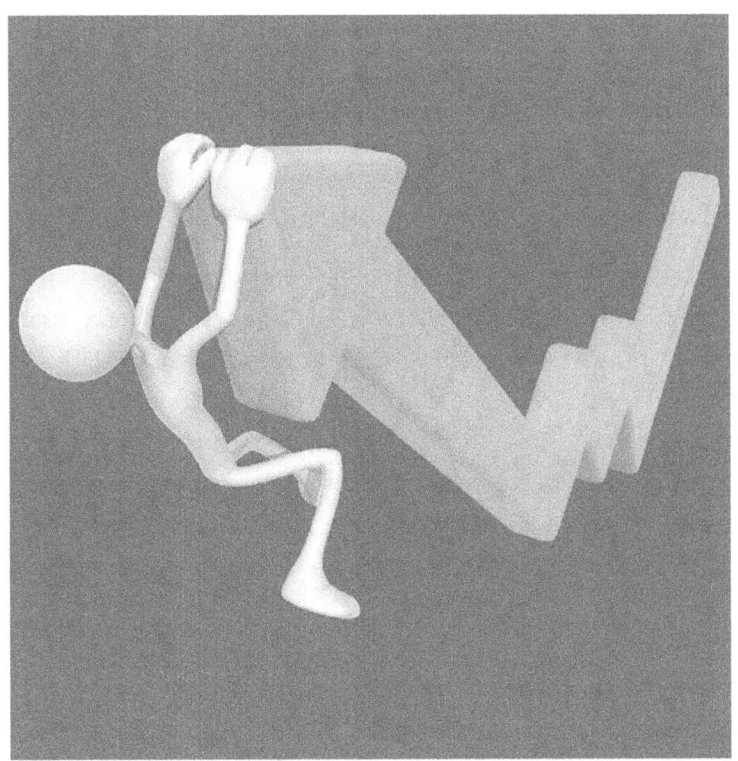

Reading the news accounts about the press conference held by Finance Minister Raya Hassan was a cause for bewilderment and even confusion. The problem does not rest only with what the minister said and what she chose not to say but the real problem is in the lack of any meaningful critical coverage of that event by the press who seem to act as cheer leaders for whatever the officials say. This dereliction of duty on the part of the media plays a seminal role is keeping the Lebanese citizen in the dark. Ms. Hassan and the Lebanese government have every right to boast for having completed rather successfully the issuance of $750 million in Eurobonds but they have no right to present the event as being a huge accomplishment and to pat themselves on the back and to act ecstatically by describing the event as an accomplishment that is unique and extraordinary.

The fact of the matter is that Ms. Hassan has chosen not to describe in any detail at least three problematic areas:
(a) Foreign ownership
(b) Foreign currency denomination
(c) Interest Rate.

(a)

Although Lebanon has one of the highest proportions of national debt to GDP in the world, the Lebanese national debt has so far been looked upon as being "manageable" simply because most of it has been issued by domestic institutions. Whenever the percentage of the national debt of any country that is held by non residents grows then that debt becomes a greater burden on the issuer if for nothing else but the resulting drain on its own domestic resources that would be required each year in order to service the foreign held proportion of the debt. Yes it is a sign of confidence when foreigners are willing to hold another countries debt but by doing so the issuer is in essence contributing to an increase in its vulnerability. All other things being equal domestic lenders should always be given preference.

(b)

The currency in which national debt is denominated is at least as important as foreign ownership and possibly even more so. The principle behind this is simple and straight forward. Whenever an individual, a firm or a government agrees to issue a liability in a foreign currency then that entails, besides all the regular associated risks of investing the proceeds productively and efficiently, the acquisition of an added risk, the foreign exchange risk. Actually most savvy investors would never hold an open liability denominated in a foreign currency without taking measures to hedge against the foreign exchange risk. It is incredulous to find out that the Lebanese government is proud of the fact that it is acquiring more risk.

(c)

And then there is the interest rate. Again it is understandable when the Lebanese authorities are glad that the Lebanese sovereign debt rating has allowed them to borrow at 5.87 % for 5 years and 7% rate for 15 years. Things could have been worse but they sure could have been much better had it not been for the weakness, whether perceived or actual is not important, of the Lebanese economy. The Finance minister is glad that the latest 5 year issue carries a 5.87% interest rate but she does not share with the press that there is lots of room for improvement and that this rate is good but is not acceptable when the going rate for 5 year notes is only 2.03%; That is less than 35% of what Ms. Hassan is proud of. The same thing is true of the 7year yield curve; the going yield on the 7 year notes is 2.74 which are under 40% of the winning bid.

The Finance ministry and Ms. Hassan have a responsibility to become more, much more transparent about the decisions that are being undertaken to finance the Lebanese national debt. We are the ones who will have to pay back this debt and so we have the right to know the rationale for the excessive foreign exchange risk, the need to increase the proportion of foreign ownership and we have to be told the unvarnished truth about the winning bid in addition to other interest rate yields in the market.

Friday, August 21, 2009

Lebanese Real Estate: A Bubble About To Burst?

What goes up must come down especially if the rate of increase has resulted in lifting real estate prices into an orbit in outer space that is beyond the reach of most mortals. This was the case when home prices in the United States were lifted into the stratosphere and the affordability index plummeted to a historical low. The results were anything but pretty. The same bubble phenomenon was observed in the 1980's in Japan with equally devastating outcomes that resulted in what became known as the lost decade. Currently the US experience is being shared by the United Kingdom, Spain, Australia and Dubai whose real estate prices have fallen by an eye popping 60 % in many cases.

Since real estate prices in Lebanon in general and in Beirut in particular are still on a steep upward trajectory it behooves us to ask whether this bubble is any different than any of the others that have already burst. Most of the Lebanese that I have posed this question to are convinced that the Lebanese case is different and that this is not a bubble , but then people who are in the midst of a bubble rarely recognize it, just ask Mr. Greenspan the ex Chairman of the Board of the US Federal Reserve.

Unfortunately statistical data on real estate in Lebanon is not readily available but then the anecdotal evidence is all over the place. Some sections of Beirut are full of new luxury high rises or renovated ones. Most of these units fetch on the average over $2000 per square meter. This means that an average apartment of say 250 square meters demands at least half a million dollars. Many of the newer luxury units are going for $6000-7000 per square meter and the newest residential tower is asking for $14000 per square meter for the ground floor units. This means that an apartment in Beirut will cost $3-

5 million. That is a princely sum for any city anywhere in the world but it obviously is problematic in a city where an annual income of $30,000-40,000 is considered to be on the high end. Many workers do not make more $10,000 per annum.

There is some truth to the argument that such buildings are not meant for the ordinary Lebanese but are being built for the lucky few at the top of the economic ladder, for the expatriates who have come back to retire among friends and relatives and to wealthy individuals from the Gulf states. This might be true but unfortunately it is also true that as prices in one sector increase then prices in all other real estate sectors follow suit. Apartments in most of the popular resorts close to Beirut are already selling for over $1000 per square meter.

What might prevent the bubble from being calamitous is the lack of leverage and speculation. Flipping apartments is not common neither are thirty year mortgages, at least not yet. There are signs that some individuals are already speculating on a continuous upward trend in real estate prices by purchasing homes in the new residential developments with the intention of renting them for a while and then selling at a huge profit. We have heard that reasoning before in Florida, Las Vegas and San Diego among many other cities all over the world haven't we?

Another worrisome trend is that of individuals who are cash poor but feel wealthy because they feel that their homes are worth so much that they can afford to splurge on cars, trips and other luxuries by borrowing money at usurious rates. This phenomenon is so similar to the home equity loans that enabled Americans to use their homes as ATM machines except that it is potentially more devastating. Even if miraculously, Lebanon manages to avoid the dire consequences associated with the bursting of a real estate bubble it will not escape the widening of the chasm between the few haves and the rest of the have not. Lebanon appears to be living the biblical admonition that says "For he that has, to him shall be given: and he that has not, from him shall be taken even that which he has".

Sunday, January 3, 2010

Sovereign Debt Crisis Indicators

The subject of national debt, its burden or its sustainability has always led to heated debates and recriminations determined by ones political views. As a general rule those that support March 14 have a more positive view of Lebanon's ability to finance its future needs while those that belong to the opposition appear to have a dim view both of the debt and its implications.

But one would have expected all observers to take a position on this all important issue based on certain objective criteria instead of the normative subjective lines of thinking that is being employed. The eventuality of default on national debt becomes unavoidable ones a set of thresholds has been crossed irrespective of the political ideology of the ruling party in the country in question. The likelihood of declaring default is very much affected by the solvency and the degree of liquidity that the country in question enjoys. There is no doubt that geopolitical developments also play a role. But even when political instability contributes to the high likelihood of a default it does that by affecting the fundamental macroeconomic variables. That is why we intend to present a summary of the most important indicators that a recent purely objective empirical study has shown to be the most common indicators that a sovereign debt crisis is very highly likely. The study was published as an IMF Working Paper and was co authored by Mr. Nouriel Roubini whose views and analysis of the recent global economic crisis has catapulted him to the top of his profession.

The following are the 10 variables that are usually closely associated with a sovereign debt crisis:

(1)Total External Debt/GDP ratio above 49.7%

(2)Short Term debt/Reserves ratio of over 130%

(3)Real GDP growth

(4)Public External Debt/Government revenue ratio of over 214%

(5)CPI Inflation

(6)Presidential election cycle

(7)US Treasury Bill rate

(8)Current Account balance + short term debt/Foreign Reserves ratio

(9)Exchange Rate overvaluation of more than 48%

(10) Exchange Rate volatility

The above 10 indicators provide a highly reliable snapshot about an economy irrespective of its size or political orientation. The above list gives the analyst an idea about a sovereign's ability to pay, its liquidity and its exchange rate risk. No one variable by itself is capable of predicting correctly the default risk associated with a country but a number of these indicators, if they breach their threshold would create a crisis-dynamic that would be difficult to dismiss.

If we are to take a quick look at the above indicators as they apply to Lebanon then it becomes very clear that Lebanon is in serious violation of (1); (2); (4);(7); and (9) while (6) and (10) can be deemed not to be applicable. Relatively negative indicators are (5) and (8) even when gold is included. This leaves (3) as the only slightly positive indicator.

This is an unambiguous record that shows a high probability of a debt crisis which will manifest itself either in a default or a restructuring of debt.

Saturday, February 6, 2010

Population, Sustainability and Fertility

Most Lebanese, that I know, are surprised when I tell them that Lebanon is one of the most densely populated countries of the world. Most cannot even accept it since they often associate, wrongly, such countries as China, India, Nigeria and Belgium with high density.

Officially Lebanon (404/sq. km) is the 25th most densely populated political entity in the world. But if one is to keep very special and small entities such as The Vatican, Gibraltar, Guernsey, San Marino and Nauru out of the rankings then Lebanon can easily become the 10th or the 15th most populated country in the planet. India has a population density of 358 per sq. km while China stands at 139. If the current population density of Lebanon is become the global average then the population of the world would have to rise to a mind numbing 60 billion individuals.

One does not need to be a Neo Malthusian to recognize that there comes a point when human population growth becomes highly undesirable to say the least. If the projected 10 billion humans by 2050 are not enough then what is? Is it another doubling to 20 billion or maybe a further doubling still to 40 billion? Does Lebanon have the right to complain about the rapid rate of growth in global population when it is one of the biggest abuser of this metric?

Most, and possibly all, of those that have looked into this issue and investigated the potential limits seriously have concluded that we are already beyond any metric of sustainability. This only means that we have overshot the carrying capacity of the ecosystem and as a result we have to take measures that will reverse our current course. Lebanese dependence on the rest of the world for its food, energy, capital, employment opportunities and energy is so clearly visible to all that no one will question it. Yet we keep on growing by increasing our dependence on other ecosystems. Is that responsible behaviour?

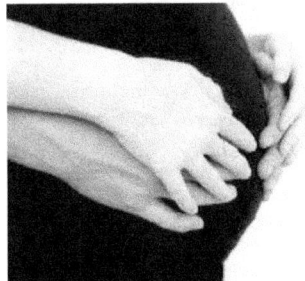

But what is it that needs to be done if we are to reduce fertility substantially? Surely we cannot stand by as idle spectators and hope that humans will decide to change their behaviour drastically just because that is good for the ecosystem? Had this been the case then they would have done so a long time ago.

So what we are left with is the absolute certainty that human population must stop growing and preferably even start to decline. Studies have shown that if the world population is to adopt the lifestyles and diet of the West then we need six planets when we have only one. Forty Lebanon's will be needed if we are to apply the same standard to the resources of Lebanon. This clearly shows that we have exceeded our limited carrying capacity and thus the current state of affairs is not sustainable.

If it is deemed to be too risky to count on a voluntary change in behaviour then the only other alternative to reduce the rate of fertility would be a direct and sustained government policy aimed at achieving lower fertility rates. There are a number of actions that the government can adopt that will act to internalize the negative externality of high fertility such as taxes, social expenditures and even outright strict limits on the number of successful pregnancies per female. But is the world ready to deal with this most basic and challenging problem? Is Lebanon ready to adopt a meaningful population policy? I will not hold my breath.

Saturday, February 27, 2010

Soak the Poor?

TAXATION ON TOBACCO

Duty on tobacco as a percentage of disposable income

Gross Income by Quintile (1998-99)

It is well known that the market fails to deliver on its promises of efficiency for many reasons such as the predominance of negative externalities; by products of activities that do not have to be recognized by the market; in addition to the prevalence of Public Goods that are characterized by "free riders"; those that will use a service without paying for it such as public education. But since society should always seek to operate as efficiently as possible the need for an institution that can correct these market failures became universally accepted. Add to the above the arguments advanced by Keynes in his masterpiece "The General Theory" in which he demonstrated clearly that the market economy does not have a mechanism that will ensure full employment of resources, quite on the contrary, the equilibrium level of output will more likely be below that of full employment. Well, all the above can be remedied through the introduction of an activist state that will impose regulations to control the externalities, make sure that there is an adequate supply of the Public goods and act as to guide the economy to reach its full potential.

The role of governments, all over the world, has grown substantially, as a result of the above. But if government is going to be asked to provide infrastructure, social services and to regulate conditions that affect the public good then the government needs a flow of revenue that it can depend upon to provide the expected services. In most cases, government acts as a provider of services and not as an owner of means of production and as a result its revenue is derived from taxing the various activities within its domain. This gave rise to the question of what are the guidelines that are to be used when the government is to levy such taxes.

One of the single most important ideas in collecting the revenue that is deemed to be necessary to further the public good is that taxes should be levied so as not to violate the principle of "ability to pay". It goes without saying that unless the above principle is adhered to then the taxing system will be unfair, unjust, will increase social inequity, aggravate social tensions and even lead to social unrest. The basic idea behind this principle has been advocated by numerous philosophers; Jean Jacques Rousseau, and JS Mill; for centuries.

Ability to pay, simply stated, is an attempt at providing essential services to those that cannot afford them by taxing those than have the ability to pay. I am sure that no one needs to be reminded that the lucky few who have accumulated a handsome fortune did not do so in a vacuum but in an environment that made that possible and so the simple idea of reciprocity implies that they should, at a minimum, help improve the productivity and equity of the forces that have made their good fortune possible.

A simple analysis based on the above means that a responsible government should undertake expenditures that would alleviate poverty, reduce inequality, decrease the prospect of unemployment and provide social services designed to improve the quality of human capital. This means that the government expenditures should be uniquely driven by the metric of how a government program impacts on poverty. Any project that does not alleviate poverty should be immediately cancelled since society can spend the same expenditures in an alternative field that will improve the quality of life for all.

It would be ironic though if the idea of expenditures does not take into consideration the impact of raising the required revenue. Would it make any sense to promise to provide a poor community with a decent school system but then proceed to tax the same people for that expense? That can be described at best as a diabolical scheme whose intent is not the alleviation of poverty but the maintenance of the conditions that have produced it.

Sales taxes; VAT is a disguised sales tax; are universally referred to as regressive taxes. This is not debatable since a household whose annual income is $20,000 pays a greater proportion of its income in VAT than a household whose annual income is $100,000. Unfortunately this is what the current Lebanese government is advancing, a 50% increase in VAT. Besides questioning the wisdom of the allocation of the expenditures we are faced with a more egregious act. Tax those that can afford it the least in order to create more benefits for those that are least in need. This policy needs to be stood on its head but what are the chances of this happening when those in charge represent the very few at the top of the economic pyramid? You decide.

Sunday, April 4, 2010

MONEY ILLUSION

The level of welfare of societies and even individuals should not be measured in purely monetary terms. This is not a proposition to be questioned since there are many other aspects that play a major role in determining the level of welfare. Income distribution, access to healthcare, quality and level of educational services provided in addition to strong protection of the right to associate and dissent are a few examples. That is in essence why the Sarkozy commission headed by Joseph Stiglitz and Amartya Sen recommended steps to avoid what it called "GDP fetishism".

Old ideas die hard. Despite all the criticism of GDP per capita as an indicator of the level of progress in an economy regrettably the idea is still prevalent all over the world and even more so among the less advantaged countries. Besides the numerous shortcomings, some referred to above, there is still a common mistake that is committed when the metric of GDP per capita is used.

Economists of all political persuasions stress the fact that when monetary comparisons are to be made across a time horizon then it is crucial to adjust the nominal unit of currency used so as to make sure that the comparisons are fair. The problem arises from the universal tendency for units of currency to lose purchasing power over time. As a result a comparison of a stream of income during one year cannot be compared to the stream of income during another year, say ten years earlier, because both streams are measured in terms of a particular currency whose ability to acquire goods and services has changed over time. In such circumstances the only way that comparisons can be meaningful and productive will be after an adjustment is made so that both incomes will be measured in terms of the same unit of currency. Please allow me to give a simple example of what the above means: If the wages of a person double but the prices of all items also double then that particular person whose nominal income has increased by a factor of 2 still enjoys the exact same level of welfare. This individual's income is still the same when measured in constant units of currency.

Many in Lebanon, both in and outside the government speak glowingly at times in the increase in the Lebanese GDP over the years. In nominal terms that is undeniable since the population has increased and since the value of the currency has shrunk over time. That is why two adjustments need to be made: the first adjustment is look at GDP per capita and not the aggregate GDP since over the years the number of residents has increased and the second adjustment is that of transforming the nominal GDP per capita into one expressed in constant purchasing power units of currency.

The above exercise, in the case of Lebanon, turns out to be very instructive as the accompanying table reveals:

...........................**GDP per Capita**..

Year	Nominal $	Constant $2000
1998	4594	4805
1999	4565	4663
2000	4421	4421
2001	4505	4416
2002	4836	4606
2003	5054	4776
2004	5414	4905
2005	5375	4768
2006	5603	4797
2007	6011	5009

Note that the per capita income of $5603 nominal dollars for the year 2006 is 22% larger than the 1998 GDP per capita of $4594 when measured in nominal dollars. But as soon as both of 1998 and the year 2006 are measured in terms of the year 2000 dollars then the typical Lebanese citizen in the year 2006 turns out to be 46 poorer than the 1998 counterpart. The implications of this are huge. The typical Lebanese has spent 9 years running on the spot when our political leaders would argue that Lebanon has made tremendous gains.

The last three years have been slightly better for Lebanon. Note that if 1998 is to be compared to 2007 then the GDP per capita in real terms would have shown an increase of 4.27 % over a period of ten years. That is nothing to write home about.

Note: Both of 2008 and 2009 promise to show net real growth but this observer did not have access to the constant $ and so decided not to use these figures for this post. All the above is based on my own estimates since such figures are not readily available in the case of Lebanon.

Saturday, April 24, 2010

Can Lebanon Afford its Current Fixed Exchange System?

There is hardly an opportunity given to individuals connected to the Ministry of finance, the Central Bank or the commercial banking system where they do not stress the substantial volume of funds that has been flowing into the country. The implication being that these capital flows are a vote of confidence in the stability, dynamism and confidence in the Lebanese economy. What they conveniently forget to declare is that capital flows are ultimately determined by a thorough analysis of the relative safety of the country in question relative to the risk premium that it is willing to pay. Very simply stated this means that any level of risk becomes attractive at a certain price.

Lebanon has had no problem of attracting capital flows into the country for the very simple reason that the Lebanese banks are paying an interest rate that is above the world interest rate. So the question should be why is Lebanon condoning this misguided policy of in essence subsidizing the deposits that are willing to flow into Lebanon and what is more important is the question of whether such a policy is sustainable. Can tiny Lebanon afford to pay a rate that is above the world rate in order to attract funds that it does not need.

It appears to this observer that the Lebanese commercial banks are willing to pay above that of the rest of the world simply because it is profitable for them. How can that be so if they are not in need of these funds? The surprising answer to this quandary is the Lebanese central bank that is willing to absorb from its member banks their excess liquidity by issuing CD's at a high interest rate. Such a policy is not sustainable in the long run and is actually damaging to the health of the Lebanese economy in the long run. The current policy attracts funds that are not needed by paying these funds a premium that makes such transactions inefficient. So why does Lebanon engage in these policies that wind up in inflicting pain on the Lebanese economy? Again the answer is rather simple. The Lebanese governments' continued need for more and more sovereign debt dictates growing the economy. But unfortunately whenever a country decides to have a fixed exchange rate system coupled with perfectly mobile capital flows then its monetary policy option becomes totally ineffective. In such a case the government will have no choice but to apply the expansionary fiscal option delivered through deficit spending. But why does the government feel the need to use deficit finance when it already suffers from one of the highest debt/GDP ratios in the world? You guessed it; the government needs to grow the economy so that it might borrow some more in order to service its sovereign debt. Under normal circumstances the above policy will eventually get the economy back to equilibrium but only once it adopts the world interest rate. And this is the rub. If Lebanon is to adopt the world interest rate then the flow of funds into the country will be greatly diminished.

A quick review of the theoretical four available options should help us get a clear understanding of this problem. Given that capital flows are perfectly mobile then Lebanon must choose from among the following policy options:

	Fixed Exchange Rates	**Flexible Exchange Rates**
Fiscal Policy	Effective if Fiscal is deficit finance + Monetary growth at world rates	Totally Ineffective
Monetary policy	Totally Ineffective	Effective if used with Fiscal based on X

X: Exports due to lower exchange Rate

Based on the theoretical options as described in the above matrix Lebanon should consider moving away from the Fixed Exchange system currently in force and should move towards a flexible system. That will make repayment of the current sovereign debt easier .will give more power to the monetary authorities and will rationalize capital flows into the country.

Tuesday, June 10, 2008

Wind Energy in Lebanon: A Win, Win, Win Proposition

At a time when the price per barrel of oil is over $130 and many believe will reach $150 in the next few months it is bewildering when electricity in Lebanon is still being produced from fuel oil. Besides the question of the large increase in the price of oil as a feed stock there is also the more important issue of the carbon footprint that is associated with the consumption of hydrocarbons.

Climate Change is a problem for all of us since nature does not recognize the artificial political boundaries that we have created neither does it care about our race, gender or national origin. Actually a change in climate will bring about devastating effects for all forms of life and not only Homo sapiens. So when we choose not to take action that will reduce the detrimental effect of our economic activities then we are acting irresponsibly and condemning not only ourselves but all species all over the world. Fortunately for us in Lebanon we are in a position to take meaningful action that will go a long way in reducing out ecological footprint in general and our carbon footprint in particular. Besides promoting the obvious policies that would encourage public transport, the greater use of efficient autos, and efficient use of electricity Lebanon is blessed in being located in a geographic region that provides around 300 days a year of sunshine and a relatively long coast line relative to the size of the country. Lebanon is abundantly endowed with the most efficient two clean energy alternatives: wind and solar. In the solar field we need to pass legislation that mandates the installation of solar hot water heat systems into all new building structures and we also need to encourage retro fitting the existing physical stock of buildings. Obviously we should also keep an eye on the rapid developments in thermal energy. This area is the most promising in the field of renewable and many new plants are expected to start large scale production of electricity all over the globe. Eventually this source of clean and inexpensive electricity could become a major source of energy for Lebanon.

But there is no need to wait for the new technological breakthroughs in thermal energy. We can and we must plan to have at least 20-25% of our electricity produced from wind turbines of f shore. Lebanon's total production of electricity is around 1500 MW annually. To produce 300 MW from wind farms is a very realistic goal and what makes it exceptionally attractive is the fact that the final product would be clean and inexpensive energy. Wind energy is currently being produced at a cost of around 4 cents per kWh and Lebanon should have no problem in securing financing for such projects at attractive terms. The Global Environmental Facility (GEF) of the world Bank in addition to the German Development Finance Group (KfW), the US Agency for International Development (US AID) and the Swedish International Development Cooperation Agency (SIDCA) plus the European Union are just a few of the International organizations that are committed to help developing nations finance alternative energy projects.

The cabinet in Lebanon has spent enough time in unproductive political grid lock over the past three years. It is high time that the cabinet take the initiative to undertake a project that will improve the quality of life of the average Lebanese citizen, a project that is self financing, that will provide the Lebanese economy with a boost and that will meet part of our moral obligation toward sustainable development. Wind generated electricity in Lebanon is the best of all possible worlds, a win, win, win proposition with no possible losers.

Sunday, February 8, 2009

Cedar Tree Island vs Clean Wind Renewable Energy

The Lebanese media has been abuzz recently with the news about the grandiose plans to construct an artificial island off the Damour coast in the shape of a Cedar tree, as if the shape of such an environmental monstrosity is supposed to make it acceptable.

No country, rich or poor, can possibly justify spending precious human and environmental resources in order to create an artificial habitat whose only purpose is to cater to the whims of the rich and privileged. Homo sapiens, at least the variety in Lebanon, do not seem to have learned the most basic of ecological principles; we are part of nature and not apart from it. This implies that we have a moral obligation to respect other species and not to act as if everything was created for our benefit. A basic environmental truth is that the more we do then the less we will have. All of that is made absolutely clear by the Second Law of Thermodynamics; entropy; which has been described by no less of an authority than Einstein as the supreme law of nature.

Lebanon is not the only country in the world that faces many challenges in practically all fields but yet it is a country whose challenges appear to be daunting whether one is to consider its political stability, economic progress, social coherence or ecological sustainability. Lebanon's political existence is challenged daily both from within and from without but what is even more essential is the fact that its social structure is fractured , its economic modus operandi rests on inequality and exploitation, its political system is tribal and its ecology is unsustainable. Such a set of circumstances must relegate the destructive ideas of building small gardens within troubled areas as totally unacceptable and ultimately selfish. It looks that the invisible hand has demonstrated its shortcomings and grotesque failure the world over except in Lebanon where the idea of individual gain still trumps the common good and that is sad.

What is even more deplorable is the complicity of the Lebanese state in the promotion of these environmentally degenerate projects. The most ardent advocates of the free market enterprise system admit that in many instances the forces of the market fail to find the theoretical optimal allocation and the proverbial efficient solution. The name of the economist Pigou, a strong advocate of traditional mainstream economics during the early part of the 20th century, will always be associated with the notion of externalities that prevent the actual market forces from performing their magic. An equally important circumstance that prevents the free market from working efficiently is that of Public Goods.

The ultimate question in regards to the Cedar Island and the Hotel opposite Saint George in Beirut is that of ownership of the sea bed on which these projects are to be constructed. Who owns the sea bed? Obviously it is not individuals, nor corporations or a handful of politicians. The closest thing to an international law regarding the ownership of beaches and waterways is the Public Trust Doctrine which simply states that the citizens are the ultimate owners of these resources and that each and every one of us has the right to protect these natural endowments even if we have to sue on their behalf. The beaches are our natural patrimony and we have an obligation to protect them on behalf of the future generations.

What Lebanon needs, and very badly for that matter, is not a Hotel on stilts in the sea or an artificial island for the rich but a serious investment in clean and renewable energy that will cut down on our carbon footprint and yet supply us with the electricity that we need. We must ask those that are running for elections about their positions on these existential issues and vote accordingly. Good citizens have no choice but to act in a manner that will promote the integrity of the ecosystem as Aldo Leopold, the great environmental ethicist, has taught us.

ISRAELI PALESTINIAN

QUESTION

Monday, September 19, 2011

Palestinian Authority: To Go To The Security Council Or Not?

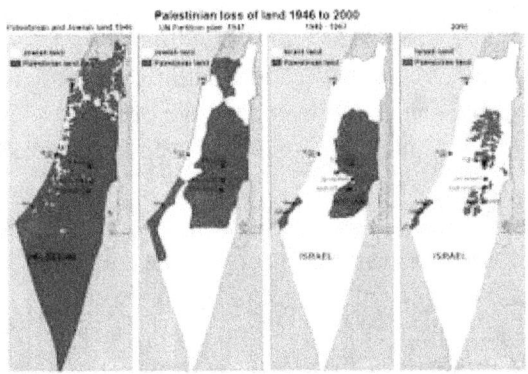

That the ongoing tragedy of the Palestinian dispossession in 1948 is still in limbo speaks volumes about the depth of the injustice that the Palestinian people have been subjected to by the whole world community. The iniquity bestowed on the Palestinians is practically unparalleled but they have come to accept the state of Israel, the power that has usurped their land, their homes, and their humanity provided they would not be prevented from establishing their own nation on the land that was taken by Israel during the 1967 war.

The sudden shock of the dispossession led to the adoption of a few unproductive policies in the hope that their acts would win back what has been taken away from them by force, their land and their right to self determination. Many have argued over the past 65 years that the Palestinians have often been their best enemies when they followed policies that guarantee negative sensational press coverage but nothing else. These wrong and misguided means are best described as pyrrhic victories. Whether it was exploding the airliners in the Jordanian dessert, massacring the Israeli athletes in the Olympic village in Germany or throwing overboard the body of Leon Klinghoffer from the Achilles Lauro the Palestinian guerrillas failed to win converts to their cause.

Eventually the Palestinian leadership agreed to renounce its claim to the whole of Palestine and to accept to live side by side with the Israeli state that has not stopped its continued incursions into the West Bank by building more settlements and by expanding the Jewish quarter of Jerusalem by continuing the acts of dispossession and disinheritance of the Palestinians. Yet the Palestinian Authority under the leadership of President Abbas and PM Fayad offers nothing but continued support for the two state solutions that the Israeli government has honored through lip service only. Their latest move is to seek recognition of a Palestinian state from both the General assembly and the Security Council of the United Nations.

It is clear that most countries in the world, with very few exceptions will vote at the General Assembly in favour of this resolution. It will pass overwhelmingly. But a General Assembly vote does not carry as much heft as one in the Security Council, and this is the rub. The US government has all but guaranteed that it will veto the Security Council resolution later on this month. Since this expected Palestinian request and US response are a practical certainty then one must ask what the potential outcome from this line of action is. One thing for certain is that the US veto will expose the US one more time as duplicitous and hypocritical as far as the Arab Israeli question is concerned. The fallout from such a vote will hurt not only the US but also all its potential allies in the region. Unfortunately, the realities of American presidential elections dictate that Mr. Obama will forget all his promises to change the world and will veto the resolution at the Security Council. Make no mistake about it, Secretary Clinton and the White House will use Orwellian language to tell us that they vetoed the resolution because of their commitment to a two state solution. If any one takes these explanations seriously then they make great prospects for those who want to sell land in New Orleans 'ninth ward.

But why should a setback for the US, as significant as it is, be considered more than a moral victory at best for the Palestinian people. In a sense such a moral victory could be construed as an empty one if not quite a Pyrrhic victory. The attempt to embarrass the US on such a large scale will undoubtedly lead to efforts by the Congress to reduce US financial aid to the Palestinian Authority at a time when its budget coffers are empty. But that in itself is not a major development. The real danger from this vote is that the intransigence of the current Israeli government will only increase and the possibilities of any progress diminished appreciably. The world media will spend a day or two maybe even a week covering this story and interviewing the Palestinian officials who will be celebrating their new status at the general assembly but as time goes on other stories, political and economic will come to dominate the news cycle. By then the Palestinians would be exactly in the same position that they are in right now and possibly they will be facing larger challenges.

Usually the argument to do the right thing wins easily. But in this case, I am afraid that the potential consequences of this act more than nullify its purely moral gains for the Palestinian people. If an act is to be judged ultimately by its consequences then the PA has nothing to gain from this line of action. Maybe what the PA should consider, rather seriously, is a declaration that they no longer want a two state solution but instead they want to demand that they become citizens of the state that has occupied them for the past 44 years. If their demands are not met then the PA will launch major civil disobedience campaigns all across Israel. Maybe it is time that the Israeli political establishment should be made to realize the consequences of its acts.

Wednesday, July 21, 2010

Palestinian Rights in Lebanon

"Lebanon will not dodge these duties, which must be crystal-clear, and not be subject to any misinterpretation" said Prime Minister Sa'ad Hariri when commenting about the most recent efforts to recognize the civil rights of the over 400,000 Palestinians in Lebanon. Maybe someone should remind the young ever traveling PM that the Palestinian refugees have been in Lebanon ever 1948 and the Lebanese authorities have yet to recognize their moral and legal obligations. Yes, Mr. PM, it is a shame when government dodges its duties but the fact of the matter is that Lebanon has been dodging its duties for over sixty years and with no end in sight.

Until the Lebanese government starts viewing the Palestinian refugees in Lebanon, both inside and outside the camps, as immigrants that are entitled to all civil rights and to access to work and property ownership then this shameful issue will not be resolved.

It ought to be emphasized again that the Palestinian refugees are entitled to unalienable civil rights guaranteed to them by the creator, UDHR as well as International law. The Lebanese authorities are not being asked to offer access as much as to recognize the right of access and stop preventing the Palestinians from getting what is legally and morally theirs. Can you imagine the outcry if say, Canada, Australia and the US are to prevent Lebanese immigrants to these countries from accessing the social services networks, jobs and the right to own property? Have we forgotten that we need to treat others the way that we expect to be treated?
And please let us not justify our bigotry and discrimination by shedding crocodile tears and by making the totally discredited argument that we mistreat the Palestinian refugees for their own

221

good. The right of return will not be diluted in any way form or fashion even if each of the 400,000 Palestinians is to become a millionaire. The right of return is not related to any developments after 1948.

Foreign ownership of property within the boundaries of the state, any state, has always been the cause of exaggerated fears and anxieties in more than one country. But if such limits are to be applied, and I do not believe that they should, then said limits are to be uniform and none discriminatory. In that case the limits that are applicable to a Saudi Arabian ought to apply also to a Palestinian or even a Marsian for that matter. One more time, if reason and common sense are to apply then it becomes very clear that the fear of having the ownership of the country in the hands of foreigners is vastly exaggerated. Lebanon already has very tight limits on land ownership by foreigners; any none Lebanese. The total aggregate area of Lebanon that can ever be owned by foreigners is limited to 3% of the country. This represents 312 million square meters. The records show that outside of Beirut only Baabda, Aley and the Metn are already more than 2% owned by foreign entities while the rest of the country is still less than 1%. This implies that foreign ownership could more than triple and yet it will not bump against the current limit on foreign ownership.

A quick back of the envelope calculation regarding the potential effect of Palestinian ownership can be very revealing. If it is assumed that the average size of the Palestinian household is 5 persons; mother, father and 3 children; then the approximate number of Palestinian households is about 80,000. Assume furthermore that ¼ of these households have the financial means to purchase land in Lebanon. If each of these 20,000 households is to buy a lot of land of 800 square meters then the total area involved would amount to only 16 million square meters, which is only 5% of the land allotted to foreign ownership. This 0.0015% of the total area of the country is not an unreasonable proportion of property to be owned by 10 % of the residents is it? Not even if that area is doubled or even tripled.

There are no valid reasons to place any restrictions whatsoever on a group of people who have been living in a country for over sixty years and who in all likelihoods will not be leaving any time soon.

Wednesday, June 2, 2010

Palestinian Refugees In Lebanon: Set Them Free

Immigration has become a burgeoning field of study as travel became less expensive, population pressure more intensive and cosmopolitanism more widely spread. As a result studies of all aspects of the impact of immigration have proliferated recently especially in North America and Western Europe. Most of the research has thus far been confined to the social and economic impact of migration with the occasional emphasis on its cultural and political ramifications. Besides the sociological studies the economic models to explain the dynamic behind immigration and its economic costs or benefits have proliferated and for good reason.

The evidence regarding the economic costs or benefits from migration is mixed. The general macro models inevitably conclude that immigration has an overall positive effect on the receiving country as a result of the additional aggregate demand that the new immigrants generate and also as a consequence of the effect that immigration has on increasing competitiveness. Most studies that deal simply with the fiscal cost seem to imply that immigration carries a fiscal cost to the host country that is heavily attributed to the expenses related to education and health care. Many of these studies, however, tend to be rather simplistic and are often driven by nativist biases.

Lebanon is a country of over 4 million inhabitants 400,000 of whom are Palestinian refugees that are roughly split between UNRWA run refugee camps and urban areas. As a result of this relatively large proportion of Palestinian refugees in the country it should not be surprising to find out that the issue of Palestinian refugees keeps dominating the political, humanitarian and economic discourse. What is surprising though is the paucity of any serious studies that would attempt to gauge the impact of the problem. Since I have spent a long time studying the effect of immigration both in Western Europe and in North America and since I am totally convinced that the Palestinian refugees can be viewed as immigrants I conclude, without any hard evidence, that those who make the argument that the Palestinian refugees imply a substantial cost to the Lebanese economy and Lebanese tax payer are grossly misinformed. The fiscal impact of the Palestinian refugees is negligible and might even be positive as a result of the UNRWA expenditures on healthcare, education and even some basic food commodities. I strongly believe that the Palestinian refugees in Lebanon do not create an economic burden on the Lebanese but just the opposite; they help ever so slightly in increasing the level of aggregate demand and they do contribute to increased labour competitiveness at the low skill end of the labour force.

So why does Lebanon persist in exploiting, dehumanizing and discriminating 10% of its inhabitants? And why is there unanimity on this subject matter? The only explanation that is used by all the Lebanese political parties and even private citizens is the hard to believe rationale that these totally unacceptable practices are designed to help the Palestinian cause. What a falsity.

The Palestinian refugees have been living in Lebanon for over sixty years, they are prohibited from owning real estate, they are not supplied with either educational or healthcare services and they are prevented from practically all the professions in addition to the fact that they have no venue to acquire Lebanese citizenship and the right to vote. It would be difficult to argue that the Palestinian refugees in Lebanon are not being treated as second class citizens and even as undesirables. And the irony is that all of these harsh measures; it is argued; are designed to benefit the victims. How can anyone make such an argument and expect to be taken seriously?

The fact of the matter is that the Lebanese are opposed to integrating the Palestinian refugees for purely narrow and selfish reasons. Based on the clear evidence one is forced to conclude that the Lebanese are driven to act as bigots for two reasons : (1) The overwhelming reason is the fear that if the Palestinian refugees are naturalized then it would be difficult in to maintain the archaic delicate sectarian balance in the rotten current political structure and (2) the totally unsupportable hypothesis that to offer the Palestinian refugees their human rights as dictated by UDHR, of which Lebanon was a major author, would weaken the argument for the right of return. This is balderdash.

Lebanon must do the right thing. If the young fragile democracy is threatened by offering an actual naturalization process then at a minimum it has to give all its legal residents including the Palestinian refugees' access to all the rights and privileges of any Lebanese short of the right to vote. The drive to extend civil and human rights to the Palestinian refugees in Lebanon is not to be viewed as an act of charity or magnanimity; it is simply a moral obligation to treat humans equally and it is an intrinsic right born by each of the refugees. Are we ever going to have the courage to do the right thing? I do not see why not especially when we are going to be the better for it.

Tuesday, June 1, 2010

The Gaza Fiasco: What Next?

There is no need to get bogged down in some peripheral details meant to obfuscate this human tragedy that was committed by the IDF opposite the coast of Gaza. At times the specific details of an act are much less important than the major principle that is to govern human actions. In the words of the philosopher, Peter Singer, it is the moral obligation of every single one in the world to do whatever is possible in order to decrease the hurt and the pain to others when such action will keep us at least at the level of wellbeing of the party being helped. Simply stated, we have an obligation to help the worst off all over the globe as long as we are not to become worse off than the party being helped. Give until it hurts is his very well thought out solution to need, misery and hunger. The fact that there are many other people in the world whose rights and human dignity is at least as much violated as the people of Gaza and yet the world chooses not to do anything about it is not an excuse to be silent about Gazans also.

Officially Israel pulled out of Gaza in 2005. Shortly after that Hamas won the elections of the Palestinian Authority and were asked to form the PA cabinet. Internal disagreements with Fatah led to a quasi civil war after which the forces of Hamas occupied the Gaza strip while the PLO maintained control of the West Bank. Hamas proceeded to allow militants, to target and shell; by rockets; some southern Israeli towns. This behviour angered the Israeli colonizing forces who launched a massive attack on the poorly equipped Hamas forces during 2008. The savage attack on the Gaza strip leveled many quarters of Gaza and killed over a 1000 Palestinian civilians during a debilitating attack in which the IDF is accused of having used new and potentially illegal weapons.

As if the utter devastation of Gaza, the potential use of illegal weapons and the international condemnation of the Goldstone report were not enough the IDF determined to continue the sea blockade to prevent; not arms and war materiel which would have been understandable; the delivery of food and any humanitarian aid to the whole population held hostage by the IDF. Yes Israel, through its intransigent policies, has imprisoned 1.5 million people, many of whom are elderly, women and children. This abominable act is a clear violation of international law and the Universal Declaration of Human Rights and in particular Section 24 which states" Everyone has the right to a standard of living adequate for the health and well-being of himself and of his family, including food, clothing, housing and medical care and necessary social services." Israel's' efforts to subdue a population by starving it is an ironic policy to be adopted by the children of the Holocaust survivors. Unfortunately their message to the rest of the world is clear: Holocaust is an ugly and deplorable act that is never to be forgotten when committed against the Jews but such genocidal measures are acceptable tools if used by the children of the Jews of that most abominable Nazi and Fascist policy.

So what is the lesson from this recent outrageous act of Israeli hubris? An act of piracy in international waters that was so badly planned and misexecuted that it has resulted in the unacceptable loss of 9 innocent lives by those who were trying to alleviate human suffering? There are two possible responses. One response is to decry the barbaric Israeli action and to use this event as a rationale to sever relations with the Israeli regime. That would be a mistake. Such a reaction would only drive the parties more apart and will result in an increase of hurt on both sides. A better path would be to use this occasion to increase the pressure on the current Israeli government to approach the two state negotiations in good faith. This dark cloud could have a silver lining but only if the international community takes a unified strong plan to resolve once and for all the Palestinian Israeli question that neither the region nor the world can afford to leave unresolved. If we show resolve, courage and creativity then this sorry chapter could become the beginning of a peaceful and comprehensive solution to what thus far has been an intractable problem.

Thursday, May 13, 2010

Arab Israeli Peace: One Last Chance.

If the Arab Jewish conflict in all its phases is to be looked upon as a continuum then its duration is getting very close to becoming the longest war in History. It could eclipse the Hundred Year Wars between the British and France which lasted from 1337 to 1453. Jews had started immigrating to Palestine under the Ottoman Empire rule late in the 19th century but the Zionist movement picked up support as a result of the Balfour Declaration of 1917.

The UN plan of 1947 recommended partition; under the infamous UNSCR 181; but on the day that the British mandate ended May 14, 1948 Israel was declared as an independent state. The Arab league declared war against the new state of Israel but its forces were defeated which resulted in having the Israeli forces in control of most of mandated Palestine and forced the Arab states to sign an Armistice agreement which still represents the internationally recognized borders of Israel. The tentative peace that followed lasted less than seven years. Israel joined the British and the French in their Suez Canal War by attacking and capturing the Sinai and the Gaza strip in October of 1956.

An uneasy peace lasted this time 11 years. On June 5, 1967 the Israeli Air Force launched a preemptive attack on Egypt followed by one on Iraq, Jordan and Syria. When the six day war ended Israel had added to the Sinai, and Gaza, the West Bank and the Golan. This was followed by the 1973 war which started with promise for the Egyptian and Syrian forces but ended up in a cease fire.

Egypt managed to get the Sinai back as a result of the Camp David Accords signed in 1979 which were followed by a Jordanian peace agreement in 1994. Meanwhile Israel attacked Lebanon in 1982 in an effort to force the PLO forces that had been thrown out of Jordan. The PLO withdrew to Tunis and Lebanon signed a ceasefire agreement with Israel in 1983.

In spite of all the misery inflicted by all of these wars there was a genuine chance for peace. Besides Camp David of 1979 the Oslo Accords were signed in 1993 followed by the already mentioned Jordanian peace treaty of 1994 NS OSLO II in 1995. Unfortunately most the promise faded when Israel, in 2003, retook some Palestinian land in contravention of Oslo II. This has been followed by Israeli withdrawal from Gaza, the Lebanon war of 2006 in addition to the Gaza war of 2008.

So what has been achieved in almost a century of conflict besides the constant change of positions? The Israelis start in accepting a partition that is rejected by the Arabs and we move to the point when the Arabs accepted a two state solution which has not been accepted by the

Israelis. The situation looks as hopeless as ever, if not even more so. But is it?

I saw today the rough outline of a suggestion by Zbigniew Brzezinski, the National Security advisor for Jimmy Carter, that is simple straight forward and I believe very promising if the political courage is found to adopt it: President Obama must declare in a press conference that the US will spare no effort to forge an agreement along the following four points

(1) Declare that the right of return for the Palestinians will not apply to the pre 1967 Israel

(2) West Jerusalem will become the capital of Israel and East Jerusalem is to become the capital of Palestine.

(3) The 1967 borders with very minor modifications are to become the internationally recognized borders. Any agreed upon modifications will be based on a one to one ratio.

(4) The new Palestinian state will be demilitarized with NATO forces on the border.

The only question that is worthwhile speculating upon: If President Obama is to make such a commitment then would the rejectionists have any rational excuse to turn such an opportunity for peace down? What do you think?

Friday, October 30, 2009

Can A Zionist Be Fair To Arabs?

There is no doubt that the Palestinian people have not been treated justly and fairly over the past sixty years or so. In a sense their problems became insurmountable with the Balfour declaration of Nov 2, 1917 (92 years ago this Monday), the development that started the saga of the establishment of Israel as a Jewish state on the land of the Palestinian Arabs of the time. Fast forward to the 1948 war and all what followed; one loss after another and then you might start to understand the rationale that the Palestinian mind set has had to adopt vis-a-vis all Jews and Zionists. That inability to differentiate between one Jew and another or even one Zionist and another has served to inflame the Palestinian Israeli problem when a more liberal and objective understanding could have helped ease the pain and maybe even hasten an end to the suffering.

To suggest that the Palestinian Israeli problem has become the opiate of the authoritarian Arab regimes is not an exaggeration. Each and every Arab ruler is constantly engaged in grandstanding and in advocating positions that would demonstrate the opposition of his regime to everything Jewish and his devotion to everything Arab and Palestinian. That is why Arab "sham democracies" are invariably opposed to anything Jewish and why they favour supporting resistance groups and even terrorist actions. Blowing up school children in Tel Aviv is to be commended while harming those in say Damascus is barbaric. Our love for the Palestinians is best demonstrated by the squalid living conditions that we have provided for them and the severe constraints that we have placed on their ability to integrate in our societies, own property and acquire citizenship. On the other hand we are constantly proud of our ability to blame the Jew for each of our problems be it social, economic, scientific or political. It has even been reported recently that a major Hollywood producer was denied the right to land at Beirut International because his private jet had some Israeli manufactured parts.

Tragic events that have befallen the Palestinian people should not be allowed to become blinders that deny us the possibility of making a case based on its merits even when we have to cast a favourable judgment on a Jew, an Israeli or even a Zionist. Two cases in point help illustrate the inadvisability of generalized condemnations. The latest events in Jerusalem subjected innocent Palestinian civilians to intolerable abuse at the hands of a few members of the Israeli police force in Jerusalem. The abuse was a reminder of the degrading incidents that took place at Abu Ghraib. In the Jerusalem case two Israeli border guards decided to pick on, torture and dehumanize Palestinians for no other reason than they were Arabs. The evidence of the abuse was incontrovertible; the Israeli guards had recorded their cruelty on their own video cameras and then proceeded to boast about it. When the Jerusalem Police force refused to prosecute the officers involved and to recommend that the matter be handled by internal investigation Shulamit Aloni was infuriated. Ms. Aloni, a former Education Minister went on the offensive berating the Israeli authorities and asking whether dignity is to be viewed as the preserve of the Jews only (http://www.ynetnews.com/articles/0,7340,L-3795648,00.html). Her courageous stand is an example of what honest and decent people should do on both sides of the aisle.

Another example that deserves lots of attention in the Arab world is that of the Goldstone Report. Judge Goldstone, a South African Jew and a Zionist led the group that issued a scathing indictment of the Israeli war machine in its most recent Gaza adventure. Judge Goldstone was also critical of Hamas and its tactics. His judgment that both the IDF and Hamas have committed war crimes and violated the Geneva conventions in the last Gaza war might still prove to be one of the most damaging decisions against Israeli racism and brutality. Arabs will do well to listen to Judge Goldstone and follow his example of objectivity and justice.

Fate of Palestinian Refugees in Lebanon: Revisited

Whenever parties that represent opposing points of view, concerning practically all matters, agree on an issue by taking even a united stand then it should be obvious that something is amiss. The Lebanese political scene is represented by all sorts of ideologies, homegrown, imported, extreme right and extreme left but yet time and again all of these discordant voices sing in harmony the tune that the over 400,000 Palestinian refugees living in Lebanon should not be given the chance to become Lebanese citizens but must be kept as aliens that eek an existence in camps that lack access to modern school, job opportunities, social safety network, decent infrastructure or even recourse to law enforcement. The residents of these camps are discriminated against in practically every single sphere only because they are Palestinians. So why do the Lebanese politicians of all stripes insist on the continued dehumanization of these unlucky Palestinian refugees? It cannot be the fear of a cultural clash since the Palestinians and the Lebanese are practically indistinguishable and it cannot be the concern of the fiscal burden associated with assimilation since most studies conducted in various countries all over the world have demonstrated that new immigrants usually more than pay for their share of the fiscal cost because of the additional jobs and economic growth that they create. So if there is no basis for an economic argument neither is there a rationale for a cultural argument why do the Lebanese parties act united in their opposition to absorbing the Palestinian refugees? The common response by all sides is that these bigoted policies are adopted because they are good for the Palestinians. Yes you heard it right. Depriving people of their rights and forcing them to live in sub human conditions is good for them, it builds character and keeps them yearning for their fatherland. This is as good as arguing that slavery was good for the slaves since they did not have to worry about their next meal. What a crock.

How come no one used this argument when the Armenians came to Lebanon and why is it that most of the Christian Palestinians have been absorbed into the Lebanese society not only without creating a meaningful fiscal burden but by playing an essential role in the economic growth and prosperity of Lebanon in all fields? The answer is clear. The only reason for insisting on the continuation of policies that deprive the Palestinians of their inherent rights is political. The real reason that the Phalange in addition to the Lebanese Forces and the Aounists oppose the integration of the Palestinian refugees is sectarian. They are very concerned that the demographic position of the Lebanese Christian who barley account for 40% of the population but are granted 50% of the parliamentary seats would become untenable. As soon as the youthful Palestinian refugees are given Lebanese citizenship then the Christians would become 35% of the population which will then highlight the absurdity of their insisting on 50% of the parliamentary seats. This absurdity should remind us of the Orwellian dictum that "we are all equal but some are more equal than others". The Lebanese progressive parties on the other hand, led by Hezbollah, and cannot bear to lose the only cause that justifies their presence. Take away from these parties the need to "resist" on behalf of the disinherited and you would have taken away their whole reason to exist. The progressives would not look favourably on any attempt to take away their power to use the Palestinian refugees as pawns in justifying their "resistance".

What makes both of these selfish positions powerful is that each of them is based on half truths. A sectarian society would not welcome policies that will throw its sectarian balance out of whack and the "Pan Arab resistance" parties cannot surrender an issue that is essential for their existence.

Fortunately there is a solution that will benefit all sides. (1)The adoption of a secular electoral system will dispense of this divisive sectarian tribal system once and for all. This can actually be a boon to all by enabling true citizenship to emerge. (2) The act of transforming the deplorable conditions in the camps will rob the "resistance" parties of their military option which has been ineffective anyway but should help them move into the potentially more productive realm of promoting civil disobedience policies. And obviously every single Palestinian will gain more self respect and a greater opportunity to fulfill their human potential.

Sunday, February 15, 2009

Gaza: A grotesque Death Experiment

New and ugly allegations have surfaced recently in connection to the recent Israeli onslaught on Gaza. The accusations are coming from many reliable sources and as such must be thoroughly investigated in order to determine their veracity.

According to a Norwegian MD who was working at a Palestinian hospital in Gaza during the recent war the type of injuries that were inflicted on war casualties ,during this campaign, were different than anything that he has seen before in a war theater and he has seen quite a few conflagrations over the past thirty years. Another Norwegian doctor named DR. Gilbert told the Oslo Gardermoen that "there is a strong suspicion that Gaza is now being used as a test laboratory for new weapons."

The suspicion as expressed by many medical doctors is the use of what the US Army calls DIME, Dense Inert Metal Explosive. This weapon was originally designed by the Lawrence Livermore National Laboratories to inflict severe damage on people but cause lighter destruction on buildings. Dr. Brommant , a German Doctor , who was also present in Gaza, describes the injuries that he has witnessed by saying that "It seems to be some sort of explosive or shell that disperses tiny particles that penetrate all organs, these miniature injuries, you are not able to attack them surgically." Those who are lucky to survive the initial injuries are most likely to develop RMS a deadly cancer related to the tungsten tiny particles.

Some observers had suspected the use of these weapons in the Lebanon war of 2006 but the intensity was nowhere close to what took place in Gaza during the first three weeks of January 2009. No one has yet accused the United States military of either deploying or using this type of a deadly weapon either in Iraq or Afghanistan but the question that begs to be asked is: Where did the IDF get these ammunitions from? If it can be shown that Israel has built its own DIME ammunition then we need to find out whether this development is purely coincidental or whether the US military supplied the Israeli government with the plans to build DIMEs. Irrespective of whether Israel bought the weapons from the US or whether they obtained the right to manufacture them the US has clearly acted as a co-conspirator in this case. If it is to be shown that the Israeli forces did use DIME explosives in the Gaza campaign then it would be difficult not to view the US as an active partner in that war. What is even more unconscionable is the idea that the whole Gaza campaign might have been designed in order to test the effectiveness of this new killing device. It is to be noted that DIME weapons are not banned by the Geneva Convention but may I suggest that the weapons have not been banned simply because they have never been used before. Many are confident that once the use of these devices is established then their use will probably be prohibited.

Citizens of good will, the world over, must make their voices heard in order to demand a thorough investigation by the international community in order to establish clearly what weapons were used in Gaza, the origin of these weapons, how was the design for manufacturing them obtained by the IDF and whether the whole Gaza affair was nothing short of a camouflaged operation whose only purpose was to run an immoral and grotesque death experiment. If the above hypothesis can be proven then, paradoxically, Hamas's naiveté was even deadlier to their Palestinian brethren than what was originally thought.

Tuesday, January 13, 2009

How to Avoid A quagmire in Gaza

It is clear that the stated objective of the Gaza operation for the Israeli government is to silence the Hamas rockets that are fired periodically from Gaza into the southern part of Israel. What is not clear though, is what Hamas is after in having provided the Israeli government its rationale for this current operation?

It is also clear that the Israeli government did not put together this complicated plan of fighting in Gaza at the spur of the moment. Israel has arguably been preparing for this onslaught for the past two years in an effort to rehabilitate its image that took a beating after the Lebanese 2006 campaign that proved to be quite ineffective if not outright fiasco. Yet, Israel wanted an excuse to move into Gaza and Hamas seems to have been more than willing to provide the IDF with a solid rationale for its onslaught. Why? Did Hamas miscalculate the Israeli ability to tolerate the Qassam rockets or were they motivated by other goals. The Hamas leadership has shown over the years its ability to be effective strategic thinkers and to be popular political players. As a result it is only fair to assume that Hamas must have known that Israel will eventually respond with overwhelming force, its own version of shock-and-awe, if you will. But yet they went ahead with their provocations by continuously firing the ineffective but irritating Qassams into Ashkelon and its environs. There are only two logical explanations for their semi-suicidal behavior: (1) Hamas was following orders issued by their financiers, military trainers and arms suppliers, the Iranian mullahs or (2) Hamas seriously believes that it is ready to inflict on the IDF major losses once the IDF is lured into urban warfare on the streets and alleys of Gaza. On both counts Hamas has either grossly miscalculated or willingly agreed to sacrifice the blood of the innocent noncombatants for the benefit of an outside non Palestinian power. Whichever is the reason for the recent provocations Hamas did not act in the best interest of the Palestinian people but seems to be merely driven to score propaganda points against the brutality of the Israeli offensive that their acts have initiated in the first place? These acts border on being criminal and must be seen as such instead of the constant media barrage from all across the Arab speaking countries that condemns the Israeli aggression but does not question the Hamas policies that in essence craved this Israeli operation.

And so who is it that has lured whom into this quagmire? Was it the Israeli policies that pushed Hamas into providing the IDF with an excuse for its forceful reoccupation of Gaza in an effort to influence the outcome of the upcoming Palestinian elections or even an effort to help Mr. Olmert; Israel's George Bush; or was it Hamas incompetence and misguided policies that handed the IDF with the rationale that it needed for its operation? It really does not matter. Both sides to this bloody conflict have shown nothing but total disregard for the rules of war, sanctity of non combatants and have persisted to misread history.

Hamas, especially its refusal to accept the existence of the state of Israel and its resort to random violence as a means to achieving its goal makes it an anachronism. It is time that Hamas, Hezbollah, PFLP and all the other resistance groups recognize that their adopted methods have proven to be ineffective and counterproductive. It is time to abandon these destructive tools and engage the adversary on a higher level. It is time to introduce into the equation pragmatism and an acceptance of reality. It is time to learn to live in peace with those that speak a different language and have a different religion. It is time to apply the idea of impermanence instead of clinging to the notion of authenticity in a world best described by contamination and flux. It is time that the Palestinian people reject the rejectionists in order to have hope for the future. Israel, on the other hand, is just as much in need of a change in its policies. Military force will not bring peace; it might silence begrudgingly the guns for a while. Peace requires policies that do not dehumanize, discriminate, exploit and abuse the very same people that Israel claims that it needs as good neighbours. It is time for Israel to demonstrate its willingness to accept a Palestinian state next door by negotiating a date certain for the total sovereignty of the West Bank and Gaza.

The current war in Gaza has entered its third week and yet it shows no signs of winding down. The rough details of the outcome of this war have been known from the outset. The IDF cannot wipe out Hamas, only the Palestinian people can do that and Hamas will have to stop firing its rockets into Israel. Is it that important who stops first? The IDF has a golden opportunity to declare an end to the Gaza operation, to remove the embargo and to start a serious economic development program with the help of the GCC in exchange for strictly inspected borders and an end to rocket firing into Israel. These acts stand the chance of moving the peace process forward. Israel and its Palestinian neighbours need desperately "change that they can believe in"'

Tuesday, January 6, 2009

Gaza Disaster= Hamas Intransigence + Israeli belligerence

The tragic events that have been in control of the Palestinian- Israeli problem for over sixty years have brought nothing but misery and suffering to both parties. It is unfortunate but true, that the continuing struggle between both sides and the ensuing "logic' applied by them has been inevitable. This is a classic tragedy that cannot be avoided since the rules of logic that are in control of the situation dictate and lock in what economists call a sub Pareto optimal solution.

It is in the light of the above that the current Gaza crisis should be evaluated. Hamas and the government of Israel are in essence the two actors in the traditional Game Theory known as a Prisoners Dilemma. According to the rules of logic where each party is concerned with improving its own welfare the solution is always sub optimal. This simply means that whenever the actors in a "game" are attempting to maximize their own welfare they inevitably make choices that are not in their best interest

Note the decision by Hamas to keep on lobbing its ineffective and rudimentary rockets on nearby Israeli towns despite the fact that Israel has pulled out its forces and settlements from Gaza over two years ago. I have no doubt in my mind that the Hamas leadership and the greater majority of the 1.5 million Gazans are convinced that these acts are helpful to the Palestinian people. Except that the real calculus makes it very clear that this chosen line of action is very costly on the Palestinian people. Actually the death and destruction brought about through these acts is ultimately a set back to the welfare and aspirations of the Palestinian people.

The same flawed logic is in control of the Israeli side. Israel appears to think that there is only one solution to the Hamas intransigence, a military solution. Israel has chosen, at its peril, not to

237

learn from history that victory at the battlefield does not translate in this case to peaceful relationships with its neighbours. Israel has not learned yet the lesson that many problems in the world do not have a technical solution.

Is it inevitable for the two persons randomly picked up by police and accused of a crime to confess to a crime that they did not commit? Not until they learn to cooperate and stop making decisions based on their own selfish welfare. Unfortunately the exact conditions apply to our protagonists in the current Gaza –Israel quagmire. Both parties need a radical transformation in their priorities, values and mores. Unless they learn to play the game cooperatively then both of them are doomed to stay in the hell that they have created.

Give Peace A Chance

June 2004

Many opportunities to move the peace process forward have been squandered by both the Palestinian and the Israeli sides over the last half a century. History must not be allowed to repeat itself yet again and the Palestinian Authority must do all in its power to bring to fruition the current Israeli plan to evacuate the Gaza strip. The usual rhetoric that the planned Israeli evacuation does not meet all the Palestinian demands and thus must be rejected is a specious argument that must not be allowed to stand.

It is clear that Mr. Sharon's efforts to backtrack on his original proposal to dismantle all the Israeli settlements in Gaza have failed. The direct pressure of the White House and the less direct one by the other members of the Quartet have for the time being, at least, compelled Prime Minister Sharon to abandon his watered down plan in favour of the original proposal for a total evacuation of the 7,000 Israeli settlers spread over the twenty-one settlements. He was even willing to sack the two ministers from his cabinet who were not willing to support the Gaza initiative.

There is no larger loss than that of letting a potentially beneficial opportunity pass by. This is true of individuals as well as any group of individuals, nations and even the international community. The biggest tragedy of poverty is not the diminution of the availability of physical consumption goods to the underprivileged but the deprivation of the chance to actualize one's potential. Any barriers that act to obstruct the access to essential amenities become nothing short of efforts to deprive people of their humanity and to rob them of what they can be.

This conflict is not confined to Palestinians and Israelis. It is a conflict that affects the life styles of all the people in the region. Over a hundred million people have allowed this wound to fester and spread for over half a century. The price paid for this neglect and intransigence has been overwhelming. The cost is not limited only to the monetary aspect; it goes beyond that to affect all facets of society. The poor have been the most affected, have had to pay the highest price and make the largest sacrifice. They have been denied decent educational facilities, meaningful job security, acceptable health care facilities, and any semblance of a social safety net, personal freedom, representative democracy and civil liberties.

Palestinians, in particular, and neighbouring Arab countries in general have justified all that sacrifice in the name of the struggle to regain sovereignty over Gaza and the West Bank. The results of these failed policies over the past fifty-six years speak for themselves. The Arab citizens of the neighbouring countries and the Palestinians of Gaza and the West Bank are some of the most deprived people in the world according to the studies released by the United Nations. As a result it makes perfect sense to abandon the failed policies of the past and to offer support to

239

what promises to deliver a significant portion of what all the great sacrifices were supposed to achieve in the first place.

If the window of opportunity of a pullout from Gaza is allowed to close then the only beneficiaries will be misery, squalor and authoritarian regimes. It is the duty of all Arab states to use their good offices to prevail on the Palestinian Authority to take positive meaningful steps that will help materialize the promise of the current evacuation plan from Gaza.

Accepting such a plan has no downside. It will improve the quality of life for 1.3 million Palestinians and will simultaneously act to improve the atmosphere within which the Palestinian-Israeli dialogue is to continue. A Gaza pull out is too precious of an opportunity to be allowed to fail without a serious and determined effort by all sides - Arabs, Palestinians and Israelis- to learn from the previous mistakes and to make it the first meaningful step of a comprehensive peace in the Middle East. Could the Arab regimes be afraid of peace because it robs them of their only justification for authoritarianism? Does the PA fear peace because it fears free, democratic elections? And could the Israelis fear peace because they do not want to be seen by some as weak?

History will not judge favourably those that squander a major possibility to start a process that could be the beginning of the end of subjugation, occupation and random violence.

Thursday, September 16, 2004

Edward Said Remembered

I am pleased and truly honored to be able to participate in such an auspicious occasion and thus to play a small part in the activities this afternoon to remember and memorialize Edward Said, truly a renaissance man.

Like hundreds of thousands, maybe millions of people, I have long been captivated by Dr. Said's charm, wit, courage, wisdom and intellect. While I have known for over a decade about his struggle with leukemia, yet when I learned of his passing away I was awe struck by the gravity of the loss. Believe me the pain was deep and profound.

Actually, one of the first things that I did last January upon my visit to my home village of Brummana, Lebanon, home also to his wife Miriam, was to visit the Friends Cemetery there where his ashes were buried on Oct 30, 2003. While he never made it back to his beloved homeland in Palestine, I had expected, unrealistically, that his final resting place would have become a pilgrimage of some sort for a grateful people who would want to pay their respect and gratitude to someone who had devoted a lifetime to their cause. That, unfortunately, did not prove to be the case. On the other hand, I was astonished by, and his family must have been gratified to see, the outpouring of love and affection from all over the world in all types of media, but in particular the electronic one. These letters and articles from all over the world were unceasing. The sheer volume prompted me to request Yahoo to cancel my subscription to one such special service.

As you have already heard many times, he was an accomplished pianist, an opera lover, a connoisseur of classical music, a world-class cultural critic, a fighter for human justice and dignity, an authority on Conrad, and above all, a story teller, a hakawati.

You see, to me, Edward Said will always be associated with the narrative of Palestine. He had succeeded more than anybody else in telling the story of truth to power, of forcing the world to take note of a people who have been abused and denied their history. Edward Said obliged the world to listen to the Palestinian story and to stop the charade that denied not only its human inalienable rights but even its existence. It is not an exaggeration to claim that the perception of and the recognition given to Palestinian identity over the last thirty odd years owes a great deal to the work of Professor Said.

Make no mistake about it; he was above all a teacher. He taught the world about the history, culture and yes, the rights of the Palestinians. He was able to construct and weave together the story of a people disinherited and dispossessed. He taught the West about Islam and the Orient and the Orient about the West.

In that regard he has fulfilled what Conrad thought was the task of the writer: "by the power of the written word, to make you hear, to make you feel- above all to make you see. That and no more". Through the writing of Edward Said we saw the injustice, felt the anguish and saw the cruelty of imperialism in all its forms.

It is often suggested that blowback, the unexpected consequence of an action, can be strong enough to at least nullify the direct product of that action. The 1967 six day war was, to my mind, such an event. What appeared at the time to be a decisive military victory by the Israeli state and a stunning defeat to the Arab states and the Palestinians may have to be rethought. It is from the ashes of this military defeat that the PLO arose to speak for the Palestinian people and it is this same stunning defeat that I believe transformed a Professor of comparative literature at Columbia University. This event led him to marshal all his intellect and energy to establish conclusively the rights of the vanquished in that war. His interest in his Palestinian identity was enhanced by the magnitude of that defeat and the way that it was reported in the press. The blowback did not stop there. The renewed interest in his homeland led him on a search for answers that culminated in the writing of the very influential book Orientalism in 1978. In it he spoke of the tendency to advocate cultural imperialism by developing a view of the other that is self serving. Many of his ideas proved to be prescient. Take for example the following speech delivered at the House of Commons in 1910: "We are in Egypt to benefit the Egyptian, we are there to liberate and educate him, we are there for his sake and that is also good for all of Europe". Now move forward 93 years and substitute the word Iraq for Egypt and the US Congress for the House of Commons.

The 1967 war provided the impetus to create an implacable critic of the Israeli state and a book that has changed the whole meaning of Middle Eastern Studies. Orientalism was nothing short of a paradigm shift. Those who did not adopt Orientalism as the only acceptable method to read the narrative used it as a corrective to the ideas of the old established masters such as Bernard Lewis. The establishment considered the ideas of Orientalism so dangerous that a Congressional bill threatened to reduce the funding to the Universities that espoused the radical and subversive ideas of Edward Said the "professor of terror". However, he was more than up to the task of responding in equal measure to his critics. You see, Professor Said did not suffer fools gladly. That is evident in many of his responses to his critics. I recall that in one of his last interviews with The Guardian, he made references to the "intellectual lackies" of the US political leadership. He never shied away from a fight.

What distinguished the work of Edward Said on the Palestine Question was its objectivity. Despite his criticism of the state of Israel, he shunned the use of such verbiage as "the Zionist entity" and acknowledged the sufferings of the Holocaust. He did not give either the Palestinian politicians or the Arab regimes a carte blanche. His numerous books, lectures and articles about the Palestine Question have informed the debate for decades. His ideas lent strength to many in the field. That is evident by the difficulty of reading serious discourses on the subject that do not make references to his work and ideas. The standards that he applied were informed by universal values of human rights, dignity and justice. He berated those that denied the atrocities committed against the Jews in Europe, he opposed the logic of the suicide bomber, and he became a vocal critic of Chairman Arafat's leadership and the undemocratic practices of The Palestinian Authority.

As for a Palestinian solution, he came full circle in his beliefs. In the 70's he advocated a single democratic state solution but then during the 80's he adopted the view that a two state solution was acceptable. That, however, changed again after the Oslo Declaration which he saw as a Palestinian Versailles. As a result, he rejected the view that separation was workable and adopted what he liked to call a bi-national state (he did not care for the term a single, secular democratic state). To him, Israel should become "a state of its citizens and not the whole Jewish people."

Edward Said's passion in his Palestine writings was clear and palpable. What might have contributed to that was a feeling that he described as "out of Place". It was an existence similar to that of an exiled person. One is not accepted as part of the social fabric of the country of residence and is equally out of place in one's homeland; in his case he was not even permitted to visit his ancestral home. It is a difficult existence similar to being in limbo, not totally rejected but far away from being accepted.

Edward Said was above all a thinker, a teacher, a story teller. Now that he has left us, the world in general is a much poorer place, but the Palestinians in particular are desperately in need of an equally eloquent hakawati to carry on the fight and the struggle, to speak truth to power.

Let me leave you with the lyrical words of another Palestinian intellectual M. Darwish the National Poet of Palestine:

"His family is now the world. Our loss is shared, and so is our sorrow. He set Palestine at the heart of the world and brought the world into the heart of Palestine".

ENVIRONMENTAL
Issues

Sunday, May 18, 2008

Chickens Of Environmental Skeptics Have Come Home To Roost

For almost two decades environmental skeptics, those who believe that there is no problem that cannot be solved through the application of a healthy dose of unfettered markets and technological innovation, have never tired from gloating over the Ehrlich/Simon wager.

Paul Ehrlich the author of the Population Bomb and a staunch advocate that planet earth is overpopulated and that there are limits to growth had a wager with Julian Simon who was just the opposite. He believed that science and technology will always deliver and that there is no limit to the level and intensity of human activity.

Mr. Simon argued that if the bleak view held by Mr. Ehrlich is accurate then the prices of commodities will go up from the resulting scarcity. But he does not think that will happen because human ingenuity will find substitutes to prevent that from occurring. Ultimately they agreed to keep track of the prices of five commodities; tin, copper, chromium, nickel and tungsten; over a ten year period. That was agreed upon during 1980 and by 1990 all the prices were lower than 10 years ago even in nominal terms. Paul Ehrlich wrote a check to Mr. Simon and suggested another bet but Julian Simon turned down the offer.

As is often the case Mr. Ehrlich turned out to be correct in his pessimism but his mistake was in limiting the bet to ten years only. A recent recalculation of what has transpired over the past 28 years shows very clearly that the prices of each of the five commodities in question has increased , both in real and nominal terms significantly. So yes Julian Simon won the wager over the first ten years while the caution about excessive demand and limits to growth as advocated by Paul Ehrlich is the real winner.

Another illustration that demonstrates the prescience of Paul Ehrlich can be found in the recent study released by the University of London's' London School of Hygiene and Tropical Disease in which they calculate that obesity is a serious contributor to Climate Change because of the additional food that needs to be consumed, the energy needed to grow the food and the additional energy required to transport obese people. Again what the authors of that study seem to have conveniently neglected is he formula developed by Paul Ehrlich and used by most serious students of environmental degradation namely that the environmental impact is very much determined by our chosen lifestyles.

Instead of discovering the detrimental impact of SUV's, incandescent light bulbs, air travel, large homes, diets, fashion, war (just to name a few) and now obesity one at a time Paul Ehrlich admonished us more than forty years ago that what is needed in order to avoid the ecological and environmental abyss is a radical change in our life styles and not one item at a time. Will we recognize the significance of the moral imperative to act and act now or are we going to wait one more time until it is too late to act.

Wednesday, September 2, 2009

No Real Global Commitment to Slow Climate Change

There is unanimity that climate change poses an enormous challenge to our specie. That is no longer debatable. But assessing the enormity of the problem is one thing and doing something meaningful about it is another. History is replete with examples of catastrophes that were hastened because of our inability or unwillingness to act. Every aspect of environmental degradation from climate change to desertification, from overfishing to deforestation, from population growth rates to malnutrition , from overproduction to overconsumption, from diminishing biodiversity to the non-abiding trust in economic growth, from unjust distribution of income to neo imperialism, from unsustainable practices to the rejection of intrinsic value and from the conviction that the whole of creation was meant for our own whimsical use to the strong belief that humans are hard wired to be selfish is a vivid demonstration that "Homo Sapiens" (wise humans) we are not. Yet we pretend that we are and furthermore we make believe that we are earnestly looking for a solution.

The upcoming COP 15 at Copenhagen scheduled for December 2009 was supposed to demonstrate our earnest desire in finally seeking a solution that is commensurate to the existential challenge of keeping climate change within an increase of 2 degrees centigrade. Well don't hold your breath. The UN Development Chief Helen Clark has just issued a statement preparing us for the upcoming disappointment. She declares: ""If there's no deal as such, it won't be a failure. I think the conference will be positive but it won't dot every 'i' and cross every 't'." That does not make you very confident in the quality and commitment of international governance does it?

Kyoto and Copenhagen are about one issue only. If we believe, truly believe that climate change must be stopped and that it is essentially the result of human activity then we need to act and act promptly. Global calamity is about to strike and we have no one to blame but us. The Pogo Cartoon said it best over forty years ago" We have met the enemy and he is us".
So what is the US, the world's largest economy, doing about this problem? The US seems to have finally accepted the idea that it is its duty, nay its obligation, to reduce its carbon footprint since it is the greatest contributor to the anthropogenically produced carbon since the onset of the industrial revolution. Give the Obama administration its due credit. It plans to submit a plan to reduce the US contribution to the worldwide carbon emission through a cap and trade program. The proposed reductions are not even close to what they should be but they are greater reductions than what the previous administration has been willing to commit to. Under the proposed system of Cap and Trade the government will set a total level of emissions and issue against that standard permits. The emitters cannot collectively exceed the level mandated by the government but they are free to trade these permits among each other as they see fit. That does not sound so bad except the reduction in overall emissions is nowhere as major as the challenge

dictates that it should be. The other problem, and may I suggest that this is just as major if not even more so, the government plans to give away gratis, for free, these permits to the corporations that pollute instead of auctioning these permits and raising the 100's of billions of dollars that they are worth. Think about it, instead of asking the polluter to pay we are asking the already burdened tax payer to subsidize pollution. That is madness. But why would anyone give away for free that which is worth billions? Well we have already answered that question. Homo sapiens we ain't, neither are we rational or even committed to the idea of biodiversity and sustainability.

And finally let me say that the US is not the only obstacle to finding a solution to climate change. China, India, Brazil and Saudi Arabia are even more adamant that they do not have to apply any restraint to their level of economic activity, let the health of the global ecosystem be damned. One can easily add Russia and Indonesia to the group of countries that have to be dragged to adopt pro-forma carbon emission reduction targets. (The combined emissions of the above seven countries is over 56% of global carbon emissions). Enough said about our real concern for sustainability and biodiversity.

Tuesday, September 15, 2009

It Is Time To End GDP Fetishism

Most common discussions, by all kinds of media outlets all over the world, of the concept of social welfare of a particular society never fail to mention the state of the Gross Domestic Product, the GDP. This all popular macroeconomic variable has grown, despite its enormous shortcomings, to become a metric of what it was not designed to be in the first place. Very simply stated, the GDP is a money measure of the value of final goods and services that are produced by a particular society. Note that the concept does not pretend to say anything about the level of welfare but is only the summation of all what is produced without even deducting the damage that ensue from such levels of production and consumption . A simple common example might help illustrate this absurdity. If during a particular year, the number of expensive medical procedures, undertaken in a state, increases then the overall size of its GDP increases also. So if the GDP is such a good indicator of the social level of welfare then why not promote cigarette smoking in order to increase the incidence of lung cancer which will keep the surgeons busy and lead to a large rate of growth in the GDP? Of course such a policy would be rejected by all. But isn't this exactly what we do when we allow firms to dump their toxic wastes into rivers and when we encourage workers to commute long distances from where they reside to their place of work. The GDP concept is rife with problems that are too many to list and that economists and environmentalists have been pointing out for decades chief among them is the inability of GDP per capita to say anything about the all important income distribution. Wouldn't it be more important to learn who had access to the increased output rather than to just say that output went up? It has often been the case that all the growth in the GDP accrues to a small group of privileged economic class while the rest of the population looses ground.

Environmentalists in general and environmental economists in particular have been in the forefront of an unremitting attack on the method of assembling national income statistics and in particular the GDP. These efforts have been helped over two decades ago by the work of Amartya Sen, the Noble laureate in Economics, through his pioneering work on how to measure poverty and social well being. His work has led, among other things, to the increasingly popular Human Development Index by the United Nations. The HDI ranks countries by creating an index that takes into consideration the level of GDP per capita but combines that with measures of literacy and life expectancy. As a result it becomes possible to rank a country with high literacy rate and a high life expectancy above one that enjoys a higher GDP per capita but lags in the other two indicators.

Two days ago Joseph Stiglitz, another Noble laureate in Economics, a Professor of Economics at Columbia University and an ex Chief Economist of the world Bank has joined ranks with the above group of advocates for a change in National Income Accounting. He called, in his capacity as a member of a group advising president Sarkozi of France, upon world economic leaders to

250

"avoid GDP fetishism and… to stay away from that." What a welcome message during these perilous economic times in a world that is clearly not sustainable. Bravo Dr. Stiglitz.

So does this apply to Lebanon? You tell me. Is a growing GDP, accompanied by a growing poverty rate, inequitable distribution of income , larger public debt, higher unemployment, less electric power, a construction boom for the super wealthy, privatized public beaches, low minimum wage, environmental degradation in all fields and rampant corruption a sign of social justice and better social welfare?

Saturday, September 26, 2009

Is Copenhagen Conference 2009 Flawed?

We are already witnessing the beginnings of a barrage of saturated media coverage about climate change and the upcoming Copenhagen conference. By the time the COP15 Conference at Copenhagen arrives it might be the only item in the news all over the world and that is good. We need to take some meaningful measures that could get us to move in the right direction. Who knows, we might even avoid the apocalypse.

The failure to reach an agreement to adopt an effective and clear plan of action to reduce greenhouse gas emissions would be a major setback to the environmental efforts to avert a catastrophic climate change, an increase in temperature greater than 2 degrees Celsius. Sea level will rise, major ocean currents would be disrupted, monsoons and hurricanes will increase both in their frequency and intensity, crop failures will become more common, desertification will increase; life as we know it will become disrupted. What is at stake is surely the greatest challenge that civilization has ever faced and a successful Copenhagen meeting is a must.

Yet if we are to act as dispassionate observers of this process we will have no choice but to note the major logical fallacy upon which Copenhagen is built. The issue is not whether the world can afford not to decrease its GHG emissions; it cannot. The real issue though is whether Copenhagen can deliver us out of this self inflicted quagmire? How can it possibly do that when we even refuse to look into the root cause of this problem? Anthropogenic emissions are simply the product of human economic activity and no one is proposing that we limit economic growth.

The position at Copenhagen is nothing else but an exercise in a combination of major logical fallacies such as "argumentum ad populum" combined with "argumentum ad baculum"; a false argument based on the appeal to the majority and to fear.

Let me explain. One of the major efforts that the nations, represented at Copenhagen, will confront is that of reducing car emissions. It is widely believed that the move to hybrid engines and electric plug-in vehicles, in addition to more efficient engines, will turn out to be a major contribution in achieving the sought reduction in carbon emissions. But would it? The world produced over 70 million new vehicles during 2007 but under the best estimates all the hybrids and electric plug-in will not amount to more than 2 million units a year by 2015. If these numbers hold then that is a miserly 2% of the new cars, not to mention that China and India alone are slated to replace the United States as the number one producers of vehicles in the world. Emissions from China and India, both of whom are neighbours of Bangladesh, will not be regulated. Climate change is the largest infringement on the sovereignty of Bangladesh and yet it goes on each day of the year without firing a bullet or creating a political standoff. Even if we are to assume, as unlikely as it might be, that by 2020 one fifth of the newly manufactured in the world each year would be powered by either a hybrid or an electric engine, what about all the raw materials that has to be mined and processed in order to build all of these cars not to mention all the tires, spare parts, accidents and highways that they will generate and require? Would supplying all of these resources by "developing" countries be without a carbon footprint?

A more efficient car is a welcome development but a more efficient car will be useless in reducing the human impact on the ecosystem unless we are to simultaneously build fewer cars and consequently fewer garages, less highways, less spare parts use less resources and conserve our natural capital.

It is not sufficient to set up a goal. We must set up a goal accompanied by a workable plan otherwise the goal would best be classified as a wish. Imagine ,if you will, that all the water bottling facilities in Fiji ; whose products are shipped to North America and the rest of the world; are to become totally powered by energy acquired through either thermal solar , photovoltaic or wind turbines, would that then make the consumption of such water environmentally friendly? You decide.

As you can see from the above the need to cut down on GHG's and carbon emissions is not questioned. What is at stake is our ability, or rather inability, to accept that climate change is nothing more than a manifestation of a systemic failure and such failures demand a total redesign of the system. If we cannot understand this most basic of all facts then all our efforts, as well intentioned as they might be will be for naught.

Sunday, October 18, 2009

TANSTAAFL

"There ain't no such thing as a free lunch" has been traced to the late nineteenth century when saloons in the US offered free lunch for their paying customers. Obviously the idea has since become a corner stone of economics by emphasizing that whenever we make a choice then we have to sacrifice something else in exchange. The same principle governs all activities in the scientific world that is governed by the entropic nature of the universe. We can never produce something out of nothing.

It is unfortunate, in light of the above, that so many thinkers, institutions and organizations have chosen to remedy what is arguably the greatest challenge to civilization; environmental degradation; by advocating policies that are not guided by that most basic of ideas. Sustainability, an inevitable phenomenon of an increasingly complex systems, is being promoted by each and every government in the world, by the United Nations and all its agencies and many think tanks and educational institutions of higher learning through arguments and models that seek more economic growth when it is very clear that sustainability came to the forefront; as an existential issue; as a result of the destructive activities of economic growth. Major concerns about sustainability, the ability to continue the current scale of operations into the future demands that we adopt a radically different methodology rather than the current paradigm that glorifies economic growth and unfettered markets. As the proverb says: "If you always do what you've always done, then you'll always get what you always got." Business as usual will only result in severe shortages and unthinkable environmental degradation.

Kenneth Boulding, the preeminent economist is reputed to have said: "Only mad men and economists believe that infinite growth is possible in a finite world". He actually went further as to characterize that kind of irresponsible behavior as a "cowboy economy" when he suggested that we need to think of the delicate balance of a "spaceship" earth. A society without limits is a fiction.

This idea of the absolute need for limits to growth has been adopted by many thinkers in all sorts of fields, physics, anthropology, biology, ecology, philosophy and economics just to name a few. But the most effective proposition has been the one made by Herman Daly who revived the old idea of the classical economists in general and that of J. S. Mill in particular, namely steady state economics. This notion has become the foundation for all environmental visions that seek to steer human activity in such a way as to avoid the imminent collapse that we are heading towards. How far are we from the abyss is debatable but many of the models such as the Club of Rome, global ecological footprint, Pimentel estimates of the limits to the size of global population or the Energy Return on Investment (EROI) speak in terms of decades and not centuries.

Add to the above the bleak Environmental assessment of the group of 1300 scientists assembled by the UN, the dreadful outlook of James Hansen of NASA about the severity of the upcoming climate change in addition to the dire predictions of James Lovelock who has been described as "one of the environmental movement's most influential figures" and one cannot help but be bewildered when we hear the politicians suggest more growth when it was growth that created the problem in the first place. When would we understand that more of the same is a recipe for disaster and that sustainability is not compatible with economic growth? It is simply one or the other.

Under the best of circumstances growth can be justified as a means to an end but it is pure madness when growth becomes an end in itself as it has become in the developed world. Why is it so difficult to connect the dots and conclude that since pollution is a byproduct of economic activity and since economic growth demands a greater scale of human activity then economic growth is the cause of environmental degradation. Maybe when all is said and done Homo sapiens (wise humans) we are not.

The world is at a critical proverbial fork in the road. We can either change direction and hope that we can avoid the abyss or we can pretend that there is a free lunch and we can have it all, economic growth and sustainability in a finite world. The choice is very clear, either follow the principles and the models that show unmistakably the absolute need for a radical change in the whole architecture or continue the pretense that we can have our cake and eat it too. Lipstick on a pig just won't cut it.

Sunday, November 1, 2009

Copenhagen, One more Time

The peace Nobel laureate Desmond Tutu sent a letter to the EU parliament in which he berated them for not acting to slow down climate change. Mr. Tutu said in his letter "The rich world is historically responsible for the emissions causing climate change and they have a moral obligation to provide the means for the countries on the front line to survive and prosper."

Mr. Tutu was in effect urging the countries of the North to overcome their differences and to live up to their moral responsibility by agreeing; during the Barcelona negotiations; to find a way out of the current impasse before Copenhagen. The developing countries have made it clear that they expect financial transfers from the developed countries of around $148 billion a year by 2020 if they are to do their part of reducing their expected carbon footprint.

But since climate change is a global issue then it does require a global solution. Again it seems obvious that we cannot have a global solution if the largest, well second largest, emitter is not ready to participate in the game. Copenhagen is exactly one month away and the US climate change bill is still languishing in the Senate sub-committee. Senator Boxer, the chair of the Environmental Committee, remains hopeful that a bill will leave her committee before Copenhagen. That is not assured because a number of the Republican senators promise not to attend the committee mark up sessions. If they do not attend then no bill can be presented to the senate at large. Even if a bill is to emerge some very powerful Democratic senators such as Max Baucus promise to hold up the measure in his powerful Finance Committee by delaying funding for the measure. What are even worse are the proposed targets. Kyoto which was initially agreed to by the US was to cut carbon emissions by 5 % from the 1990 level by 2012. The US is estimated to have released around 5 Billion tons of carbon in 1990 and thus the implicit target by 2012 would have been 4.75 billion tons. The new bill is aiming for a 20% reduction from the 2005 levels by 2020. Since the 2005 emissions are estimated to be 6 billion tons then the 20% reduction will take the US back to 4.8 billion tons by 2020. That is irresponsible behviour besides being a cruel joke on the aspirations of those that take these existential matters seriously. The US is targeting to potentially reach by 2020 a level of carbon emissions that it was supposed to have hit by 2012 and yet they want the world to call such measures responsible action. Go figure.

Mr. Yao de Bar, the UN Climate Change Secretariat said it best when he stated the need to "Step back from self interest and let common interest prevail" Nothing else will work.

Wednesday, January 6, 2010

The Flat Earth Society Is Alive And Doing Well In Saudi Arabia

As the world, at least most of the countries in the world, express concern and even regret over the failure of the Conference at Copenhagen to come to a meaningful conclusion the Saudi Arabian chief negotiator at the talks expressed Saudi Arabia's glee and satisfaction that the Copenhagen Conference failed to take any positive steps towards meeting the most important challenge that civilization has ever met. Mr. Mohammad Al-Sabban went further as to predict that the world seems to be heading towards a stalemate on the question of anthropomorphic global warming, AGW. Mr. Al-Sabban proceeded on an interview on the BBC to predict that the action on climate change will become similar to that on the Doha round of the WTO. The WTO members have been engaged in negotiations for the past ten years with no resolution in sight.

It is shameful that a country takes pride in the fact that it is not likely for the world community to make any progress on the climate change issue for at least the next ten years and furthermore Saudi Arabia is proud of its record on AGW because it was essentially the work of a China-Sudan-Saudi Arabia cabal that sank the Copenhagen Conference. Saudi Arabia's obstructionist role in Copenhagen earned it the moniker the" most likely villain in the awkward squad".

When the world was initially presented with the problem of AGW, many countries, institutions, scientists and individuals were skeptical until the world scientific community has practically united in adopting the view that human activities are the culprit behind climate change. It has been estimated by the scientific community that any change greater than 2 degrees Celsius will have profound global catastrophic implications that range from disease, to storms, higher ocean levels, food shortages and extinction of specie. The fact that human civilization has become a major evolutionary force can be seen in numerous scientific studies.

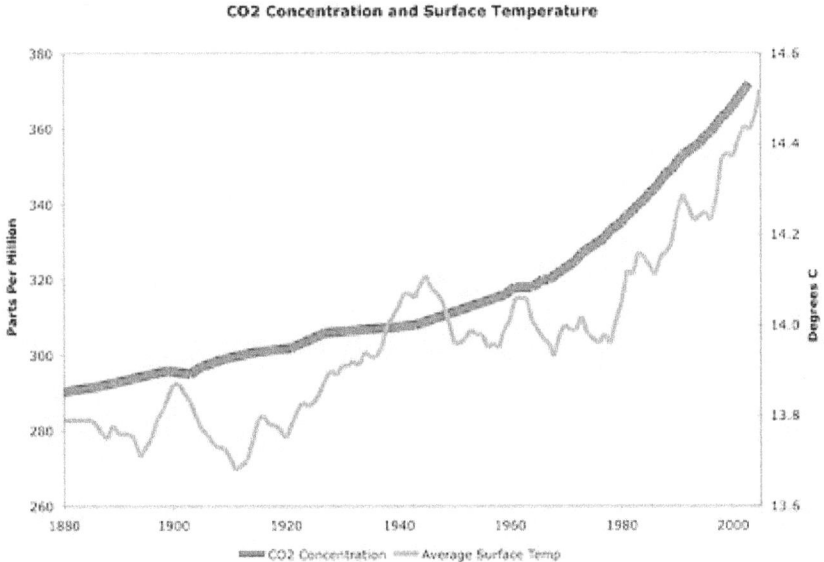

The Proceeding of the National Academy of Science concluded that "Since 2000, a growing global economy, an increase in the carbon emissions required to produce each unit of economic activity, and a decreasing efficiency of carbon sinks on land and in oceans have combined to produce the most rapid 7-year increase in atmospheric CO2 since the beginning of continuous atmospheric monitoring in 1959. This is also the most rapid increase since the beginning of the industrial revolution."

And the Intergovernmental Panel on Climate Change, IPCC, has also said that:" Warming of the climate system is unequivocal, as is now evident from observation of increases in global average air and ocean temperatures, widespread melting of snow and ice and rising global average sea level. Observational evidence from all continents and most oceans shows that major natural systems are being affected by regional climate changes, particularly temperature increases."

In light of all the scientific evidence from all over the world that climate change is a fact, that its effects will be dramatic, that it is our duty and obligation to try to mitigate it Saudi Arabia is glad that we are not planning any action. But that position is to be expected. Would we expect the drug pusher to support measures designed to decrease drug usage? Of course not. To allow Saudi Arabia and China to have a major say in how to deal with global warming is similar to the proverbial image of putting the fox in charge of the hen house. I am not sure that Saudi Arabia and possibly all other major exporters of fossil fuels should have a say in what is to be done in order to implement strong steps that are bound to create major withdrawal symptoms but that are necessary if the addict is to be given a chance to overcome the addiction. Saudi Arabia and all the other 25 countries in its camp have prevented the global community from making any progress towards rehabilitation and sustainability by insisting that the world is flat. Such a position is demonstrably evil and unethical. But that fact that the global community allowed the "Awkward squad" to carry the day is a powerful statement about our lack of resolve. Shame on all of us.

Sunday, February 14, 2010

Sovereign debt and Pigouvian Taxes

Sovereign debt, as a potentially crippling fiscal problem worldwide, has risen to the forefront over the past few months. Whether it is the US, Europe, Japan or many other developed and developing countries the sovereign debt watch is on.

The major metrics of a pending sovereign debt crisis that have been in vogue for decades used to be applied only to developing countries. Unfortunately this is no longer the case. The Herculean efforts by governments all over the world; the developed in particular; to avoid a repeat of the debilitating depression of the 1930's has forced these countries to increase substantially their fiscal stimulus programs. In a sense the monetary and fiscal policies adopted by the officials of all of these countries have been very successful. A worst case scenario has been avoided.

But as economics has always taught us, "There Ain't No Such Thing As A Free Lunch"; TANSTAAFL. Yes we avoided a deep recession and the top officials can pat themselves on the back for this. But maybe not. Is the cure at least as expensive as or maybe even more so than the ailment that it saved us from? That is, currently, the $64,000 question or maybe I should say the $64 billion question? :-)

Often, our efforts at prescribing remedies are counterproductive because of what is inherent in problem solving. We always seem to target the symptom rather than the disease. As a result we inevitably move from one crisis to the next as a result of the law of unintended consequences.

In our efforts to save the system and to prevent a major economic depression we proceeded to throw money at the problem in order to generate more final demand and thus put more people to work. What we did not stop to consider is the major question of how are we going to pay back all of these funds that we have borrowed? It seems that we did what we always do; shift the burden onto the future generations. The debt will not come due for some decades, right? Wrong. Well informed individuals know that more debt implies more taxes in the future and so they take corrective by refusing to own the highly risky debt. Once we find out that the debt service is too large and that we cannot keep on rolling the debt unto the future then we will have no choice but to become deadbeats. That is where we are at the moment. The question is which country is going to go under first? Would it be Greece or would it be one of the other PIIGS? How about the UK, or even Japan or the US? If any of these countries default would they set up a contagion that will devastate all the current international financial system as we know it?

Believe it or not there is a potential mechanism that if adopted could go a long way towards addressing the real cause of this issue and not only the surface phenomenon. The solution that I am about to propose is not new, actually, N.G Mankiw wrote about it in 2007.

"The scientists tell us that world temperatures are rising because humans are emitting carbon into the atmosphere. Basic economics tells us that when you tax something, you normally get less of it. So if we want to reduce global emissions of carbon, we need a global carbon tax. ...

The idea of using taxes to fix problems, rather than merely raise government revenue, has a long history. The British economist Arthur Pigou advocated such corrective taxes to deal with pollution in the early 20th century. In his honor, economics textbooks now call them "Pigovian taxes."...some taxes align private incentives with social costs and move us toward better outcomes."

I would love to see a carbon tax levied not only in the major industrial countries but all over the globe with all the proceeds dedicated to lowering the sovereign debt. Such a tax could be a first step towards internalizing the negative externalities of all the production in the world economy. If that leads to less and more efficient production then all of us will be winners.

Note: Lebanon has already reached the point of no return. The current sovereign debt burden is so large that it will be impossible to avoid a cataclysmic crisis if we do not seek an immediate renegotiation of some of the debt and at least a partial write off. If we do not change course then we will get where we are heading, the financial abyss.

Monday, February 22, 2010

It Is Not Too Late If We Act Now

It is not very often that we get credible ecological news that is not full of bad news and projections. Well, I am glad to say that the following is a recent study that actually suggests that humans have not lost the race yet. Yes we are on our way towards catastrophic outcomes but we are not there yet and interestingly enough we can avoid the worst outcome if we are smart enough to change our ways and work meaningfully towards redemption.

The Stockholm Resilience Center, at Stockholm University is self described as a center of Research for Governance of Social-Ecological Systems. The Centre released a few months ago a major study undertaken by 28 world renown scientists in which they have established a new area in planetary management. Their first study describes nine planetary boundaries (listed at the bottom of this entry) that they believe humanity must not cross. The study goes on to say that human activity has thus far resulted in breaching three of these boundaries (the stared ones)but not the other six.

We are currently living in the geologic era known as the Holocene which started around 10,000 years ago. As we all know, it was during the Holocene that agriculture was developed, civilization prospered and industrialization became the norm. But unfortunately we are entering the Anthropocene, a new geological age in which human activities have grown as to form a major threat to the health of the earth.

Will we have the wisdom to adopt the right policies and change our behavior so as to avoid catastrophe? Yes we still can do that but time is quickly running out.

The nine Planetary Boundaries:

1 Strategic ozone layer
2 Biodiversity
3 Chemical Dispersion
4 Climate Change ***
5 Ocean Acidification ***
6 Freshwater consumption & the global hydrological cycle
7 Land System Change
8 Nitrogen & Phosphorus inputs to the biosphere & ocean ***
9 Atmospheric aerosol loading
*** Transgressed boundary.

Monday, March 22, 2010

The Mother Of All Leaks.

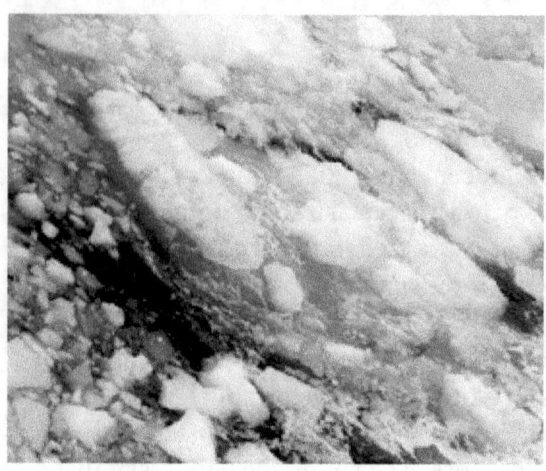

In a recent study published by Science magazine in the March 5 2010 issue it was announced that a group of scientists from over 12 different institutions has found a leak in the Siberian permafrost.

The methane, an estimated 1.5 trillion tons of frozen carbon, was thought to be sheltered by an impermeable barrier is being emitted through perforations. Natalia Shakova, the lead scientist of the research team went on to warn that "Our concern is that the subsea permafrost has been showing signs of destabilization already," she said. "If it further destabilizes, the methane emissions may not be teragrams, it would be significantly larger."

It is important to note that methane is a GHG that is 30 times deadlier than carbon dioxide and that each teragram is equivalent to 1.1 million metric tons. If this leak is to proceed and if only 1 % of the methane is released then the research scientist predict that the effect on climate change could be catastrophic. This leak might be the event to confirm that the world has already passed the tipping point since such a release would be expected to accelerate substantially the rate at which global temperature would rise.

Are there still any skeptics out there? Will we ever act, not to save the ecosystem but to save ourselves? Don't bet on it.

Thursday, April 22, 2010

<u>Earth Day 2010</u>

Forty years ago Earth Day was born and it validated what is perhaps the most promising social movement of the last century and arguably at least the last two centuries. Earth Day did not give rise to environmentalism as an idea but it sure helped spread the awareness and the concern that the nascent field of ecologism had fostered.

A popular movement, especially one whose concern is not limited by geography, ethnicity or religious belief does not just happen. It evolves as a result of deteriorating conditions in the status quo and it attempts to deliver a synthesis, if you will, of the conflicts that had arisen. In this case humans had been exploiting nature, abusing the natural endowment that is so critical for their survival as well as the survival of other species both in the plant and animal kingdoms. Human hubris had dictated to us, at least in the West, that we were created in the image of God, who gave us dominion over all other things on earth. These religious beliefs had become so well established that they contributed towards the creation of science, capitalism, colonialism and ecological degradation on a massive scale. Senator Nelson, the main organizer behind the first Earth Day celebration was merely attempting to provide a forum for individuals to express their concern about the direction in which the world was evolving and thus to empower people to challenge the prevailing orthodoxy that has already been challenged by Rachel Carson, Murray

Bookchin, Arne Naess and others.

The world was very receptive to the idea that something radical needs to be adopted in order to meet the existential challenge that was facing all of us. Major environmental thinkers, like the ones already mentioned, to their credit saw the challenge not only in terms of open spaces, green grass, fresh water and clean air. They spoke of the need to create a just social order, a society that respects the individual rights but that is guided by the common good as well as global justice. They aimed for a world that is free of gender, religious, racial, ethnic or sexual exploitation; a non hierarchical structure. They argued and rather convincingly that we can never free nature unless we free ourselves of all the prejudices that dominate our relationships with each other.

Forty years ago a serious social movement became well established and even entrenched to save the world, to save us from ourselves and many of us responded with enthusiasm and energy. But only to be disappointed. The vision has been shattered and the accomplishments have been few.

What happened? What went wrong? The simple answer is that we have allowed the establishment, the one we were determined to fight, the order that we were supposed to challenge to co-opt us. Capitalism which was the nemesis of a healthy environment metamorphed into "green capitalism" the saviour , Incentive Based policies were adopted to restore health to an eco system devastated by the markets very own failures, affluence and affluenza are being promoted as a silver bullet for all what ails us despite the fact that over consumption is one of our seminal afflictions, complexity is still being promoted as a tool to become sustainable when the evidence is exactly the opposite and we persist in our belief that all of this was created for us, for the pleasure of the human species.

So far we have failed to address the issue of human population growth, we have made no progress in cleaning the polluted water that we have, climate change has reached a tipping point , grain stocks are the lowest they have been, conventional and non conventional energy are rapidly facing lower EROI; energy return on investment, the world is full and we are way above carrying capacity but what is most painful is that we have thus far allowed a revolution, a paradigm shift, to slip away from us for the simple fact that our concern is not genuine enough otherwise why would we have agreed to be sold for thirty of silver?

Thursday, July 15, 2010

<u>Peak oil: World Crisis, Arab Benefit</u>

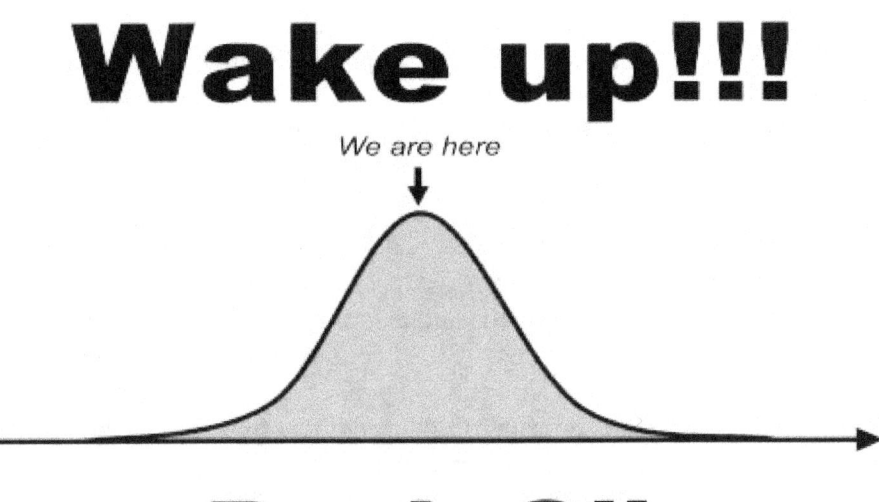

Energy is best defined as the "capacity to do work"; there cannot be life without it. That is simply what is meant by saying that life on planet earth will come to an end when the sun becomes so hot in a billion years or so that water on earth would evaporate and life on its surface will become impossible. Meanwhile the energy flows from the sun to the plants that sustain herbivores that in turn are eaten by carnivores and then at the top of this food pyramid the omnivores. This was the case for 100's of millions of years. A most significant change started with the industrial revolution and it is still going on unabated, the use of machines powered by various forms of terrestrial energy. All machines are in essence dependent on coal, oil or electricity which is produced in most cases from fossil fuels.

The global economy consumes about 500 Quadrillion BTU's each year and this level of consumption is projected to rise at about 1.4% every year for the next 20 years. Over 86% of all this energy comes from the three major fossil fuels of oil, coal and natural gas. All other forms combined (nuclear, hydro, biomass and all other renewable) account for less than 14% of energy consumption.

Oil supplies the largest proportion of energy in our industrial society and its role is looked upon as being the most crucial for civilization, so much so that a few are already predicting collapse of society as we know it when oil becomes scarce. Peak oil is the term used to describe what some of the best known geologists argue is inevitable. Peak is the point in time when the world would have used half of all the available oil reserves in the world. Whether we have passed the peak as of 2008 or whether we are to pass it in the next couple of years or even decade is not materially important. What is significant is that many, but not all, geologists, energy traders, oil company executives, academicians, environmentalists and common citizens have adopted the new paradigm of peak oil.

Even if we are to leave the issue of climate change aside for the purposes of this post yet it is clear that peak oil is a game changer. The world oil production is about 86-87 million barrels a day and the prestigious and mainstream IEA, International Energy Agency, projects the need for over 110 million barrels each day by 2030. If the world is already at peak then where is the additional oil going to come from? A quick survey of plans by the major oil companies of the world shows clearly that we are digging deeper and in more difficult terrain than we ever did simply because the low hanging fruits have already been picked, so to speak.

There are at least two important implications associated with peak oil. (1) The less the availability of conventional oil then the greater is the incentive to exploit the non conventional oil reserves like Venezuela's heavy oil, Canada's tar sands and eventually Colorado's shale. Each of the above produces oil but at a much greater cost. (2) As conventional oil becomes less abundant; we have already lifted half of all the oil reserves; then again the energy return on investment ; EROI; will decrease and continue decreasing to the point whereby it would require more energy to lift a barrel than the energy embodied in that barrel.

The implications of the above two facts that result from peak oil are very clear. As the world demand for energy increases and the supplies cannot keep pace the resulting imbalances will play havoc with the price of oil. We have already witnessed what a slight shortage could do in 2008 when the price per barrel rose parabolic ally to over $140. Under the scenario of peak oil towards the end of this decade that previous price will be appreciably overshot. There are some who project a price of over $300 per barrel given the tight market conditions predicted by peak oilers.

Arab countries can very easily be producing about 30 million barrels of oil each day by 2020 if Iraq is to achieve its planned goal of 8 million barrels per day. Furthermore it would be easy to project exports of about 22 million barrels each day. If the above scenario is to play out and if the resulting economic crisis does not lead to the use of military force then the Arab oil exporters can expect an annual cash flow of over $1 Trillion. Could peak oil, a major challenge for most of the world be exceptionally beneficial to the Arab countries? And if so are they ready to absorb such flows of funds in order not to clog the international flow of funds.

Saturday, July 17, 2010

Hybrid cars cannot save us, only less population can.

We are often told that one major consequence of industrialization and modernity is the resulting climate change and its deleterious effects. We are further told that if we value planet earth then we should avoid all the activities that result in a major reallocation of carbon in the world. Note that based on the first law of thermodynamics no element is ever destroyed, all what we can do is to release carbon from being locked in fossil fuels to be released as a gaseous compound in the atmosphere. Is such a minute reallocation important for the planet? If we are to recall that this planet has been hit by a meteorite travelling at a tremendous speed, has experienced a cooling process and has a tremendous capacity to adapt and heal itself. In the words of James Lovelock the earth is a "homeostatic super organism" that will constantly change and adapt as to ensure its survival. So does the planet care about our reallocating carbon or any other element for that matter? Physics and common sense tells us that the answer is an unequivocal no. But that does not mean that climate change is not the biggest challenge that humans have ever been faced with. The operative word in the previous sentence is human.

In order to fashion a real and meaningful solution to any problem requires a clear understanding of what is the problem all about. Climate change is not about maintaining a carbon balance for the sake of the earth but it is a purely anthropocentric concern about life for the human species. No one can deny that human civilization has evolved to become an evolutionary factor. A major by product of human activity is climate change which will result in putting into motion a process that many ecologists are calling the sixth extinction. Climate change combined with the growing needs for more roads, buildings, deforestation have radically changed the nature and characteristics of the habitat and thus is leading to more and more extinction.

If we do value these changes, and we should value them, then the solution is not to develop an alternative to the internal combustion engine, although that is desirable, but what is required is a recognition that the biggest threat to human civilization and biodiversity as we know it is the human species itself. The threat is not purely that of numbers, although numbers do count but it is a combination of numbers and levels of affluence. The expression I= PAT as developed by Paul Ehrlich emphasizes clearly the relationship between environmental degradation (I), pure number of humans (P), lifestyles (A) and the level of technology (T). Note that if we are to constantly seek a higher level of affluence, for a larger and larger population then the inevitable outcome is greater and greater ecological degradation.

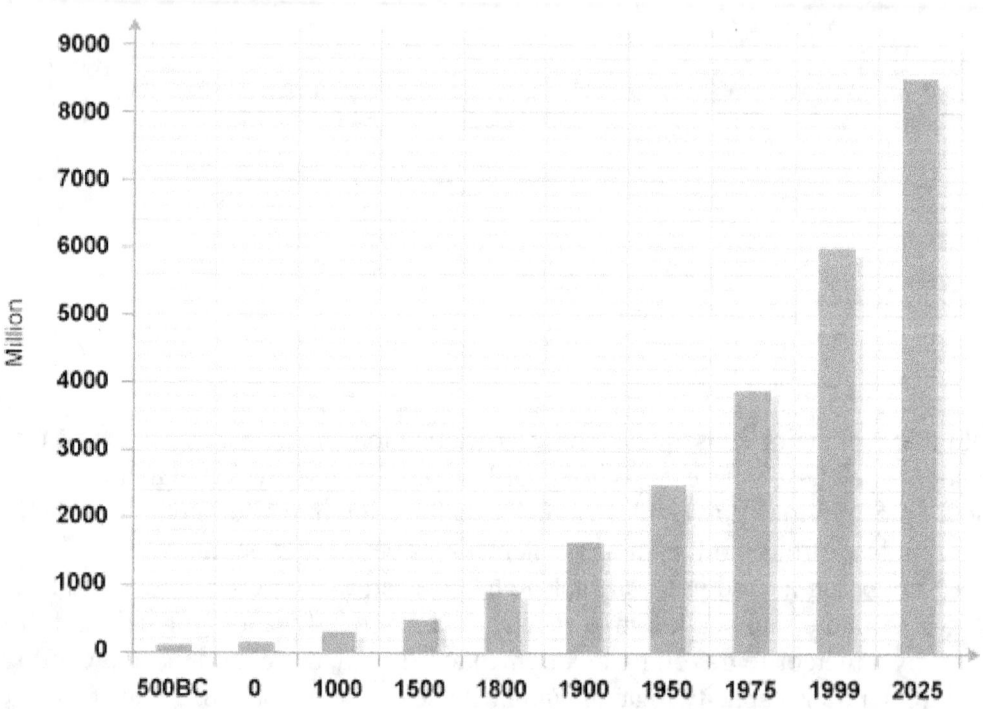

There are a number of studies that show conclusively that the planet is already beyond its carrying capacity. A popular and easy to understand measure is the estimate of how many global acres are required to provide a particular life style. Such estimates vary from one country to the other and from one household to the other. A simple back of the envelope application of the above shows that if a Western life style is to be adopted by the 7 billion inhabitants then the resources of six planets will be required.

Sustainability is everyone's concern, large countries, small countries, poor countries and rich countries. Since sustainability does not recognize artificial political boundaries then it must be dealt with on a global level and coordinated policies. Yale University in cooperation with Columbia University have developed a rather sophisticated Sustainability Index based on 76 variables and 21 indicators that shows a weak relationship between GDP and Sustainability Index of each of the 146 countries sin the study. For example, three of the top ten most sustainable countries are not OECD member (Uruguay, Guyana and Argentina). Other rankings that are of interest: Japan is the 30th while the US is the 45th and the UK is the 65th.

Unfortunately, but understandably Lebanon ranks as the 129th most unsustainable country out of the group of 146. The other countries in the region are slightly better but all are very highly unsustainable. An application of the ecological footprint to Lebanon would not make things any better. The average footprint for an individual leading a Western life style is over 22 global acres when the world has on the average only about 6 global acres and Lebanon offers an average of just over ½ a global acre, a deficit of over 21 acres per Lebanese.

Sunday, August 8, 2010

Nuclear Power Is Far From Optimal For Arab States

No matter how the nuclear impasse between Iran and the international community is eventually resolved there will definitely be an unwelcome byproduct of this controversy that will affect the life of all inhabitants in the region for decades to come. Electric power generation in many of the GCC countries in addition to other Arab states is regrettably going nuclear. Many contracts have already been signed and a few others are in the discussion phase.

Iran has been at odds with the international community over what it calls its peaceful nuclear initiative and what practically the whole world regards as a nuclear program for the production of atomic bombs. The Iranian program to enrich uranium and its adamant refusal to agree to have international inspection of its facilities and to cease the local enrichment efforts in exchange for imported enriched uranium 235 have served to heighten the contention that Iran's' nuclear efforts are not peaceful.

Iran, a signatory of the Nuclear Non-Proliferation Treaty, NPT, was found in 2003 to be in non compliance of its obligations under the treaty. As a result the International Atomic Energy Agency, whose Director General at the time was Mohammad El Baradei reported this violation to the United Nations Security Council in 2006 which has resulted in sanctions against Iran and on and off negotiations regarding its right to enrich uranium.

The suspicion that Iran is pursuing nuclear weapons has heightened international commitment that the world has to act decisively to stop nuclear proliferation and enforce the 1970 NPT statutes. This current nuclear standoff between Iran and the international community is further complicated by the nature of unfriendly relations between Iran and Israel where some Israelis regard an Iranian atomic bomb to be an existential threat to the state of Israel.

It is hoped that ultimately cooler minds will prevail, Iran will find a way to pursue its peaceful nuclear program without the need for local uranium enrichment and that the palpable level of tension with Israel will be brought under control. But even if all goes well and all the nuclear issues between Iran and the rest of the world are resolved the neighbouring Arab states have become directly involved in a different kind of a nuclear race. The UAE, Saudi Arabia, Egypt, Jordan and possibly Kuwait have either embarked on programs to generate electricity from nuclear power or are seriously considering it.

So why shouldn't these countries generate electricity from nuclear power? That does not contravene any NPT regulations. What is most ironic is that probably none of these programs would have been given the approval to proceed had it not been for the Iranian nuclear program. Most of the Arab countries and the GCC in particular feel uncomfortable with an assertive nuclear Iran and so felt that they would respond the best way that they can by adopting peaceful nuclear technology. Nuclear power became the new status symbol in the region and the major providers of the technology; US, Japan France, S. Korea and Russia; welcomed the prospect of tens of billions of dollars for the proposed plants.

But do nuclear power plants make sense? Nuclear power is risky, dirty and inefficient. No one in the world has any workable solution for disposing of nuclear waste, an accidental meltdown of a nuclear core is within the realm of possibilities, the uranium deposits are limited and the cost of producing electricity through a controlled nuclear reaction is competitive only because of the fuel subsidies and the limits on liability to make insurance affordable. Then there is the question of huge capitalization and the prohibitive price of decommissioning.

It's ironic that when the countries who have the technology and the know how to go nuclear have decided not to. The US has not built a nuclear power plant in over thirty years and there are major public outcries whenever renewing the license for any of the existing ones comes up. Germany has even gone further than the US. Germany is on a process of phasing out all its current nuclear power plants and is replacing them by renewable clean energy.

Sunlight is for free and is very abundant in each of the Arab states that are going nuclear. Besides the abundance of the sun there is also abundance of land close to the final demand for electricity. All of these factors combine to make concentrated thermal solar a clean, inexpensive energy source that will be difficult to beat. Where else would one get a guarantee for the price of the fuel for decades to come? Many of the plants in the Mojave Desert in California and the plans for 2 gigawatts of solar thermal in China show that electricity can be produced through this technology for about 6-7 cents per kilowatt hour.

It is not too late for the UAE to shift gears and change its nuclear plants into solar thermal ones and obviously Saudi Arabia, Egypt and Jordan should reconsider seriously the long term implications of nuclear power and whether it is worth the risk and the additional cost. Investment decisions especially costly projects that are expected to last for decades should not be undertaken on the basis of fads and status symbols they should instead be undertaken on the basis of efficiency, safety and communal good. Under fair conditions solar thermal will win against nuclear every time. It would be regrettable if the only legacy of the current Iranian standoff is the unwise adoption of electric nuclear power in the Arab states of the region.

Thursday, August 5, 2010

Food Insecurity in Arab Countries

Many of the Arab countries have large reserves of fossil fuels that make them the envy of the world. Saudi Arabia is the largest oil producer in the world, it is estimated that Iraq carries the same potential as Saudi Arabia and has embarked on a plan that could make it the second largest oil producer in the world within less than 10 years. Obviously there is also Kuwait, UAE, Oman, Libya, Algeria and others. All of that is well and good especially since in most cases the reserves are expected to last for decades and possibly centuries to come. The assured continued presence of such an important resource guarantees a substantial flow of funds that will go a long way towards footing the bill for economic and social development not only of the specific countries with the deposits but also for the whole region.

No one can doubt that energy is the basis without which civilization could not exist. But what is at least as important, if not even more so, is the availability of food. Modern society requires ample energy supplies but without food there would be no one to inhabit the world and demand the energy. The good news is that there is even an apparent tenuous balance, on global bases, between the world's ability to provide energy and food and the global demand for these two essential commodities the bad news is that the most severe case of food insecurity in the world happens to be the Arab world.

A United Nations study speaks in very unambiguous terms about the absolute need for Arab governments to take major steps in order to contain the expected effects of a major food crisis in the Arab countries. Studies by FAO; Food and Agriculture Organization; show that the Arab world imports over 50% of its caloric import every year and furthermore, this gap is expected to increase substantially at least until 2030.

The Arab countries, as a group, are the largest net importers of cereal in the world; larger than Asia. Arab countries imported around 60 million metric tons of cereals during 2008. One reason; not the only reason; for that huge dependence on cereal is the Arab diet. On the average the typical Arab gets 35% of his/her daily calories from wheat. This problem could be partially addressed through a different and more varied diet but above all the major reason for the continued growth in the gap between production and consumption is the above average growth in population. That is one reason why family planning, if encouraged by government policy would be expected to make meaningful contributions in this area. Lower population growth rate should make it easier to manage poverty, hunger and malnutrition. It is currently estimated that over 31 million Arabs are classified as hungry that is almost 10% of the population.

It would be very difficult to foresee a scenario that would eliminate food insecurity in the Arab countries for the very simple reason that the Arab world has already overshot its carrying capacity. It is true that the Arab countries do not exploit enough of the available arable land; Arab countries use only about 12% of the estimated 550 million hectares available; but water shortage poses a huge problem. Renewable water resources form almost an insurmountable problem. Water places a real constraint that is very difficult to overcome. But improved agricultural techniques would help contain the resulting food insecurity gap since the average yield in the Arab world is much below the world average. This is where investments in machines, water management and research could pay dividends.

Food insecurity is essentially felt by the poor. Hunger does not occur only because of lack of food but is primarily the result of lack of access. It does not do the poor any good to have shelves stocked with food if they do not have the financial resources to purchase food. That is why the substantial rise in food prices two years ago is estimated to have created over 6 million new hungry Arabs.

Unfortunately the global conditions that led to the price increases of two years ago have not been addressed. The world grain reserves are at an all time low, the world population is still adding almost 65 million new mouths to feed each year, the biofuels programs are still being encouraged and above all the level of income in China, India and other developing countries is increasing. Economists have known for a long time that more income leads to greater demand but since the food stocks are rather limited this additional demand is manifested in higher prices. This is the problem of the poor; expensive food but low wages. Lower income Arabs have to allocate up to 65% of their income for food. That is unacceptable.

Sunday, August 22, 2010

Water Insecurity in MENA

"Water water everywhere ,Nor a drop to drink" from the Rime of the Ancient Mariner is an adequate description to the water insecurity that is threatening the world as a whole but that is a practical certainty for the countries of the Middle East and North Africa. It is true that many an Arab country is blessed with an excess of Black Gold but the serious scarcity of fresh water availability could make Blue Gold much more important in determining the future of these lands.

Fresh water scarcity is a global problem but in some regions it is much more severe than others. The Middle East and North Africa are classified by the United Nations as the ones with the most water insecurity in the world. Although 75 % of the surface of the planet is water only 2.5% of that is fresh water and ¾ of that is not available since it is frozen icebergs. What is left is less than 1 % of the volume of water and even that 1% is not totally available since some of it is hard to get to and others are just soil dampness. What is important is to note that the amount of fresh water availability is fixed but it is, like most other resources, not evenly distributed. Many regions in the world have access to over 12000 cubic meters per capita per year while others have only a few hundred. Actually, the United Nations considers countries with 500 cubic meters of water per capita per year to be suffering of absolute water insecurity.

Unfortunately, many Arab states are already there, such as Kuwait, UAE, Qatar and Gaza. Furthermore it is estimated that the first world capital to run out of water will be Sana'a by 2020. Water availability is so scarce in MENA that the FAO projects that by 2025 17 Arab states will have to be classified under "scarce water supplies". In order to put this in perspective the average water availability/consumption the typical Arab will be just 700 cubic meters per year when the global average is ten times as high in availability and 3-4 times in consumption. The situation for the most essential resource for life is so critical in MENA that less than 0.5% of the renewable water resources are in this region of the world. The stability of the water resources is even more acute if one is to remember that 75% of the water in this region originates from outside its political boundaries.

Given the expected increase in population in the region in addition to climate change and its attendant increased demand for water for irrigation the availability of water will be halved by 2050 which will imply severe water insecurity for the whole region. Whether these expected shortages translate into political instability and water wars is a potential outcome that needs to be taken seriously. That is at least one reason that calls for a major highly coordinated effort by all the countries to invest heavily in water infrastructure including modern irrigation techniques.

Lebanon is in a slightly better position than the average Arab country but definitely not in an enviable position of any water excesses. The best that can be said about the Lebanese situation is that it is less severe than Jordan, and the GCC to name a few. Estimates of water availability in Lebanon are rough and they vary between a conservative estimate of 2200 million cubic meters per year and almost 4000 million cubic meters of fresh water per year. As it is clear even the upper estimate provides each of the 4.5 million Lebanese only about 900 cubic meters per year. Lebanon is expected to be consuming just about 3000 million cubic meters of water by 2015. As the above figure makes it clear that would then imply that Lebanon needs huge investments in the next few years in order to gather a lot of this water that is wasted every year by flowing into the sea. More than half of the water usage in Lebanon is needed for irrigation while about 30% goes for domestic uses. The remainder is used by industry.

The warning by Minister Gibran Basil about the impending water crisis in Lebanon must be taken very seriously. Arguably the crisis has already begun and is visible from the constant failure of the water authorities to deliver adequate amounts of water to its clients. One reason is the antiquated infrastructure and another is the lack of awareness to conserve this most precious of resources. Lebanon cannot afford not to construct a series of dams and to build a modern facility to supply Beirut, where half of the Lebanese reside, with the estimated 250 million cubic meters of water that it needs while it is currently getting less than half of that amount. It is also hoped that the impending water shortages will impel the Lebanese government to adopt a meaningful population policy. Lebanon is simply beyond its physical carrying capacity.

Sunday, October 10, 2010

Climate Change: Global Civilizational Challenge.

The Kyoto Protocol, the only international agreement to fight climate change, will come to an end in two years, 2012. The world, including the US who is not bound by Kyoto, has been trying frantically for over a year to come to agreement on what is to replace Kyoto. The Copenhagen conference, last year, turned out to be totally unproductive. Yet the major players have not given up hope for reaching an agreement that would be legally binding to all its signatories.

Unfortunately the progress has been very slow to nonexistent. The meeting at Tianjin, China ended up last week in total disarray. The meeting which was expected to resolve a few of the obstacles preventing an agreement was described by participants as being full of bickering. "At times it has been like watching children in a kindergarten," said Wendell Tio from Greenpeace International.

Although the talks are scheduled to move to Cancun, Mexico, next month not many are hopeful that the level of disagreement between the US and China will diminish. Kyoto divided the world into two groups, the developed and the developing, with the former subject to strict legal limits on its emissions of carbon dioxide while the latter is subject only to voluntary restraints. And that is the rub.

Officially China has become the largest emitter of carbon in the world, replacing the US but by all conventional metrics China is a developing country and so is refusing to abide by the US demands that China and other large developing countries should be subject to strict emissions quotas also. Obviously the Mr. Su, the Chinese representative at the talks, would have nothing of these demands. Mr. Su likened the U.S. criticism to Zhubajie, a pig in a classic Chinese novel, by saying "It has no measures or actions to show for itself, and instead it criticizes China, which is actively taking measures and actions."

It is this inability to view climate change as a global problem that demands a global solution that has wrecked Copenhagen, is threatening Cancun and will probably doom the final resolution to a meaningless gesture that will do nothing to control climate change. As long as various players are attempting to guard their own selfish interest then no meaningful solution is to be expected. This is a classic case of the tragedy of the commons whereby individual actors believe that they are doing what is good for themselves but wind up in hurting themselves and all other players as well.

Climate change is arguably the most important challenge that civilization has faced. This is not a regional problem but one that would affect everyone and everything. No one has the right to neglect this issue, not even the Arab countries who do not think of themselves as being large emitters of carbon. The data says otherwise. The largest emitters of carbon on a per capita basis are the five Arab gulf countries and these are joined by Saudi Arabia as the 14 largest in the world and then Oman as the as number 20. The Arab states as a whole emit over 1.5 billion tons of carbon dioxide annually which amounts to around 5 % of the global footprint. The Arab League has failed to take any measures to either control or diminish the carbon footprint of emissions in the Arab world. Actually, the record indicates just the opposite. Saudi Arabia has joined forces with China in order to torpedo any agreement in Copenhagen. Isn't it time that the Arab world demands that its governments face their ethical and moral responsibilities squarely?

What do you think: Should the less developed be exempted from strict limits on emissions so that the developed will shoulder the greater part of the burden of emission reductions? Does nature discriminate on the basis of the national origin of carbon emissions? What would be a fair allocation of the burden and how heavy should it be?

Sunday, April 3, 2011

Ecological Footprint of the Arab World: Disasterous

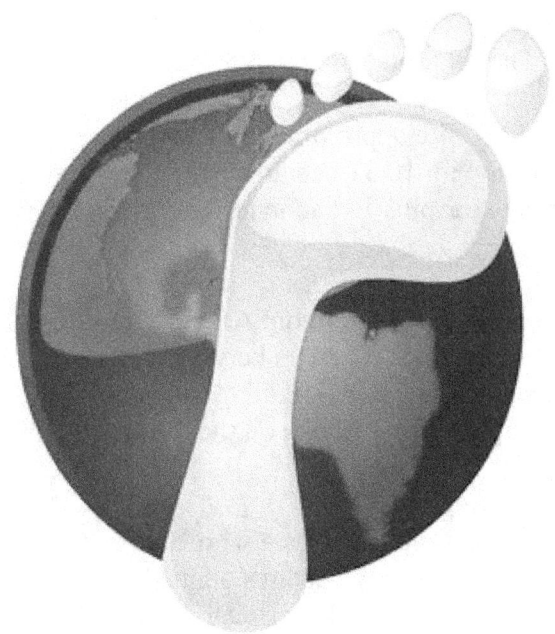

It is so common to speak about environmental degradation but unfortunately no country or group of people seem to be willing to do anything meaningful about the single most important challenge that humanity has ever faced. The problem does not manifest itself in the area of prognosis. A large number of studies by individuals, universities, governments and the UN have concluded as a result of numerous detailed studies that the world is full and that business as usual will only lead to disastrous outcomes, possibly collapse, and total collapse of civilization. Furthermore if collapse is to be the outcome then it would not be the first time that the human inability to take decisive corrective action has resulted in ruin. Just ask the Incas, the Mayans and the inhabitants of Easter Island.

Obviously the adoption of meaningful sustainable measures is in everyone's interest. But yet we have failed to undertake a single measure anywhere in the world that would move us in the right direction. Why? The answer is very simple. Capitalism cannot accept a no growth economy irrespective of the fact that all our studies tell us that the world is full and cannot accommodate any more growth. Actually we know that the present level of economic activity is beyond the carrying capacity of the globe and so sustainability demands major significant cuts in the level of economic activity if we are to have a shot at preventing a climate change of over 2 degrees Celsius.

One of the most common measures of sustainability is that of the ecological footprint. That is simply an estimate of the resources consumed by each person in order to lead the average life style in each country. Studies have shown that at the present the global resources available per person are less than 2 hectares. It follows therefore, that whenever the average footprint per capita of the citizens of a nation is above 2 hectares then that country is operating at a global deficit. This simply means that these citizens are maintaining a life style that we cannot afford, as a planet and that this state of affairs can only result in disastrous outcomes for everyone. That is the message of the Tragedy of the Commons that Hardin has popularized almost fifty years ago.

The Arab world appears to be split into groups. The oil producers in addition to Lebanon, Syria and Tunisia consume at a level that much above the global average. Ironically, the largest ecological footprint in the world belongs to the UAE with approximately about 16 hectares per person. The 3rd highest footprint belongs to Kuwait with 10.31 hectares per person then Saudi Arabia ranks 17th in the world with 6.15 hectares per capita. Lebanon ranks 52nd in the world with a footprint of 3.19 hectares per capita.

Not all of the Arab countries belong to the group of overconsumption. Algeria, Iraq, Jordan, Egypt and Morocco have a per capita ecological footprint that ranges between 1.79 and 1.56 hectares. This implies that each of these countries could increase slightly its level of consumption and yet stay within the global carrying capacity. Sudan on the other hand has an ecological footprint of only 1.14 hectares per capita.

A simple calculation of the total deficit created by the Arab world as a whole reveals the uncomfortable fact that we are in a deficit of about 200 million hectares annually. If we, as a region, are to take our responsibilities towards a sustainable world seriously then we have no choice but to:

(1) adopt strict population policies that would result in decreasing the size of the human population of the region. Stabilizing the population is not acceptable and to continue, unchecked, the current rates of growth in population are immoral and irresponsible.

(2) The level of consumption in the region as a whole is excessive and steps must be taken to limit it to levels that would correspond to a sustainable level.

(3) No doubt that a few are consuming too much and many do not have enough and this calls for strong redistribution efforts.

(4) And lastly we have to confront head on the question of whether any of the above can be realistically achieved under capitalism?

Since it should be clear that the answer to #4 is clearly a resounding no and since we will not change the current societal structure then we should not be surprised when the inevitable collapse takes place. We have no one to blame but ourselves.

ARAB WORLD

Friday, November 20, 2009

Would The Wall Ever Fall In The Arab World?

The whole world has been celebrating one of the most momentous events of the latter half of the 20th century, the fall of the Berlin Wall in 1989. What a triumph for the human spirit, for democracy, individual freedom, human dignity and personal freedom. The events that followed the collapse of that symbol of oppression were as exhilarating as the event itself. The fall of the wall set in motion a liberation tsunami that washed over all of Eastern Europe, parts of the Soviet Union and Central Asia.

It was only Africa and MENA (Middle East and North Africa) that have been "spared" the move towards liberal democracy. Not even Russia was able to resist the tide to democratize and introduce some reforms, albeit not as successful as in most of the other countries. Yet the gulag has been exposed and discredited and the hope is that it will never be able to make a comeback. Despite all of this the one region of the world that seems to be immune to the trend to liberalize and democratize seems to be the Arab World. In a sense the region that has resisted rather successfully until now the forces of liberation and freedom includes the whole of MENA with the possible exception of Turkey.

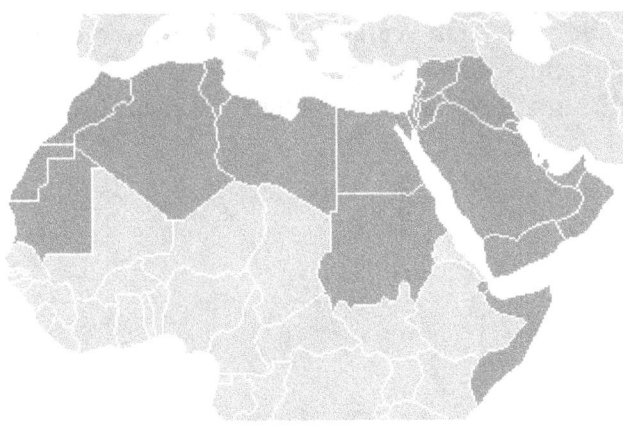

Many are by now familiar with the Arab Human Development Reports commissioned by UNDP but authored by independent Arab thinkers. The results of these studies have been anything but flattering.

The Arab countries as a group are home to over 300 million people and yet the total number of translated books every year is less than the books translated by Greece. It is not only education that is lacking but so is science and development. The Arab countries, as a group, managed to register in the US less than 400 patents when South Korea had registered in the same time period over 15,000 and Israel over 7000. A recent global happening illustrates the "backwardness" of the Arab masses best. When what promises to be one of the greatest discoveries, that of ARDI, a 4.5 million year old skeleton was announced the few mentions of this phenomenal discovery in the Arab press were devoted to the wrong interpretation that Darwin was wrong. They had missed the fact that ARDI is one of the most impressive pieces of solid evidence about the truth behind the Darwinian theory of evolution. Furthermore a survey conducted in Egypt revealed that less than 30 % of the public had even heard of the name Darwin. Such examples abound in every field. The fact of the matter is that the Arab region lags behind the rest of the world in practically every single area and field.

But many individuals of Arabic decent have succeeded in practically all fields and in all sorts of countries. Obviously this suggests that the fault is not that of the individual but it is of the oppressive, dictatorial backward exploitative political environment in each and every one of the 21 countries including the 22nd Occupied Palestinian Territory. A cursory look at the map of MENA from the Atlantic Ocean to the Persian Gulf reveals countries that are ruled by absolute monarchs, Emirs, Sultans and dictators. Muamar Kaddafi has been in power for 40 years and is preparing the ground for his son, Egypt is about to become Mubarak land, Syria was inherited by a young optometrist, Yemen has had the same president for 30 years , Tunisia just reelected its president for the sixth term with an 87% plurality and the beat goes on. Lebanon is the only country that has a claim to democratic institutions but in reality they are just as hollow and rotten as those of its neighbours. Political feudalism masquerading as democracy.

It is obvious that in a wired up world and one with more travel and interactions than ever before the role of the authoritarian regimes is becoming more difficult. But the size of the Mukhabarat keeps on growing, and indiscriminate fear continues to spread in an attempt to thwart the inevitable move to personal freedom and democracy. An Arab Wall shall fall and when it does it shall sweep all throughout Mena to topple these regimes. That we can count on, that is how history unfolds. I just hope and pray that when the time comes we are mature and smart enough to have a velvet revolution.

Monday, July 12, 2010

Arab Philanthropy: MIA

One of the better ways to understand a society is to look at the way it treats its poor. Unfortunately the practically universal adoption of capitalist principles of production has created a world with a highly inequitable distribution of income. This should not be surprising because capitalism rests on two seminal ideas that are constantly at odds with each other; efficiency and equity. The belief in equality and democracy is based on the notion of equality and what is described in economic terms as perfect competition. In the Microeconomic model of perfectly competitive markets, the various actors are numerous and none of them can exert any influence on the market. What that implies is a in which each actor behaves in such a way as to improve its welfare and by doing so it does not influence anybody else since no one has the heft to influence other decision makers. This is a perfectly competitive society guided by an invisible hand to always promote the communal good through promoting self interest.

The above is true in an idealized world, it is a fiction. In reality we live in a world whose environment is best described as one of market failures, a world of imperfect competition. In such a world of monopolistic tendencies the strong take advantage of the weak and the concern with efficiency leads to gross inequities and huge concentrations of wealth and consequently deprivations. Different societies have chosen to adopt different approaches to correct such inherent negative outcomes. In the final analysis these proposed solutions become defined by the strength/weakness of the role assigned to government in each of these respective societies. Besides the crucial role performed by income tax progressivity and the strength of governmentally financed safety net there remains an important function for philanthropic institutions in alleviating the social and economic problems brought about by the failures of the market to be equitable. Philanthropy can and does help remedy some of the injustices brought about in the name of efficiency by the market forces. Philanthropy can help fund research, improve access to educational institutions, help protect valuable ecological resources, provide access to essential heath care, housing and nutritional food.

A major change in the role of philanthropy took place as a result of the beliefs of John D. Rockefeller Sr. who is credited with having institutionalized the view that wealth carries with it a sense of responsibility to give back to the community. It was Mr. Rockefeller who helped establish the view that wealth carries with it a huge social responsibility since wealth ought to be looked upon as nothing more than a privilege to help do Gods work. That was when the idea of stewardship became established.

This is exactly what Bill and Melinda Gates with the help of Warren Buffet are trying to revive. As the world already knows Bill and Melinda gates have already given away to their foundation most of their wealth. The same is true of Mr. Buffet how has already committed to give away his almost $50 billion. The Gateses and the Buffetts have joined forces to encourage the US billionaires to give away at least half of their wealth either during their lifetime or in their final wills. Luckily for the world, since most of these philanthropic efforts are global in scope, many billionaires such as David Rockefeller, George Soros, Pete Peterson and Oprah Winfry have agreed to this proposal. As of 2010 the US millionaires are estimated to be worth at least $1.2 trillion. If the gates-Buffet plan is to succeed then philanthropic activities are to receive at least $600 billion from the current crop of billionaires.

And now we get to what really concerns us. According to the records compiled by Arab Business Magazine the wealthiest Arabs have a wealth that is almost $200 billion. Wouldn't it be fair to expect our wealthy to be as socially enlightened as those in the US? If these privileged few are to be held to the same standard of stewardship and they must then that implies that Arab philanthropies should be the recipients of $100 billion over the next few decades. A cursory analysis of the wealthiest 50 individuals in the Arab world finds that over 60 % of the aggregate wealth belongs to 25 Saudi Arabian citizens followed by 8 billionaires from the UAE whose wealth is almost 15 % of the total Arab wealth in question. The third largest wealth by nationality belongs to 6 Kuwaiti citizens who collectively account for almost 11 % of the combined net assets of the 50 richest Arabs. The remaining 14 % is spread amongst 2 Egyptians, 2 Palestinians, 2 Iraqis and one from each of Bahrain, Lebanon and Qatar.

Not everyone is a big fan of philanthropy for the misguided idea that the poor are poor because they want to be poor. As if privilege and the accident of birth has nothing to do in determini9ng who gets what. But above all the wealthy need to give even more than half of their accumulated wealth if we are to be reminded of the conditions that made that accumulation possible in the first place, a system that pays lip service to equity but gives efficiency a free hand, a system that does not encourage the government to address the resulting inequalities. A sense of fairness, a belief in Rawlesian justice and a commitment to fair play dictate that we have to give until it hurts. Isn't it preferable to live rich and die broke and whenever that is not possible to at least give away half of the would be legacy for the benefit of less privileged individuals.

Thursday, August 26, 2010

Religious Freedom vs. Religious Phobia

Utopias are perfect societal structures that are goals to be attained. They are dreams that will never be fulfilled whether they are based on Plato's Republic or Thomas Mores' ideal economy. These are dreams that provide us with targets to aim for but that we will not attain. If a utopia is to be achieved then that would be the end of history, a stage of perfect homogeneity and no conflict.

No world society is at that stage, although some have argued that certain states are closer to the end of history than others. Democracy, when seen in the above light, is such a conception that is to be approached asymptotically and so obviously never reached. That is true of all societies and all states including the experiment that we know as the United States. We all know of many severe challenges that the US system is constantly struggling with such as the relatively major income inequality, the presidential electoral system, the role of money in all elections and the corporate influence in shaping the legislative process. It is clear that given such challenges the resulting democracy is nowhere close to perfect but yet it can be argued that in many areas such as the principles of separation of church and government in addition to the tremendous seriousness given to the issue that is commonly known as "first freedom" make it very difficult, even impossible, to violate the principle of freedom of religion as spelled out in the first amendment:

"Congress shall make no law respecting an establishment of religion, or prohibiting the free exercise thereof; or abridging the freedom of speech, or of the press; or the right of the

people peaceably to assemble, and to petition the Government for a redress of grievances. "

A democratic system might not be perfectly equitable or perfectly just but it cannot afford to violate personal freedom of expression and religion. There ought to be no room whatsoever in the public square for religious affairs since these are best viewed as issues of personal faith. I have every reason to believe that the United States looks upon this issue with the utmost seriousness it deserves and will not knowingly violate any persons' right to worship whoever she wants anyway she desires provided that such an exercise does not impinge on any other persons rights.

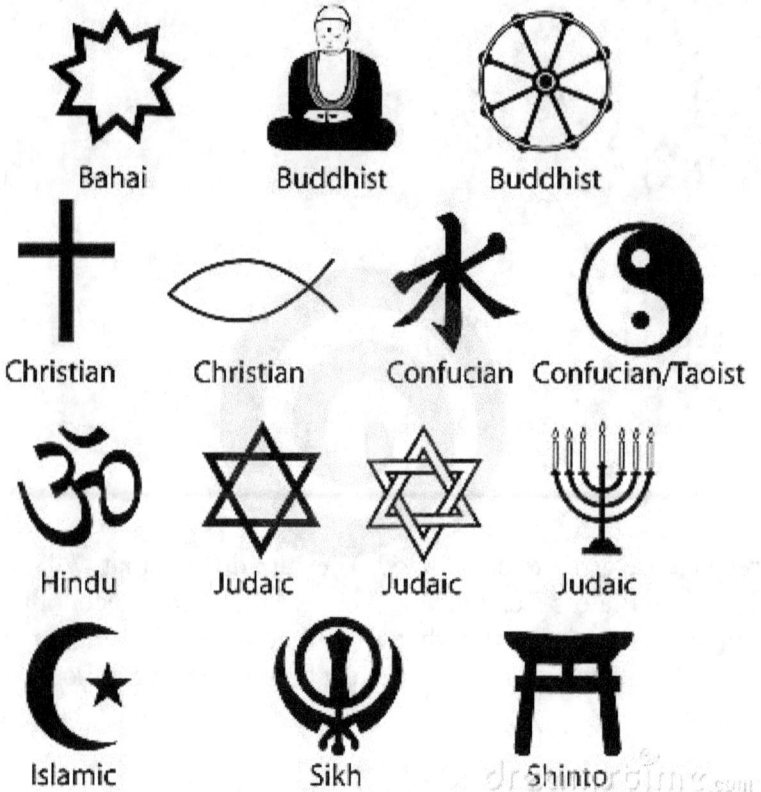

The controversy regarding the issue of the construction of a mosque close to ground zero in New York City must be seen within the above parameters. Ideally this means that any individual or group of people should have the right to practice their faith anywhere they want as long as that does not impinge on the rights of others. No one in Manhattan has said that the group of Moslems does not have the right to worship or to build a mosque; the only objections raised are based on the appropriateness of the location. The Mayor of the city, Mr. Bloomberg, has given his unqualified support for the construction of the Islamic center where it is proposed since it meets all the zoning requirements and I believe that the center would be built where proposed.

If for any reason the planned Islamic center is relocated then that unlikely event would be a reflection of Islam phobia and not a violation of the seminal constitutional principle embodied by the first amendment. Fellow Muslims will still be free to pray and build their houses of worship but not in that particular location which will be a tragedy but not a constitutional catastrophe.

If it ever comes to that , which I doubt that it will, then the most obvious question that should be raised by Arabs and Moslems alike is Why did so many of the well educated and enlightened United States citizens develop an Islam phobia but not a Buddhist phobia or a Hindu phobia? Is there something that we can do as a community to allay these fears, as unreasonable as they might seem? Could it be that when so many terror attacks were carried in the name of Islam that not enough was done to denounce these attacks? Could it be that the small groups of fundamentalists have been allowed to hijack Islam without any major rebuttals from the mainstream Islamic power structure? But above all are there many Arab countries that can truly object to religious discrimination by pointing out to religious freedoms in their countries?

The controversy in lower Manhattan does not rise to the level of being a violation of the first amendment. The Islamic center should be built as proposed but if for one reason or another a zoning justification is found to move it to a different location then Islam phobia would be the reason.

If that is to transpire then it would be the duty of every US citizen to analyze in a detached manner the unfairness and the injustice of such a selective judgment. May this controversy also lead to serious soul searching in the Arab countries also? We need to recognize that when we place severe restrictions on the religious practice of non Moslems in our countries and when we prohibit the building of non Islamic houses of worship or place restrictions on the use of religious symbols then we would have abandoned the right to criticize others when their acts infringe on the rights of our fellow religionists. In a perfect world there should be no restrictions on anyone to believe or not believe but in an imperfect world we need to find out the reason for popular phobias.

Monday, December 8, 2008

Islamic Banks:Have They Eliminated Interest Or Just Changed Its Name?

"Those who charge usury are in the same position as those controlled by the devil's influence. This is because they claim that usury is the same as commerce. However, GOD permits commerce, and prohibits usury. Thus, whoever heeds this commandment from his Lord, and refrains from usury, he may keep his past earnings, and his judgment rests with GOD. As for those who persist in usury, they incur Hell, wherein they abide forever" [The Koran]

The rise of Islamic Banking over the past 40 years into an institutional financial structure spread over the globe has been a phenomenon that has attracted lots of interest. As is often the case whenever a new idea arises it s rise is associated with many falsehoods, half truths and unfulfilled promises. The whole concept of Islamic Banking rests on 4 Qoranic verses that speak against Ribaa (2275-81; 3:130-2; 4:161 and 30:39). Although the Arabic word Ribaa does not mean interest rate yet the four schools of Islamic jurisprudence have interpreted Ribaa to imply interest rates. In the opinions of many that interpretation could easily have been usury. In that case the idea of "Islamic Banking" would no longer appear to be inviolable.

The Islamic Development Bank, the largest Islamic Bank, is a breath of fresh air in the stultified field of economic development. How appropriate it is to give interest free loans to the developing nations instead of burdening them with huge debt service and strict conditionalities a la World Bank and the IMF. But this idea of interest free banking which rests strongly on the two sources of (1) Ijma, Consensus, and (2) Qiyas, analogy, becomes more problematic in other areas.

It should be clear from the above that the basis on which interest free banking rests does not sanctify the idea but in fact is an attempt to replace the interest rate income with a substitute that achieves the same objective as the banished instrument. This is nothing short of a process that seeks conformity with the letter of the prohibition against Ribaa but not its spirit. Since income that flows from trade and risk sharing is considered to be Hallal, lawful, Islamic Banks have adopted Profit Loss Sharing (PLS) as a replacement for the Lender-Borrower Haram, forbidden, relationship.

The Mudarabah and Musharakah, the most popular methods to avoid interest rate income are structured so as to yield the same income that traditional interest rates would have produced in traditional banks. Such a cumbersome structure makes Islamic Banks less competitive than traditional ones. It might be instructive in this regard to recall the words of the Islamic Pakistani economist Ahmad: ""No single Moslem country is running its financial institutions without resorting to interest... no one knows how to do it...they resort to some kind of subterfuge..change the name of interest and you have abolished interest".

An even more scathing criticism is delivered by Dr Hasanuz Zaman who writes:
".. many techniques that the interest-free banks are practicing are not either in full conformity with the spirit of Shari'ah or practicable in the case of large banks or the entire banking system. Moreover, they have failed to do away with undesirable aspects of interest. Thus, they have retained what an Islamic bank should eliminate. "

The current Sharia prohibition on Ribaa renders consumption loans very difficult to structure and as a result the practice of financing trips and personal purchases under Islamic Banking rules becomes harder to structure and implement. Furthermore, a real challenge of Islamic Banking is the ability to develop effective tools that Central Banks can employ in transacting their monetary policies.

Equity and justice, the hallmarks of an Islamic society, do not have to be incompatible with a banking system that charges interest rates. All what is needed to make traditional banking acceptable to the Moslem believer is an act of Ijma, consensus, by Islamic fiqh whereby a distinction is made between usury and a regular interest rate. Once the Islamic Ulamah agree to equate Ribaa with usury then the often cited reason for the prohibition of Ribaa in the first place, ruinous borrowing and the need for Adl, justice, in protecting the weak and the poor would have been met.

Moslem societies do not have to invent financial instruments to perform the function of what is already being done but albeit under a different name. Islam can enrich us all by emphasizing the importance of ethics in the economic sphere but it does not need to reinvent the wheel in order to accomplish that.

Wednesday, November 3, 2010

Civil Rights of Non-Moslems In The Arab World

Logical internal consistency is a fundamental characteristic of a model that has withstood the rigours of investigation both empirical and otherwise. The advocates of an internally inconsistent model, especially one that suffers of an apparent logical fallacy are often chided for their position and for their inability to promote rational thinking. Such is the case when those that make a habit of disregarding say the rights of nature; make an issue of the failure of their neighbours to act in an environmentally friendly manner. Of course the corporation that seeks governmental relief is not in a position to be taken seriously when it opposes the extension of such a program to cover its competitors.

The above fatal fallacy could easily be avoided through the incorporation of the ideas embodied in the principle of the Golden Rule. This simple but profound idea has been traced to practically all cultures all over the world, although one of its most popular and common manifestations are encompassed in the saying: Do unto others what you would like others to do unto you. As it is obvious it would not be difficult to suggest that this ethics of reciprocity is the foundation upon which human rights and fair treatments are based.

What often goes unnoticed, in the Arab world, is that this simple but yet elegant idea about justice and equality has been traced as far as the middle kingdom of Egypt, 19th century BC, as well as the Code of Hammurabi not to mention the Torah and Confucius. Furthermore it is also important to note that The Parliament of World Religion during its centenary held in 1993 adopted the idea of reciprocity found in the Golden Rule as the common belief in all religions. This document of Global Ethics declared to the world:

We are interdependent….We take individual responsibility for all we do. All our decisions, actions, and failures to act have consequences.
We must treat others as we wish others to treat us. We make a commitment to respect life and dignity, individuality and diversity, so that every person is treated humanely, without exception. We must have patience and acceptance….
We consider humankind a family…We commit ourselves to a culture of non-violence, respect, justice, and peace. We shall not oppress, injure, torture, or kill other human beings, forsaking violence as a means of settling differences.

We in the Arab world seem to have conveniently decided not to adopt and apply the above principle despite the admonition by the prophet Mohammad, PBUH, that such a principle of respect and reciprocity to others is essential as can be seen clearly in more than one Hadith:

"None of you [truly] believes until he wishes for his brother what he wishes for himself." An Nawawi

"No man is a true believer unless he desires for his brother that, what he desires for himself." Forty Hadith

"Hurt no one so that no one may hurt you". Muhammad, The Farewell Sermon on Mount Arafat in Mecca.

"Woe to those . . . who, when they have to receive by measure from men, exact full measure, but when they have to give by measure or weight to men, give less than due"
—Qur'an (Surah 83, "The Unjust,"

The principle of justice and reciprocity is as seminal to Islam as it is to other cultures and we choose to neglect it at our peril. This is not the place to describe in full details the practices in separate countries against non Moslems.But it should be clear that when we close our eyes on discriminatory practices by our neighbours and friends then that amounts to acquiescence in these wrongful and hurtful practices.

The Arab world has paid dearly for the inequities that its non Moslem population is subjected to. Why is it not evident that the time of the dhimmis is gone forever and that if we consider ourselves to be part of this global community then no one has the right to deny any other person the right to self expression and the freedom of thought and religious belief? Why can we not see that when we discriminate against others then we automatically give up our right to complain when others discriminate against our fellow co religionists? Saudi Arabia could not possibly object to a rule preventing school girls from wearing a Moslem headdress when a non Moslem is not allowed to practice her religion openly in the kingdom. Egypt was not in a position to complain against the Swiss rule that regulates the size and location of minarets when even minor repairs to churches in Egypt require almost presidential approval. The Arab league could not join in the important dialogue about the advisability of building a Mosque close to ground zero in Manhattan when many Arab countries have strict prohibitions against the construction of Churches and other non Moslem houses of worship.

Yes this is a different world than it was 1500 years ago in many respects but the principles of justice and universal humanity and equality are still the same. Many of the Arab governments that claim that they are only doing the work of Allah and that of his Prophet, PBUH, would do well to review the treaty of Medina which L Ali Khan argues could serve as the basis of treating minorities justly and offering them equal rights under Islam. And most importantly we cannot disapprove of the acts of others when we sanction these same acts either in our countries or we are silent when these same human rights violations are committed by our neighbourly countries. There ought to be no prejudice or partiality in civil rights.

Friday, April 9, 2010

Ali Sabat: What about His Human Rights?

Ali Sabat, a Lebanese citizen, was arrested by the Religious police of Saudi Arabia while he was on a pilgrimage to Mecca during 2008. There is nothing wrong in arresting an individual for committing an offense in a country that he /she is visiting or travelling through. I do not believe that many people will disagree with the proposition that travel does not entitle the traveler to break the laws of the country that one is visiting. But what is clearly, in this case, an abuse of human rights as spelled out in the Universal Declaration of Human Rights, UDHR, and a major infraction of international law is the arrest of Mr. Sabat for having performed a vocation, albeit part time, in Lebanon where fortunetelling is neither a crime, nor a felony or even an infraction of any kind.

Relevant Articles from the UDHR

Article 5.

• No one shall be subjected to torture or to cruel, inhuman or degrading treatment or punishment.

Article 9.

• No one shall be subjected to arbitrary arrest, detention or exile.

Article 11.

• (1) Everyone charged with a penal offence has the right to be presumed innocent until proved guilty according to law in a public trial at which he has had all the guarantees necessary for his defense.

• (2) No one shall be held guilty of any penal offence on account of any act or omission which did not constitute a penal offence, under national or international law, at the time when it was committed. Nor shall a heavier penalty be imposed than the one that was applicable at the time the penal offence was committed.

The Saudi religious police used entrapment methods to get Mr. Sabat to agree to read the fortune of a caller but the fact of the matter is that Mr. Sabat, the father of five children in Lebanon, did not use any talisman in Saudi Arabia. He was arrested by the police for having indulged in a practice that they do not approve off but he did not commit the alleged act in Saudi Arabia. As a result the obvious question to be raised is whether Saudi Arabia has the power and the legal authority to hold a Lebanese citizen for having practiced fortunetelling in Lebanon? The answer to the above question is a simple and clear one; the Saudi Religious police have no jurisdiction whatsoever to apply its laws and morality to acts committed outside its geographical jurisdictional space. Otherwise they should probably arrest and execute every Saudi citizen who has either gambled, drank alcohol, used drugs or sought sexual favours anywhere in the world. The travail of Mr. Sabat gets even more bizarre. As if it was not enough of an insult to arbitrarily arrest him for having done nothing to warrant his arrest, the Saudi police and legal system made things worse, much worse, by convicting Mr. Sabat of the charges he is innocent off and by having the audacity to trample international law and Mr. Sabats human rights by issuing an order to have him beheaded.

The relatively positive development thus far is that Mr. Sabat has not been beheaded yet although he is still in Saudi prison where he has been for over a year and a half and where he is kept alive but under the constant threat of being beheaded at any time.

Many organizations both within Lebanon and outside it have take up the case of Mr. Sabat by demonstrating and writing about the case. But Isn't it rather strange that the issue was not covered adequately in the Lebanese press, as if Mr. Sabat does not have any rights and privileges for being a Lebanese citizen especially when Lebanon had voted for the adoption of the UDHR at the General Assembly of the United Nations on December 10, 1948.

I wonder whether the ownership of a large number of Lebanese media outlets has anything to do with this lack of coverage. This is another sad example about how seriously disadvantaged is civil society whenever a truly free and independent media does not exist. Only an independent and responsible press would speak truth to power.

Sunday, March 28, 2010

Mothers Day and Honour Killings

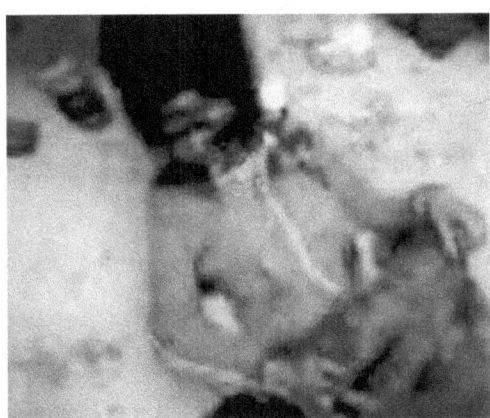

Last Sunday Lebanon and all the Arab countries recognized March 21, the first day in spring, as Mothers Day. On this day every year we pay tribute to the person who has given us love and attention from the moment of birth. Mothers are celebrated for the sacrifices that they happily make for the welfare of their children. Motherhood is arguably the best example of what it means to be noble and to and human.

Isn't it though hypocritical when we claim to uphold mothers for all what they do for us but structure our laws and behavior so as to deny women their basic human rights. So far we have not elected any women to a position of political leadership and we have denied the female sex their right to be treated as equals as any other citizen in our society. Lebanese women are not permitted to convey the Lebanese citizenship to their children when the father is not a Lebanese national and many live in fear of physical abuse, possibly death, if the males in their family do not approve of their behavior. Males boast of their nights on the town, their sexual "achievements" but look down and even punish the females in their household if they dare fall in love and be seen holding hands or necking with the boy next door. This must be the epitome of double standards.

Although the right to vote has been granted to women, in most cases the local tradition still dictates that females cast the ballot that the males in the household approve of. Unfortunately women are treated as second class citizens, as individuals whose legal stature is on the same level as that of a slave. She has, in most cases, no choice but to accept the husband that her parents have picked for her. Is that the woman that we celebrate once a year, the one that we choose to oppress abuse and manipulate for the next 364 days every year?

Sadly the rights of women in our region are as distant to the females as democracy and human and modernity are for society at large. It is time that we realize that none of us is free as long as one of us is

299

oppressed. We can never claim to be liberated when half of us are denied legally their social, political and economic freedoms. The empowerment of women is an essential ingredient in an equitable, free and liberated society. If we fail to liberate women then we will always be enslaved.

Yet we can be thankful that despite all the above listed injustices we have thus far resisted the heinous practice of stoning to death as this barbaric practice is still carried away and condoned in Saudi Arabia, Sudan, UAE, Iraq, Jordan and Iran to name just a few of the countries that celebrate Mothers Day but treat women otherwise as a commodity at the disposal of the males in society. But the question must be asked what is the difference between stoning to death and honour killings? Not much, I am afraid.

Friday, June 18, 2010

Hezbollah, Lebanese Defensive Strategy and the Arab League

"Pacta sunt servanda" is the major principle behind all international treaties and accords be they unilateral or multilateral. The fact that "Pacts must be respected" should not come as a surprise since a treaty between sovereign states is essentially similar to a contract between two parties. And we all know that contracts are binding otherwise why enter into them? In the business world as well as personal one hardly anything is done without a contract whether it is explicit or implicit. Honoring a contract forms the solid foundations upon which personal and business relationships are based. Individuals borrow from banks for all sorts of purposes by agreeing to certain contractual conditions, we buy cars and appliances and expect them to perform to certain standards specified in the contract embodied in the bill of sale. The same is true for corporations and businesses of all types and sizes. They rent or lease their premises by signing contracts, they honor the patents obtained by other firms and protect their own patents with contracts and they negotiate with labour unions the terms of employment by also signing contracts. Obviously the same is true for governments. They finance their deficits to the tune of trillions of dollars only because we have trust in their ability to deliver on their contractual obligations. And when nations form customs unions, free trade areas, monetary associations and mutual defense treaties they do so with the full belief that the counter party will honour its obligations.

The fact that contracts and international treaties are sacrosanct does not mean that they are always honored or that countries can depend on the execution of the provisions specified in the treaty in question. Unfortunately, in the same way that individuals do not always perform as per the contract s they enter into neither do countries. There is a major difference though between an individual who violates a contract and a state or group of states that fail to live up to their promises. Individuals can be forced to make the other party whole while states can literally speaking get away with murder and they do.

Lebanon has been preoccupied with finding an acceptable solution to its dire need for a defensive strategy since the security concerns in its neighbourhood are grave. It is not the intention of this post to analyze or deal with the specifics of the current Lebanese deadlocked domestic search for a solution to its security problem. What I would like to highlight, however, is a massive contractual failure on the part of the Arab League to honor its sacred obligations toward each and every single member.

Lebanon was one of the countries that helped establish the Arab League in 1945. The Arab League that still masquerades as if it is an effective organization of 21 states has let down many of its members and in this case Lebanon in particular. Hezbollah arose as a result of the Israeli aggression on Lebanon during 1982. What happened then and several times after that, not to speak about the daily Israeli violations of Lebanese air space should have triggered automatically a coordinated response by the Arab League to counter the Israeli offensives. It is not being suggested that the Arab League should come to the aid of a member state out of sympathy or as an act of magnanimity. The Arab League had entered into a contractual obligation as of sixty years ago called "Treaty of Joint Defense and Economic Cooperation between the states of the Arab League on June 17, 1950.

The above treaty was signed at the time by Jordan, Syria, Saudi Arabia, Iraq, Egypt, Yemen and Lebanon. Article 2 of the provisions of the treaty states:

Article 2
The Contracting States consider any [act of] armed aggression made against any one or more of them or their armed forces, to be directed against them all. Therefore, in accordance with the right of self-defense, individually and collectively, they undertake to go without delay to the aid of the State or States against which such an act of aggression is made, and immediately to take, individually and collectively, all steps available, including the use of armed force, to repel the aggression and restore security and peace. In conformity with Article 6 of the Arab League Pact and Article 51 of the United Nations Charter, the Arab League Council and U. N. Security Council shall be notified of such act of aggression and the means and procedure taken to check it.

The said treaty goes on to speak in greater details about the steps that need to be adopted in order to implement this mutual defense strategy. Alas, the Arab League has been a total failure and has not even made any pretence to fulfill its legal and moral obligations under a treaty signed by all its members at the time. Had the Arab League lived up to its duties then Israel would not have acted with abandon as it did neither would Lebanon be in the unbearable situation it finds itself in. The rise of Hezbollah and the spread of Iranian influence to Lebanon would not be nearly the problem that they are had the Arab League, the embodiment of political pan Arabism, not been the total failure that it is. Contracts that are not honored are ultimately dissolved; it is time to put the Arab League to rest.

Human Development in the Arab World

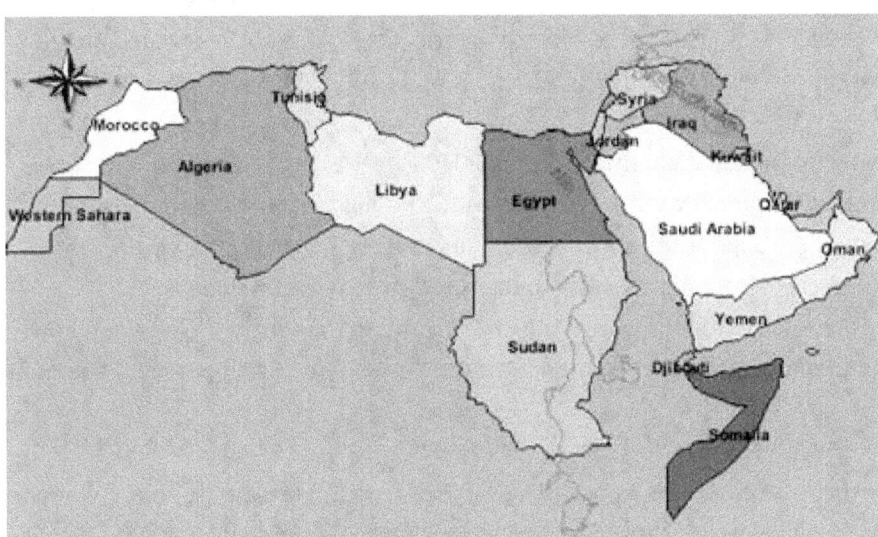

The Human Development Index for the year 2010 was released by the UNDP on the 4th of November. This is a grand issue. It reintroduces to the public both Mahbub Al Haq and Amartya Sen whose ideas and enthusiasm for a multidimensional development index resulted in the HDI in 1990. Ever since then this measure has continued to grow and evolve into the very informative data set that it has become. During the past twenty years this measure has become so popular and common that it is hard to find a textbook of economic development that does not teach it in lieu of the rather simplistic approach that used to rank countries by the level of income per capita.

It is especially noteworthy that the last iteration of the all successful HDI has introduced a number of improvements on the older methodology. It has become quite simple to rank countries by their non-income HDI is one is so inclined and to even rank them by an Inequality Adjusted Human Development Index. The newest edition has also introduced a Multifaceted Measure of Poverty that incorporates many of the seminal ideas of Mr. Sen, a Noble laureate in Economics.

So how did the Arab group of countries fare? Not so good. The Arab states as a group were below the world average in every single category. Life expectancy at birth averaged 69.3 years for the Arab states when it was at 69.3 for the world while the mean years of education for the world was 7.4 years compared to only 5.7 years for the typical Arab citizen. Even the per capita income measured on a PPP basis was only $7861 compared to a global average of $10,631.

A close examination of the individual Arab states' individual statistics is quite revealing and at times even surprising. It might be easy to explain the good performance of the top ranked two Arab states; UAE (32) and Qatar (38); as a byproduct of their high per capita income but that would not be the case for Bahrain whose income per person is less than 10% above that of Saudi Arabia but yet Bahrain outranked its larger neighbor by 16 (Bahrain 39, Saudi Arabia 55). Then there is Libya whose performance among the Arab countries would rank it close to the top of the heap on a Non income basis. The performance of Jordan is even more compelling in the group of Arab countries. Although its per capita income was a modest $5956 which is below that of Algeria ,Egypt and not that much above that of Syria, yet it outranked each of them (Jordan (82), Algeria (84), Egypt(101), Syria(111)).

The conclusion of the relative performance of countries during 2010 is rather revealing. The Arab world is still mired in inefficiencies and poor human capital. It is apparent that high income is helpful but is not sufficient. Many other countries all throughout the world had managed to outperform us by a wide margin despite their lack of a natural endowment similar to oil. Is it a stretch to conclude our authoritarian political systems are our major impediment to change and to modernity? When would we wake up from our slumber and demand our individual human rights to self expression personal freedom and responsible government?

The following is the ranking of the Arab countries as per the 2010 HDI report: Please note that Lebanon, Iraq, Palestinian Authority and Somalia are not ranked due to lack of data. My personal estimate is that Lebanon would have been around 70 since its data resembles that of Iran.

Rank	Country	Index	Life Expectancy at Birth	Mean Years Education	Personal Income $(PPP)	Non Income HDI Index
32	UAE	0.815	77.7	9.2	58006	0.774
38	Qatar	0.803	76.0	7.3	79426	0.737
39	Bahrain	0.801	76.0	9.4	26664	0.809
47	Kuwait	0.771	77.9	6.1	55719	0.714
53	Libya	0.755	74.5	7.3	17068	0.775
55	Saudi Arabia	0.752	73.3	7.8	24726	0.742
81	Tunisia	0.683	74.3	6.5	7979	0.729
82	Jordan	0.682	73.1	8.6	5956	0.755
84	Algeria	0.677	72.9	7.2	8320	0.716
101	Egypt	0.620	70.5	6.5	5889	0.657
111	Syria	0.589	74.6	4.9	4760	0.627
114	Morocco	0.567	71.8	4.4	4628	0.594
133	Yemen	0.439	63.9	2.5	2387	0.453
154	Sudan	0.379	58.9	2.9	2051	0.373
	Av. Arab States	0.588	69.1	5.7	7861	0.610
	WORLD	0.624	69.3	7.4	10631	0.663

NOTE:

15......Israel......................0.872...............81.2...................11.9.................27831......................0.916

Saturday, April 16, 2011

What Happened to the Arab Spring? Ask Saudi Arabia

The Arab countries, each and every one, have the distinction of being ruled by undemocratic and illiberal regimes. This has been the case at least since the era of independence that started almost a century ago. Even prior to WWI the Arab Middle East, under the Ottoman rule, did not experience a major revolutionary movement demanding sovereignty, and personal liberty despite the fact the Turkish rule was ruthless and exploitative.

Many a study has concluded that the Arab countries have failed to actualize their potential and that the region as a whole has trailed practically all parts of the world in economic, political and social development save for sub Saharan Africa. This is why so many in the region as a whole and in the rest of the world were elated when the Tunisian popular uprising was followed by the one in Egypt. These promising and exciting developments led so many to talk about an Arab Spring that has finally arrived to transform the region and deliver on the promise of economic, social and possibly environmental development.

The euphoria was contagious. Demonstrators went to the streets of Yemen, Bahrain and Libya. The last four weeks have even witnessed popular movements all across Syria. Is the Arab Spring here to stay? Is it a historical moment similar to the annus mirabilis of 1848 in Europe?

The Arab Spring appears to have been overwhelmed by a deep frost that might just kill all of the revolutionary buds. With the exception of Tunisia the revolutionary zeal has been either co-opted by the old established ruling class, Egypt is currently ruled by a 75 year old general who has never shown any predilection for democracy and individual freedom. The army has actually imprisoned a blogger for having assumed that it was his natural right to express his point of view.

In Libya it is even worse, much worse. The Libyan dictator or mad man Qaddafi would rather carry a civil war, orders the army to strafe civilian protestors and unleash savage artillery bombardments of those that dare ask for an end to the cult of personality rule. Colonel Qaddafi's efforts to subdue brutally civilian demonstrators were halted, at least temporarily, by the United Nations Security Council who came to the rescue of the besieged civilians. The French, British and US aerial support has given way two weeks ago to NATO who has not been able to keep up the pressure on the Qaddafi loyalists. It appears currently that what looked to be another victory for the popular masses has been brought to a standstill. Qaddafi might still be defeated but this does not mean that democracy and freedom are about to follow.

Then there is Syria and Bahrain. Two nascent revolutionary movements struggling with established dictatorships. In Syria the Assad regime of the Baath party has promised a modicum of reforms, not the least of which is the lifting of the emergency rules that have been established almost half a century ago. The demonstrators in Syria were initially encouraged by the UNSC resolution on Libya calling for the protection of the peaceful demonstrators. These hopes were squashed when Saudi Arabia in conjunction with Hillary Clinton gave the present regime in Syria the moral support that it needed to deal brutally with the demonstrators. Thanks to the efforts of the Saudi King, the world s' sole absolute monarch, the aspirations of the people of Bahrain and Syria have been dealt a serious setback. He has offered his moral support to the Syrian dictator and sent his troops to silence the calls for reform in Bahrain under the guise of the GCC. When you have such friends you don't need any enemies.

Under the best of circumstances, the chances for an Arab Spring were never overwhelming. But the possibility of success has been dealt a major blow by the unholy union of reactionary forces led by Saudi Arabia whose king was not in favour of even allowing the Egyptian masses to remove the corrupt Mubarak regime in Egypt. Unfortunately these reactionary forces cannot be dismissed since Saudi Arabia controls the daily production of 10 million barrels of oil in a world described best by Peak Oil scarcities.

Yet, despite all of this, the blame for the failure of the Arab Spring does not lie totally on the shoulders of the reactionary Saudi regime and the dictatorships that it supports. How can the Saudis support democratic representation when they are the antithesis of such societal make ups? The real ultimate reason for an Arab Spring is the same one that has haunted the Arab world for centuries. It is the lack of a strong personal commitment to the ideas of personal liberty, freedom, equality and secularism. It seems that we are destined to continue offering our allegiances to local tribes instead of cultivating the notion of citizenship and equality.

Wednesday, May 4, 2011

Arab Illegitimate Regimes.

If it is to be argued that the act of acknowledging, in a realpolitik way, the power of an oppressor when the exploited have no means to rise and demand their rights, is not clearly immoral then this moral ambiguity vanishes when an oppressor is offered support, moral and otherwise, against those whose human rights are being abrogated as they struggle valiantly and against great odds to free themselves. Sitting on the fence in the former case might be justifiable while taking a clear position against the humanitarian rights of the masses, in the latter, is an immoral act.

This is exactly what is currently going on in many an Arab country. Each and every regime in the Arab world, with the possible exception of Lebanon, is an illegitimate one imposed on the will of the people by force and repression. Many have decided that to oppose say Bashar Assad in Syria, and Mubarak in Egypt, and Saleh in Yemen, and Qaddafi in Libya would not have been productive when their respective subjects were not willing to rise in defense of their rights. But no one could ever claim to be for freedom while offering support to repression. Illegitimacy cannot become legitimate no matter what are the reasons applied. Illegitimacy is an innate characteristic that cannot be whitewashed

A major principle of international jurisprudence is to define a rational person as being the one who can foresee the consequences of his/her acts. Obviously those that resort to twisted logic in their efforts to rationalize acts of oppression and dehumanization should know better since it is crystal clear that opposing liberty and freedom will only result in greater exploitation and greater violations of all principles of dignity and freedom. If fence sitting in one instant is to be seen as not deleterious then favouring oppression against demonstrators and protesters is pernicious to say the least. To offer advice, solace and instructions on how to become a more effective dictator is a nefarious incorrigible act.

All parties, whether from the East or the West, poor or rich who have failed to advance the rights of the oppressed and who are busy acting as regime apologists must be held accountable for their despicable acts. There is never a justification for a dictatorship and no set of circumstances should be used to justify terror and human rights violations not even when the rising masses fail in establishing an "ideal" robust democracy. Revolutions seldom achieve their stated goals but that does not mean that we should not give the masses the chance to learn from their mistakes and to restore a semblance of dignity to themselves and their fellow citizens.

We ought to be reminded of the saying that if the only thing necessary for the triumph of evil is for good men and women to do nothing then the results of advocating for more repression are bound to be diabolical. How can we wish freedom for ourselves and injustice for others?

Illegitimate regimes, wherever they happen to be, cannot be justified and obviously are never to be encouraged. There is nothing, absolutely nothing, that can justify dictatorships even enlightened ones since they are based on the principle that citizens have no say in determining their welfare and that despots know better than we do what is good for us.

The current Arab spring might fall flat on its face and replace the authoritarian one man rules with periods of uncertainty and instability but to stumble while learning how to walk is superior to being tethered to a leach controlled by a slave master. It is clear that liberation could be postponed but it is one thing that can never be denied. The masses of all countries and especially of those in the Arab countries shall rise to be free again. The day when we are all living in accountable democracies or constitutional monarchies is bound to happen because that is the way history unfolds. No Assads, Mubarak's, Kaddafi's, Salehs or kings and emirs can stand in the way. It is a question of time.

Monday, February 21, 2011

Lebanon, An Arab re Awakening and Economics.

Joseph Schumpeter one of the greatest minds in economics coined the term "creative destruction" in an effort to describe how capitalism moves forward by encouraging innovation and creativity. I believe , rather strongly that this idea applies rather neatly to the field of political science in general and to what is taking place in the Middle East in particular. What appeared to be hooliganism to Mr. Mubarak and his entourage and what is described as mobs and criminals by Saif Al Islam are anything but. This apparent spontaneous chaos is in effect nothing but the most creative of destructions that could give birth to a new free and democratic MENA.Two down and seven to go might soon become three down and six to go. Wouldn't it be grand if the move towards democracy, diversity and freedom is to finally take root in the Arab world?

Many of us have been calling for an "Arab awakening" a Gdansk moment or an Arab Berlin wall for a while. But if the revolution is to uproot the ruling structures in each of the Arab countries then why do we count only 9 dictators instead of 21? Well, in my case, at least, I think a radical change in the big 9 will force the others in the Gulf including Iraq and Lebanon to change also. The smaller countries are more dependent on their surroundings and none of them is strong enough to impose its beliefs but each of them will not be able to resist the tide to change and reform once that becomes the dominant form in the region.

Yet in spite of all of this I have been struggling to explain the difference between what is going on in Egypt, Tunisia, Libya, Yemen and the lack of any change in Lebanon. After a lot of soul searching I believe that to a large extent one can explain the respective differences between any of the major players and Lebanon in terms of another economic principle. In a major country such as Egypt or possibly Libya the power is concentrated in one person at the top of the pyramid. That single person embodies all powers in the country. This concentration of power is akin to that of a pure monopolist who is free to exploit and abuse the consumers/citizens. Lebanon on the other hand is closer to what Galbraith called the "counter vailing power" structure. This would be the fact when a pure monopolist in one field is not free to exploit, restrict and abuse since this monopolist faces an equally powerful monopolist on the other side of the enterprise. The interaction between these two monopolists will result in a solution somewhere in between what each of them would have liked to do. Theoretically the solution could be a total negation of the power of each and thus the citizen/consumer will contend with a solution that could be rather beneficial. A good example of this would be say an automotive giant who would have liked to impose its will on tire manufacturers but if the automotive giant faces a rubber giant then none of them would be in a position to exploit the other and the consumer will benefit.

Michael Young, of the Daily Star, has dealt with the issue of relative personal freedom in the Lebanese public square by attributing that relative freedom to the inability of any of the major sects to impose its own will unhindered. That is exactly what a countervailing power does. This argument, however, is not to be construed as one in favour of sectarianism.

But this above argument, although it does lead to good outcomes, is just as badly in need of reform as any of the other single power dictatorships for the simple reason that the solution of the interaction

311

between the oligopolists can never be determined in advance and if it does turn out to be efficient then that would be purely accidental. The system cannot guarantee efficiency/freedom and so the need to change and the need to adopt a fairer more competitive system are just as acute as in the case of a pure monopolist/dicatorship. As a result the revolutionary task in Lebanon is even more difficult than it was for the Tunisians and the Egyptians who had to organize against the person on top of the pyramid in an effort to uproot the regime that he represents. In Lebanon, we do not have that luxury, we have to organize against and get rid of the people at the top of a number of smaller pyramids whose individual constituents regard only the opposing pyramids as corrupt and inefficient. Each constituency appears to be relatively satisfied with its own mini pyramid and concentrates on blaming the opposing power structures. This problem fits very well the line from Luke:

"How can you say to your brother, 'Brother, let me take the speck out of your eye,' when you yourself fail to see the plank in your own eye? You hypocrite". Is there any hope for a radical revolutionary reform in Lebanon? Only if we can shed our religious tribal affiliations and act as one. Unfortunately for us in Lebanon, Mouwatinieah and secularism are alien ideas.

SYRIAN

UPRISING

Monday, May 9, 2011

Syria Needs a Revolution.

So many of the regime apologists in Syria have stumbled on the phrase "evolution and not revolution" and have used it to great effect in scoring points against the critics of the Baath establishment. What is most unfortunate is the almost unanimous refrain that they get from those with whom they are debating, "of course evolution would be the better solution".

The above, sadly, does not reflect positively on either group since the two words represent completely different ideologies and since no one should be allowed to pretend that both means will reach the same end. They will not. If that was the case then there will never ever be any rationale for revolutions in any field and in any area of knowledge anywhere in the world.

Given a certain vision of reality and a set of beliefs in how the world works practitioners; high priests; proceed to use these ideas in an effort to spread that particular vision or model. Obviously any vision or model can be marginally improved upon, within its broader self imposed constraints of its zeitgeist.

Thomas Kuhn, in his highly influential "The Structure of Scientific Revolutions" described the epistemological vision that is dominant, at any point in time, as being a paradigm. It is to be noted that what is crucially important for this discussion is that as an accepted paradigm is being articulated by its believers it will always run into anomalies and paradoxes. The natural reaction of the practitioners is to reject the anomalies as false hoods and to go on with business as usual.

In all fields, these anomalies grow until it becomes impossible to dismiss them as being non essential. It is then that the youth; those that do not have a vested interest in the status quo; will rise and yell the emperor has no clothes. Once that happens then that specific field would have undergone a paradigm shift, a radical change in thinking, a revolution. It is also noteworthy not to lose track of the fact that different paradigms are "incommensurable" since each is based on a totally different vision of reality.

What the, much abbreviated, description of the above implies is that once the potential imbedded within a certain understanding of the dynamics required by a certain vision are exhausted then the only possible way to move forward is to reject the past paradigm and adopt a totally different one. This method of explaining the accumulation of knowledge is not linear. It is based on quantum leaps, on discontinuities and on having the courage to adopt a new way of thinking. This is not an evolutionary process but is actually an understanding that we move forward only through revolutions since sooner or later any accepted paradigm, set of values or system of beliefs will fail to explain the inevitable anomalies that arise.

Copernicus and Galileo provided an understanding, a vision if you will that is not related at all to that of Ptolemy. They posited that the earth revolves around the sun instead of the idea that our planet was the center around which everything revolved. That revolution changed the way that we understand our place in the universe and it was not an evolutionary movement. It was based on a total rejection of all what came before it.

The same process is true when one views social, political and economic evolutions. Feudalism does not evolve into capitalism just as much as capitalism will not evolve into ecological societies. Dictatorships and authoritarian rule will never evolve into democratic structures based on the idea of human rights and personal liberty. These ideas are diametrically opposite and to pretend that one can evolve into that which is its antithesis is groundless. The only way to shift from one phase to the other is to have a revolution. It must also be emphasized that a revolution does not mean violence to individuals but it must mean rejection of old established ideas and values that serve only the interests of the high priests. Revolutions will not cease until we get to the end of history.

The current regional applications of the above simply mean that no dictatorship will ever evolve into a democracy since that means evolving into its negation, into what it is not. Another relevant example of the above is the impossibility of transforming Lebanon into a modern democratic state without getting rid of all its traditional tribal leaders. Revolution means an abrupt change that anchors a system on principles and ideas that would never be acceptable under the current paradigm. You cannot evolve a system into a revolution since they simply represent the antithesis of each other and since a revolution is called for only once the current dominant paradigm has totally failed. It has both in Syria and in Lebanon regionally, and so has the obsession with economic growth globally.

Sunday, August 21, 2011

Bashar must go: No Legitimacy for the Illegitimate

One of the most popular expressions of the Lockian idea of "natural rights" can be seen in the preamble to the US declaration of independence written by Thomas Jefferson: "We hold these truths to be self-evident, that all men are created equal, that they are endowed by their Creator with certain inalienable rights, that among these are life, liberty and the pursuit of happiness."

The above simply means that it is not up to government to offer its populace personal rights since these are among the bundle of rights that cannot be alienated from the individual. No government can take away that which is embedded into citizens by virtue of birth and to act otherwise is a gross act of hubris and egregious exploitation. When the state adopts policies to take away from people part or all of their natural rights then the state is acting against the will of the governed whose welfare it is supposed to enhance. Such acts of diminution of the rights of citizens are best described as immoral, unethical, exploitative and constitute justifiable uprisings against the ruler whose acts have violated all accepted responsibilities of a governor.

Unfortunately, history is replete with states that have acted as authoritarian rulers, absolute monarchs, brutal dictators and autocrats. Yet the movement towards more democracy and responsible government got its biggest boost with the American and French revolutions of over 235 years ago. Many philosophers and political scientists have argued that the spread of democracy is probably the single best achievement of the 20th century. Alas this glorious trend appears not to have found even a toe hold in the Arab world until the onset of the Arab Spring that started in Tunis, spread to Egypt, Libya and Yemen then Bahrain and Syria not to mention the defensive moves in Morocco, Jordan and possibly Iraq and Palestine.

Tunis and Egypt have already started the hard work of establishing working democracies as soon as their previously strong autocratic regimes collapsed, Yemen and Libya seem to be close to uprooting the dictatorial regimes of Qaddafi and Saleh while the Bahraini demand for reform appears to have been squashed by the Saudi monarchy with the acquiescence of the rest of the GCC. But besides Bahrain, the real paradox so far has been the courageous and popular Syrian uprising. It has been over 5 months since the people of Dara'a took to the streets to send a message to the Syrian Ba'ath that forty years of suppression, exploitation and expropriation of natural rights is enough. The spark of Dara'a spread like a wild fire to the suburbs of Damascus, to Homs, Hama and their environs, to Deir Ezorr, Jisr Alshughur, Banias and Latakia among other places. The civilian protestors were met in all cases with the full force of the Syrian army whose tanks have demolished many residential quarters and whose snipers and military has already killed over 2000 civilians; men women and children, not to mention the tens of thousands of injured and the over 10,000 rounded up for interrogation and torture. It is ironic that the same army that has failed to fire one bullet in almost forty years to liberate the Golan Heights was willing to butcher its own citizens in the name of resistance. As all this blatant brutality by the Syrian dictatorship was going on not one of the Arab governments issued as much as a statement of moral support to the insurgents when each of these regimes did not hesitate to support the Tunisian, Egyptian, Yemeni and Libyan uprisings. The deafening Arab silence was finally broken a fortnight ago when Saudi Arabia issued a statement asking the Syrian authorities to stop the bloodshed. This lukewarm support by Saudi Arabia was followed by expressions of support for the Syrian insurgents by other Arab governments and the Arab League but not by Lebanon. The West on the other hand has continued to pressure Syria to stop the killing through the Presidential Statements of the Security Council, through more severe economic sanctions and through an outright call for Mr. Assad to step down.

The official Lebanese position vis a vis the Syrian uprising will come back to haunt it but it was to be expected from a country whose President was unconstitutionally elected and who has often made it clear that his allegiance to the Damascus is his priority. In addition to the above the current PM, Najib Mikati and his brother Taha, are known to have strong financial ties to the Syrian regime through Syriatel and Sami Makhlouf president Bashars' cousin. Obviously no one needs to be reminded that Mr. Mikati is the symbolic head of a cabinet that came to power through the machinations of Hezbollah whose military and financial strength depend on smuggled missiles and other ammunition originating in Iran through Syria.

Despite all of this less than overwhelming support of the Arab regimes for the Syrian people in their greatest hour of need the Syrian Revolution is still gaining strength and the autocratic and brutal dictatorship led by Bashar Assad is struggling to find a way to survive by promising all sorts of reforms including a multiparty political system. How convenient to become a reformer when your survival depends on it, this is political expediency par excellence. Mr. Assad fails to understand that there is no such thing as legitimacy of the illegitimate.

Dictatorships are often born in blood, fear, exploitation and usurpation of that which cannot be stolen since it is inalienable. Every single dictatorship will eventually end ignominiously simply because all are rooted in illegitimacy and sooner or later the people will lose the fear of the ruthless security machine that is set up to protect the dictator by pretending that the authoritarian regime knows best what is good for the multitudes when in effect all of the states' acts are dedicated to the glory of the dictator and his entourage. Mr. Assad is not loosing legitimacy since he never had it to begin with and the governed have the legal right and the moral authority to establish a regime that respects their "natural rights"

It is a foregone conclusion that the Syrian uprising will eventually free itself from the inhumane grip of the Syrian Ba'ath but the price of that liberty is subject to the acts of Bashar Assad. He will either drag Syria into a Libyan style conflagration or he will decide that it is time for the Syrian people to rule themselves. Bashar Assad must go, all dictatorships must end and this is the time to end a forty years old cruel dictatorship.

Saturday, August 27, 2011

Invalidity of the Defense of the Syrian Regime

The fall of the USSR and the official establishment of the Russian federation in 1991 was a major turning point in the political make up of what was known as the Soviet Union and all its European and Asian satellites. The rise of Boris Yeltsin to power of a free, and independent Russia that has renounced 70 years of Communism effectively marked the end of the Cold War. The occasion was welcomed by most people all over the globe if for nothing else but for the potential peace dividend that it carried and for the apparent freedom and liberty that it had bestowed on the people of Russia as well as all the Soviet satellites from Kazakhstan to Latvia, Georgia, the Ukraine, Hungary, Romania, the unification of Germany... Yet some people on the extreme left blamed the Russian citizens and the residents of each of the satellites for wanting a better life. They blamed them for their uprising and for throwing the yoke of their exploiters and corrupt politicians who deprived the citizenry of its rights but made sure to bestow all kinds of privileges upon themselves. Many leftist party members in the West argued that the citizens of the ex Soviet Union should have never demanded what is rightfully theirs but should have allowed the oligarchs and their security forces to go on abusing them for personal gain. Obviously that line of thinking is laughable as any visitor to any of the liberated countries can document.

Move forward twenty years and in particular to the uprising that started in Syria over 5 months ago and you run against the same tired, self serving, hackneyed and superficial logic. Many of the Syrian regimes supporters know better than to make a straight forward argument in favour of a brutal dictatorship and so they twist themselves into unwieldy shapes trying to argue that the regime is needed because without it then Syria would degenerate into sectarian warfare. Obviously none of those that advance this line of thinking would provide any shred of evidence why such an outcome is inevitable. We are also told that Bashar Assad the scion of the cruel dictatorship that has been ruling under an emergency law and through a single political party rule for over 40 years need more time to introduce the legitimate reforms that the unarmed civilian protestors are calling for. Isn't almost half a century long enough to come up with a package of reforms? And if it is true that the current regime is intent on reforms then isn't it a coincidence that this matter became apparent only when its monopoly on power was challenged. Is it rational then to question the sincerity of such reform proposals while the tanks are demolishing neighborhoods and the prisons are full of political detainees? It is very clear that all of these are nothing else but excuses for those that are happy with the status quo of no elections, one party rule and promotion of Soviet style personal celebrity rule.

This unfortunate use of inverted logic is not left only for the domestic supporters of the dictatorship. Similar logic has been used by Egyptian thinkers as well as Lebanese writers. The most glaring such example, however, is that taken by Hezbollah. Sayed Hassan Nasrallah has stated the position of his party clearly one more time in his latest speech on the occasion of the International Day of Jerusalem. He, as expected, lavished nothing but praise on the Syrian regime but was sure to justify that by highlighting the steadfastness of the Syrian government against Israel. His premise is that the single most important issue in the Arab society is the position against Israel and in favour of the Resistance movements and since the Syrian Baath has supported Hezbollah, Hamas and PFLP-GC then any movement by the people against this regime is suspect and must be defeated. The very clear weakness of the above, even for those that share the believe in the preeminence of the Arab-Israeli position is the fact that Mr. Nasrallah assumes that the replacement government will not take the same position against Israel. He makes that assumption and asks the listeners to accept it on faith. That is purely an exercise in tautological thinking. The other weakness in this strange logic is the assumption that Mr. Nasrallah knows best what is good for the Syrian people. They do not have a say in self determination. Could that kind of thinking be influenced by the principles of Welayat Al Faqih?

What is especially pernicious about the above illogic is that its promoters were very highly critical of the doctrine of "preemptive strikes" as articulated by George W Bush. That principle allowed the US to take action/wage war based on suspicion that an act was being planned, no proof was necessary. That is identical to what supporters of the Syrian regime are claiming, deprive civilians of their rights, use ruthless force to put them down only because you suspect that they will propose a policy that you disagree with, no proof needed and their rights be damned even if they chose to enact such a policy. What imperious hubris.

As if all of the above is not enough, many of the same groups that are defending the Syrian killing machine are applying the same logic to downplay the tremendous accomplishments of the Libyan revolutionaries that have spared no cost to free themselves from the dictates of the mad man Qadaffi. Obviously it would be unacceptable to defend such a mad person and his entourage directly and so it has become common for this group to apply its strange logic by claiming, that the courageous and brave Libyan people were manipulated by foreign powers. That is simply just as grotesque of an insult to the intelligence of the Libyan as the above thinking was an insult to the intelligence of the Syrian people.

Why cannot we accept the simple fact that the Soviet masses as well as the Tunisian, Egyptian, Libyan, Yemeni and Syrian have risen against their exploiters because they have had enough. They prefer to live in dignity rather than be used and mistreated by oligarchs bent on accumulating personal wealth and power?

The days of the Syrian dictatorship, like all other dictatorships, are numbered irrespective of its disingenuous efforts to save itself.

Sunday, November 13, 2011

Syrian Suspension And The New Reality In Lebanon.

The reaction of the Syrian regime to the recently announced suspension of the Syrian membership by the Arab League reminds me of the story about the proud mother during a military parade who was jumping up and down with joy and yelling to whoever can hear her: "Please take a look and note how all the brigade is out of step with my Amer, bless his soul"ϑ

A few months ago when the European Union announced a set of measures against Syria and some Syrian oligarchs in conjunction with Washington Mr. Al Moualem, the Syrian foreign affairs minister announced with bravado that Syria will act as if neither the US nor the EU are part of the world map. Two days ago the Syrians decided to erase another part of the world map; this time they said "Toz" to all the Arab countries. Russia and China have, so far, shown some lukewarm support for the Syrian regime although both countries have stressed that they expect Mr. Assad and his Syrian minions to stop the use of force and to implement genuine reforms immediately. Maybe it is time for the Syrians to dismiss another major chunk of the world map. It looks very highly likely that pretty soon the Syrian regime will operate in a shrunk world of its making composed of Iran, Venezuela and North Korea. Obviously they can always count on the unquestioned support of their Lebanese subordinates: Hezbollah, Amal, FPM, Marada, Talal Arslan and Wiam Wahab. The support of Mikati and Safadi will be ambiguousϑ

The relatively wide official Lebanese support for the Baath killing machine is problematic at best. The Tower of Babel, better known as the Lebanese cabinet, is one more time trying to take a position and its opposite at the same time. The PM, Najib Mikati, has never tired of telling the world that Lebanon honours all its international obligations and will obviously pay its dues to the STL. Unfortunately he forgot to relay that message to the largest bloc in the cabinet, FPM, and the real power behind the throne Sayed Hassan Nasrallah. Mr. Nasrallah, an unelected official who acts as the PM, Speaker and President; all rolled into one; has declared a few days ago that as far as he is concerned the STL does not exist, as if reality is something subjective. (If a tree falls in a forest and no one hears it then does it make a sound?) I guess not. If SHN decides not to see something then irrespective of the scientific proof that an entity exists Mr. Nasrallah feels that he can act as if it does not. Does the Emperor have cloths on or is he naked? Ask SHN or Bashar Assad before you answer that one. Their views are what counts, the truth be damned.

Then there is the Lebanese position Vis a Vis the decision of the Arab League to suspend Syrian membership. Lebanon dispatched its foreign minister to support the Syrian position and argue that Syrian demonstrators do not exist, the 3500 deaths of unarmed civilians are the fabrication of Western media, tanks and the full might of the Syrian armed forces have not been used against unarmed civilians in Homs, Hama, Dara, Latakia among numerous other places all across Syria. But to top it all the Lebanese President, Michael Suleiman, himself elected unconstitutionally, called Bashar Assad to tell him that Lebanon did not vote for Syrian repression but only to protest the punishments being doled to Syria9 What a joke. When would we ever learn that to take a position and its opposite simultaneously is a logically bankrupt exercise and what is more important that it is an insult to the intelligence of the public.

It is time to shout it from the hill tops. The Emperor has no cloths. This Lebanese cabinet is a sorry excuse for a government. Lebanon is ruled according to the diktats and personal whims of a certain unelected clergyman, Sayed Hassan Nasraalah, who does not recognize the right of Lebanon to sovereignty and independence. No one in this cabinet would dare take a position on important issues without seeking in advance the blessings of SHN. This charade has gone as far as it can. But what is equally clear is that the Syrian Baath has already lost even if, against all odds, it manages to stay in power. The minimum changes coming to Syria are a new constitution that does not recognize the Baath as a special party, free and popularly elected members of the parliament and a freely contested and elected president. Who would have even dared suggest such changes a few months ago? The new reality is that Syria will become more democratic, that all the Baath lackeys in Lebanon will have to adjust their vision to see the new reality including SHN.

Monday, November 21, 2011

The Fall of Bashar and the Rise of Democracy in Syria and Lebanon

Often reality is difficult to accept and especially for the ideologues whose understanding of development and their advice is rarely, if ever, to be taken seriously. Ideologues are not to be confused with principled individuals because their positions are dictated not by the rationality of a circumstance but by a predetermined notion of which party to oppose and which one to support. They act as if one party has a complete hold of the truth all the time while the others are always misinformed even if they are to adopt views that are associated with their opponents. A perfect example of an ideologue is the expression of utter bewilderment on the face of the head of the Ba'ath party in Lebanon, Mr. Shukur, when his debate opponent, Mr. Alloush, stated that he does not believe the statements of Bashar Assad. The priceless expression was what one would expect to see on the face of a 4 year old when told for the first time that there is no Santa Clause.

The reaction of Bashar Assad and his entourage to the declarations of the Arab League and other nations all over the world are not any different. They refuse to accept the clear inevitable conclusion of the ongoing Syrian revolution. It would be practically impossible for Bashar Assad and the Syrian Baath to stay in power. They have already lost and the longer it takes them to internalize this reality the costlier will be the final synthesis. The Syria that the Assads have ruled for over forty years as a fiefdom has finally had enough humiliation, abuse and exploitation. It has risen to and has demonstrated tremendous courage in facing the unbelievable odds to standing up to the security apparatus and the army. These actions would not have been called for had MR. Assad acted responsibly by showing that Syria is above party and it transcends family and business cronies. Alas Mr. Assad, just like an addict, could not bring himself to admit that the Ba'ath has abused the trust of the Syrian people and that the continuous mismanagement of the economy have transformed Syria into a paper tiger and a backward and bankrupt economy that is rapidly moving towards an environmental abyss as well as an economic meltdown and a social disintegration.

Instead of doing the right thing of listening to the clear and legitimate demands of his people Mr. Assad has decided to bunker down and to defy the world by threatening that if he is to be constantly reminded of reality and legitimacy then he might have no choice but to lash out at his unarmed civilians. Pity the man that thinks of himself as a modern leader but acts as a tin horn dictator. But our biggest sympathy goes out to the brave Syrian civilians who have decided that freedom is not free and that they are willing to pay the price.

The tipping point has already been breached. Syria will be free from the Ba'ath. What is not certain is how dear the price will be. Mr. Assad is still the dominant factor in this equation. He can act responsibly by accepting the new facts and start immediately the negotiations for an orderly and peaceful transfer of power or he can persist in his obstructionism by bringing down the temple on himself and the Syrian people. Time is running short and unless he acts decisively in the next few days to avoid a Syrian Armageddon to save himself and the country that he claims that he loves then he would be committing an abominable act that history will not forgive for centuries to come, if ever.

A corollary to the above is the major transformation that will engulf Lebanon when the cruel Syrian dictatorship is finally booted out. The ramifications on Lebanon will be as seminal as the changes in Syria. Lebanon will finally get a chance to exercise its independence and sovereignty. Its people will be able to rule themselves as any democracy should and the new realities will finally help bring to an end the Mafiosi rule of Hezbollah and all those that have helped and abetted its nefarious acts. It should also usher in a tide of new, young and committed youth who reject sectarianism and corruption. A new era of citizenship will take hold in Lebanon as soon as the divisive and backward Syrian Ba'athi minions are swept away from the official offices that they have exploited and profiteered from for decades. The only question that stands as an obstacle in the face of the historical movement in both Syria and Lebanon to enter a new post Assad era is whether the celebrations will take place in late 2011 or early 2012. I can hardly wait.

Monday, December 12, 2011

Syrian Dictatorship, Israeli Occupation and Civil Disobedience

It can be argued that dictatorship is not that different than outright occupation by a foreign military. Actually it has been suggested by many commentators that occupation is the ultimate dictatorship. What is important for us in this column is the similarity between the two forms of rule. Both deprive the people of their personal rights, both are non democratic, both are not elected, both maintain control through armed forces and both violate the most fundamental principles of human rights as expressed by the Human Declaration of Human Rights. It is rather obvious that both occupation and dictatorship are two different forms that accomplish the same end: rule against the consent of the governed. Whenever such rule is present then it is an invitation to rebellion and revolution. The above describes very well at least two political entities in the Arab world; Syria and The West Bank, the former is occupied by the Assad family and the latter by Israel. Both of these forms of government are cruel, discriminatory and exploitative.

The Palestinians have resisted occupation and have tried a number of policies over the past 44 years but they have not succeeded in attaining their objective yet. They are possibly the last remaining colony in the whole world unless one considers China a colonizer of Tibet and the Russians as colonizers of Chechnya. The valiant Palestinians have not however committed themselves to the principle of non violence through organized and wide spread civil disobedience. I, and many others, have often argued that the Palestinians have no choice but to adopt the Gandhian method of civil resistance. That is the only way to "disarm" the cruel Israeli machine of occupation and deliver the Palestinian people to the "promised land", the land of self determination, sovereignty and democracy.

It must be also very clear that the same methodology suggested to the occupied Palestinians on the West Bank is also the one that promises to be very effective in delivering Syria out of the clutches of the Assad regime and into the phase of representative democracy and self respect. The current Syrian regime has resisted the legitimate demands of its populace by constantly denying the facts on the grounds. The whole administration has acted over the past ten months exactly as one would have expected dictators to act. Deny, obfuscate and pretend that the unelected rulers, those that impose themselves by the power of hired thugs otherwise known as "security forces" are the only ones that know what is good for the country.

This irrational logic is so wanting that it does not deserve to be addressed except to say that if pretenders were so sure that they have the good of the people at heart then why fear an open and free election? Why insist on a system that depends on random fear and on expropriating everything of value to the integrity of the individual. Obviously dictators, all throughout history, have dreaded the moment that the oppressed find the strength to stand up and claim their stolen rights. Dictators have always lived in fear of the moment when the regular citizens will shout that the emperor has no cloths, that the regime is bankrupt and illegitimate.

The Syrian uprising that started nine months ago is all of the above and then some. The Syrian people have demonstrated great courage in standing up to the might of the dictatorship thugs and have offered the greatest of sacrifices without any hesitation. The Syrian people have given all of us, the world over, a lesson in sacrifice and commitment. They have faced the organized "shabiha" hoodlums and their supporting tanks with smiles on their bare breasts, bravery and heroism. They have already offered over 400 martyrs, many of whom are children and women and they have managed to keep up the pressure on the killers and criminals in power. They have simply set an example of audacity and boldness that has rarely been seen, if ever.

Yet the regime continues with its lies and distortions. It fabricates stories about undisciplined armed gangs that are in the employ of foreign powers when arguably it is the present regime that has often served the Israeli occupation of the Golan best. An excellent example of the cluelessness of Bashar Assad, the head of the ruling pyramid, was demonstrated in his disastrous interview with ABC where he claimed that he has never ordered any killings and that he is not in charge of the armed forces in Syria. Isn't this a perfect fit for what is a psychopath?

"Superficially charming, psychopaths tend to make a good first impression on others and often strike observers as remarkably normal. Yet they are self-centered, dishonest and undependable, and at times they engage in irresponsible behavior for no apparent reason other than the sheer fun of it. Largely devoid of guilt, empathy and love, ...psychopaths routinely offer excuses for their reckless and often outrageous actions, placing blame on others instead. They rarely learn from their mistakes or benefit from negative feedback, and they have difficulty inhibiting their impulses."

The current monstrous regime in Syria is intent on showing that the uprising is essentially driven by petty religious rivalries and revengeful acts. That is why the present Syrian dictatorship will stop at nothing that will help it provoke a violent uprising. The courageous Syrians will commit a fatal error if they fall for this trap that is being set up for them. They should spare no effort to show both the depraved Syrian regime and the world that they are above sectarian hatreds, petty politics and random violence. What better way to show that they are cut from a different cloth than the present killers and exploiters of the Syrian people than to adopt wide scale acts of civil disobedience and non violence. Let the authorities arrest, if they dare hundreds of thousands and maybe millions of citizens, let the few thugs run the schools, the factories and the shops. Civil disobedience has worked wonders in India, South Africa, the Czech Republic, the Ukraine and has even partially succeeded in Egypt, Tunisia, Yemen and even Lebanon among other places.

Syria is obviously in need of a revolution and there is nothing better than what Henry David Thoreau called "peaceable revolution" in his essay about Civil disobedience. A peaceful and non violent Syrian revolution is the best option for the Syrian uprising. I am certain that it will succeed and once it does then it would have set up another example of the efficacy and attractiveness of "civil disobedience" for the whole world in general and for the West Bank in particular. When the people ask for freedom, respect and integrity then no dictatorship can possibly deny them their intrinsic rights.